A HISTORY OF THE FRENCH LANGUAGE

Modern Languages

Editor

R. AUTY
MA, DR.PHIL.

Professor of Comparative Slavonic Philology
in the University of Oxford

A HISTORY OF THE
FRENCH LANGUAGE

Peter Rickard

Fellow of Emmanuel College, Cambridge,
and University Lecturer in French

HUTCHINSON UNIVERSITY LIBRARY
LONDON

HUTCHINSON & CO (*Publishers*) LTD
3 Fitzroy Square, London W1

London Melbourne Sydney Auckland
Wellington Johannesburg Cape Town
and agencies throughout the world

First published 1974

*This book has been set in Times,
printed in Great Britain on smooth wove paper
by William Clowes & Sons, Limited,
London, Beccles and Colchester, and bound
by Wm. Brendon, Tiptree, Essex*

ISBN 0 09 118740 0 (cased)
0 09 118741 9 (paper)

CONTENTS

PREFACE

As the vehicle of a culture and of a literature of the highest order, French has been for centuries the foreign language most widely known and studied in Great Britain, and its influence on the development of the English language has been considerable. Those who study it as it is spoken and written today are probably aware that it derives from Latin and therefore belongs to the Romance group of Indo-European languages; and some may have wondered by what process or processes an ancient language becomes a modern one. English readers of seventeenth-century French texts will have observed that some words now have a different meaning, while others have fallen into disuse, and they may also have noticed vestiges of older grammatical constructions today considered impossible, incorrect or at best archaic and quaint. Such differences will strike the reader even more forcibly as he goes further back, through the French of the sixteenth century to that of the Middle Ages. The French reader, too, finds the language increasingly opaque and baffling as he goes further back through its abundant literature. Indeed, unless he is a specialist, he will have to read such masterpieces as the *Song of Roland* and the *Romance of the Rose* in modern translations.

What were the immediate Latin antecedents of French? What was the earliest French like? What were the circumstances which favoured the emergence, from a welter of dialects, of a language which gradually spread over the whole country, and was subsequently carried to other continents? What were the factors, internal or external, spontaneous or contrived, which shaped its evolution? What are its dominant characteristics today, viewed in the light of its past? These are the questions I have tried to answer, in the hope that this book may serve as an introduction to more detailed or specialised studies in this field, a vast one which has been intensively investigated, by no means exclusively in France, for well over a hundred years.

A work of the modest scope of the present volume is obviously not intended to be an historical grammar: it is intended simply to provide, in English, a concise survey of a type already long available in French, and to indicate main outlines and significant developments, without going into so much detail as to hold the reader up as he tries to follow the broad sweep of linguistic evolution. If, for instance, I have endeavoured to characterise Old French in its dominant features, it was precisely in order not to have to describe it in detail. The reader who wishes to learn Old French as a grammatical system in its own right should turn to a more relevant book: in this one, Old French is regarded merely as a staging-post.

It is a great pleasure to record my gratitude to Mlle S. Dayras of Paris-III and Dr T. G. S. Combe of Pembroke College for their kindness in reading Chapter 7 in typescript, for their extremely valuable criticisms and for the most helpful corrections and additions they have enabled me to make.

P.R.

Cambridge

ABBREVIATIONS AND PHONETIC SYMBOLS

adj.	adjective	nom.	nominative
adv.	adverb	obl.	oblique
Cl.L.	Classical Latin	O.F.	Old French
Ed.	edited by	O.Prov.	Old Provençal
fem.	feminine	phon.	phonetically
indic.	indicative	pl.	plural
inf.	infinitive	repr.	reprinted
Lat.	Latin	sing.	singular
masc.	masculine	subj.	subjunctive
Mid.F.	Middle French	subst.	substantive
Mod.F.	Modern French	V.L.	Vulgar Latin

  *   postulated (i.e. unattested) form
  >   'becomes'
  <   'comes from'

The sounds of *Modern* French are as follows:

vowels

[i]	[fini]	*fini*	[y]	[lyn]	*lune*
[e]	[ete]	*été*	[ø]	[dø]	*deux*
[ɛ]	[pɛ:R]	*père*	[œ]	[malœ:R]	*malheur*
[a]	[sak]	*sac*	[ə]	[pəti]	*petit*
[ɑ]	[pɑ]	*pas*	[ɛ̃]	[pɛ̃]	*pain*
[ɔ]	[alɔ:R]	*alors*	[ɑ̃]	[vɑ̃]	*vent*
[o]	[mo]	*mot*	[ɔ̃]	[bɔ̃]	*bon*
[u]	[fu]	*fou*	[œ̃]	[œ̃]	*un*

semi-consonants

[j]	[pje]	*pied*	[ɥ]	[nɥi]	*nuit*
[w]	[wi]	*oui*			

consonants

[p]	[paRi]	*Paris*	[v]	[vɔl]	*vol*
[t]	[tɛt]	*tête*	[z]	[zo:n]	*zone*
[k]	[kɑ]	*cas*	[ʒ]	[ʒœn]	*jeune*
[b]	[bɑ̃]	*banc*	[l]	[laRʒ]	*large*
[d]	[dam]	*dame*	[R]	[Ra]	*rat*
[g]	[gaRsɔ̃]	*garçon*	[m]	[matɛ̃]	*matin*
[f]	[fœ:j]	*feuille*	[n]	[nɔ̃]	*non*
[s]	[sal]	*sale*	[ɲ]	[ɔɲɔ̃]	*oignon*
[ʃ]	[ʃa]	*chat*	[ŋ]	[smɔkiŋ]	*smoking*

In addition to the above, the following sounds existed in earlier stages of the language: it is emphasised that they did not all exist at the same time.

vowels

[ĩ]	[vĩn]	*vin*	[õ]	[dõn]	*don*
[ẽ]	[fẽndrə]	*fendre*	[ỹ]	[ỹnə]	*une*
[ã]	[vãn(t)]	*vent*	[œ̃]	[brœ̃n]	*brun*

consonants

[h]	[hardi]	*hardi*	[ts]	[tsɛ̃nt]	*cent*
[r]	[rɛrə]	*rere*	[tʃ]	[tʃastɛl]	*chastel*
[dz]	[dodzə]	*doze*	[θ]	[pieθ]	*piet*
[dʒ]	[dʒɛ̃nt]	*gent*	[ð]	[viðə]	*vide*

diphthongs

[ái]	[fairə]	*faire*	[yí]	[nyit]	*nuit*
[ao]	[aotrə]	*autre*	[uǿ]	[buøf]	*buef*
[áu]	[faukõn]	*faucon*	[ãi]	[mãin]	*main*
[eo]	[eo(ə)]	*eaue*	[ẽi]	[ẽimə]	*aime*
[ié]	[fier]	*fier*	[iẽ]	[biẽn]	*bien*
[ói]	[foi]	*foi*	[õi]	[lõin]	*loing*
[óu]	[souder]	*souder*	[uẽ]	[kuẽns]	*cuens*
[ǿu]	[nəvøu]	*nevou*	[yĩ]	[dʒyĩn]	*juin*

triphthongs

[eáu]	[beaus]	*beaus*	[iéu]	[tsieus]	*cieus*
[uéu]	[dueus]	*duels*			

I

FROM VULGAR LATIN TO THE RECOGNITION OF
THE NEW VERNACULAR

The prehistory of the French language begins with the colonisation of Gaul by the Romans. The Celts who inhabited Gaul when the Romans came were Indo-Europeans, related to the Greeks, Romans and Germanic peoples in both culture and language. They appear to have lived originally in central or eastern Europe, but began to move westwards around 500 B.C. and settled in Gaul some two hundred years later, displacing the other peoples whom they found there, notably the Iberians, who were driven towards the south-west, and the Ligurians, who were driven towards the south-east. By this time there were also important Greek settlements on the Mediterranean coast at such places as Marseilles, Nice and Antibes, which have preserved their Greek names. In the second century B.C. these Greek settlers, harassed by the Gauls, asked for Roman aid against them, and thus brought about the first Roman campaign in Gaul, a campaign which, spread over thirty years from 154 to 125 B.C., led to the conquest of what the Romans then called the *Provincia* or province, a name which survives today as Provence. At first the Roman colony extended from the Alps to the Rhône, then the frontier was pushed south-west across the Rhône to the eastern Pyrenees, taking in what is today Roussillon. In 57 B.C., Julius Caesar undertook the conquest of the rest of Gaul, a process which was virtually complete by 52 B.C., for the Gauls, essentially a loose confederation of tribes, lacked political unity.

In the newly conquered territory, Gauls of any rank who had anything to do with administration and supply soon found that they had an incentive to learn Latin. Moreover, the only kind of education available was the Roman one: indeed, the Gauls could not write at all until they learned the art from the Romans, and this explains why those few monuments of the Gaulish tongue which have come down to us are mostly written in the Roman alphabet. Even so, Romanisation and Latinisation were a very gradual process. The bestowal of Roman citizenship on all free-born inhabitants of the Empire by Caracalla in A.D. 212 probably made no very great difference to the linguistic situation in Gaul, and it would not be unreasonable to suppose that in the second or third century A.D., in areas remote from Roman supply routes, Latin would be seldom heard and even more seldom understood, and Gaulish the normal language used. For this very reason, perhaps, Gaulish eventually lost much of its former prestige, and came to be looked down on as the speech of rustic underlings. Even so, it seems to have lingered on in places until as late as the fifth century; while Greek, in the Rhône delta, lasted even longer, and finally died out only in the sixth century.

It is important to realise that the Latin which was introduced into Gaul with the legions and which, after the conquest of the region, continued to be influenced from without while undergoing modifications from within, was significantly different from what we understand by 'Classical' Latin. There is perhaps in every language an appreciable difference between the polished literary form of it and what people actually say in everyday life, however literate they may be. Spoken Latin is generally termed Vulgar Latin, but this term is also applied to those forms of written Latin which by their lateness and their divergences from the known standards of Classical Latin are believed to be closer to the spoken language—but only closer to it, by no means identical with it. It therefore follows that even the most strikingly non-classical text is not, to say the least, an ideal record of the spoken language, and much has to be deduced by combining the study of Vulgar Latin texts and inscriptions with the comparative study of the Romance languages in their earliest attested forms, if one is to attempt to reconstruct the broad features of spoken Latin. Even so, the picture is anything but complete. There are a great many texts in Vulgar Latin, from all over the Empire, and they suggest an almost suspiciously homogeneous language which, while it diverges in a great many ways from Classical Latin, seems to have firm rules of its own and to rise, artificially of course, above such regional variations as may have already existed. Most students of Vulgar Latin, however, are reluctant to believe that there was any substantial regional differentiation before approximately the sixth century A.D.

In its essentials, the Latin spoken in Gaul in the second, third and fourth centuries A.D. is unlikely to have been more than superficially different from the Latin spoken in other parts of the Empire. What were the common features of this spoken Latin, so far as we can deduce them negatively and positively from the texts and from the evidence of early Romance? A detailed characterisation of Vulgar Latin lies outside the scope of this book, but a few significant features may usefully be mentioned here. Distinctions of vowel quality become more important than the classical distinctions of vowel length, although distinctions of length by no means disappear; *h* has no phonetic value; the diphthongs [æ] and [œ] have been reduced to [ɛ] and [e] respectively; in the verbal system there is widespread analogical redistribution of conjugation; the classical neuter plurals in *-a* are often treated as though they were feminine singular, while masculine substantives in *-us* and neuter substantives in *-um* are frequently confused; the synthetic passives of Classical Latin are badly known and comparatively little used; new compound tenses involving the use of *habere* with a perfect participle come into being; there is much confusion in the use of cases, accompanied by a more liberal use of prepositions making the case-distinctions less necessary. The vocabulary contains many neologisms and lacks, to an increasing degree, certain classical terms: thus *ictus* 'blow' tends to be replaced by *colaphus* (Mod.F. *coup*); *tergum* 'back' by *dorsum* (*dos*); *ignis* 'fire' by *focus*, originally the hearth (*feu*); *vir* 'man' by *homo* (*homme*) —this last already classical, but more restricted in use. Early Christianity too influenced the vocabulary of Vulgar Latin, notably through the introduction of Greek loan-words which had already taken on a Christian meaning, whatever their original associations had been: hence *angelus* 'angel' (*ange*); *ecclesia* 'church' (*église*); *diaconus* 'deacon' (*diacre*); *episcopus* 'bishop' (*évêque*); *presbyter* 'priest' (*prêtre*); *martyrium* 'martyrdom' (*martyre*); *hymnus* 'hymn' (*hymne*); *monachus* 'monk' (*moine*).

Such was the kind of Latin current in Gaul and thus available to its inhabitants two or three or four hundred years after the Roman conquest. It is impossible for us to tell to what extent, if at all, those Gauls who spoke Latin, at first as a second language and later as their only language, carried over into it habits of articulation deriving from a long tradition of Celtic speech. A regional pronunciation of Latin may well have developed, but it is not likely to have made any very profound changes during the period in question. We must remember that the Latin of Gaul was still in steady contact with the language of Rome: not until appreciably later was it left largely to its own devices, and at no time was the isolation absolute. What is much more easy to demonstrate is the influence of Gaulish on the *vocabulary* of the Latin spoken in Gaul and, though far more rarely, on the vocabulary of Latin in general. Some aspects of Gaulish daily life may have appeared to the Romans so characteristic, or so quaint, that no existing Latin word seemed adequate to describe them, or it may have been that the Gauls, in learning Latin, clung tenaciously to some terms which were dear to them for one reason or another, or which seemed untranslatable. Whatever the reason, it is certain that many quite common French words date from this period and are of Gaulish origin. Naturally, when they are first attested in writing (as some of them are) they are given a Latin spelling and a Latin termination, e.g. *riga* 'furrow' (*raie*—now also 'parting of hair', 'stripe', 'crease'); *rusca* 'bee-hive' (*ruche*); **soccus* 'plough-share' (*soc*); *carruca* 'plough' (*charrue*); **cambita* 'felloe' (*jante*); **liga* 'dregs' (*lie*); **multonem* 'sheep' (*mouton*); **bucco* 'buck' (*bouc*); **bertium* 'cradle' (O.F. *bers*, Mod. *berceau*); *alauda* 'skylark' (O.F. *aloe*, Mod. *alouette*). Gaulish names of trees, types of landscape and soil, measures of distance and area, have also left their mark, **betullus* 'birch-tree' (O.F. *boul*, Mod. *bouleau*); **brucaria* 'heather' (*bruyère*); *ivos* 'yew-tree' (*if*); **sappus* 'fir-tree' (*sapin*); **cassanus* 'oak' (*chêne*); **cumba* 'small valley' (*combe*); *talutium* 'bank of earth' (*talus*); *caio* 'embankment' (*quai*); **baua* 'mud' (*boue*); **grava* 'strand' (*grève*); **margila* 'marl' (*marne*); *leuca* 'league' (*lieue*); *arepennis* 'acre' (*arpent*). Other borrowings include *bodina* 'boundary-mark' (*borne*); *beccus* 'beak' (*bec*); **sudia* 'soot' (*suie*); **druto* 'strong' (*dru* 'dense', 'luxuriant'); *cerevisia* 'malt beer' (O.F. *cervoise*); and such useful verbs as *glenare* 'to glean' (*glaner*) and **brisare* 'to break' (*briser*). Most of these words were peculiar to the Latin of Gaul, but a few others, borrowed early, subsequently spread all over the Empire, wherever Latin was spoken, e.g. *caballus* 'horse' (*cheval*), replacing the classical *equus*; *bracae* 'breeches' (*braies*); *camisia* 'tunic', 'shirt' (*chemise*); *cambiare* 'to (ex)change' (*changer*); *camminus* 'path', 'way' (*chemin*); *carrus* 'wagon' (*char* and derivatives).

It will be seen that these words cover a limited though useful range: they are almost exclusively homely, even earthy words connected with husbandry, with the soil, with the landscape, with rough-and-ready garments. There is a conspicuous lack of abstract terms, but Latin was after all well provided with these. As for place-names, the Romans usually added typical Latin endings to the Gaulish names and declined them according to the rules: only exceptionally did they rename Gaulish localities. Many names of towns derive from the name of the tribe which inhabited the district, inflected in the ablative or locative plural of Latin; thus *Remis*, the home of the tribe known to the Romans as the *Remi*, gives rise to Reims (Rheims). This explains in many cases the *-s* ending of modern French towns, for example Angers, Limoges, Nantes, Poitiers, Sens, Tours and Troyes. Paris takes its name from the *Parisii*, the tribe whose capital, now l'Île de la Cité, was originally called *Lutetia*. Many Gaulish place-names ended in *-dunum*, a suffix which originally suggested a fortified place. Verdun and Lyon(s) derive from this type. *-acum*, too, was a common termination for place-names, in north and south alike, and the development of these names offers a striking example of the wide divergence there has since been, phonetically speaking, between north and south. The more conservative south preserves *-acum* as *-ac*, as in Armagnac, Cognac, Jarnac, etc.; whereas in the north, the same suffix became *-ai*, as in *Camaracum* > Cambrai, and indeed often *-i* (usually written *-y*) if it was preceded by yod [j]: *Cluniacum* > Cluny; *Clippiacum* > Clichy. There were two localities named *Aureliacum*, one in Cantal, the other near Paris: the former has developed to Aurillac, while the latter, as Orly, has given its name to the well-known airport.

River-names are notoriously conservative. The names of the principal French rivers, Seine, Marne, Garonne, Loire, Rhône, Allier, Saône, Isère, still perpetuate their old Gaulish names.

So much, then, for the positive contribution of the Celtic language formerly spoken in Gaul, to Latin, and through Latin to Mod.F. In assessing the Gaulish element, we must of course make allowance for other words which were borrowed, but which fell into disuse during the Middle Ages, or which have survived to the present day only in dialects, and not in what has become the standard language. As for an influence on pronunciation, this can be assumed only in a very small number of well-authenticated cases where the phonetic change in question is not organic but a matter of substitution—the result of contamination of a Gaulish word with a Latin one, e.g. *tremere* 'to tremble' + **krit-* > **cremere*, hence O.F. *criembre* 'to fear', Mod. *craindre*; or the change of *articulum* 'joint' to **orticulum*, whence *orteil* 'toe'.

By the end of the fifth century, the Gaulish language had died out and had been replaced by a form of Latin still very close to the forms of Latin spoken elsewhere in the dying Empire, but containing numerous local words and possibly already showing phonetic tendencies which might eventually have differentiated it from Latin as spoken elsewhere, *even if no other factor had supervened to accelerate and accentuate the process.* With the collapse of the Roman Empire the unifying, centralising force of Rome collapsed too, and the different provinces were to an increasing extent cut off from each other. Christianity, however, had in the meantime made considerable progress throughout the Empire, though its influence was very much at the mercy of local secular rulers, who might or might not be Christians. Nevertheless, such formal education as was available continued to be on Roman lines and the tiny, almost exclusively ecclesiastical, literate minority continued to write a Latin which in intention was classical, but which fell increasingly short of classical norms. This written Latin continues to reflect the spoken language but dimly, and apart from the by now thoroughly assimilated Gaulish words which occurred in it, resembled nothing so much as the written Latin of other parts of the Empire. In other words, it was still suggesting far more homogeneity and uniformity than existed at the level of the spoken language and, to that extent, was artificial. Even a truly vulgar text like the *Peregrinatio ad loca sancta*, written at the end of the fourth century or the beginning of the fifth by a nun known variously as Silvia or Aetheria, could have been written in *any* part of the Empire: there is nothing truly local about it. It must be added that even later, when the vernaculars had diverged from each other yet more, we shall find this state of affairs reflected only remotely in the Latin texts of the regions concerned. In other words, we shall be disappointed if we suppose that written Latin, however 'corrupt' (i.e. non-classical, a less emotive word), is going to reveal to us all the secrets of the early stages of French, or indeed of any other Romance vernacular.

This is an appropriate place in which to mention the introduction into the area now known as Brittany of a Celtic language related to Gaulish but by no means identical with it. From about A.D. 430 until the end of the sixth century, large numbers of refugees from Britain, displaced by the Anglo-Saxon invasions, settled in Brittany. So, at a time when Gaulish was rapidly being replaced or had already been replaced by Latin, a substantial Celtic-speaking area resisted Latin, and only very gradually, centuries later, came under its influence or the influence of the emergent vernacular. As for the later influence of Breton on French, it was insignificant, being confined to a small number of loan-words, a contribution greatly outweighed, from the Middle Ages onwards, by the number of French loan-words in Breton.

Although in the fifth century Gaul was the most thoroughly Romanised of all the provinces of the Western Empire, there occurred in that century the Germanic invasions which were to have a far-reaching effect on the Gallo-Roman population and on its language. The Roman army in Gaul had shrunk, by the end of the fourth century, to a dangerously inadequate size. On the other side of the Rhine, Germanic tribes, themselves beset by the Huns further east, were massing threateningly. In A.D. 406 they surged westwards across the Rhine and sacked Amiens, Thérouanne and Tournai. This was the first invasion: it was followed in the course of the century by a whole wave of invasions and settlements, amounting to a major racial migration. For about seventy years, Gaul was torn by violent conflicts between Franks and Gallo-Romans, Franks and Franks, Franks and Burgundians, Franks and Visigoths, and not infrequently Gallo-Romans and Gallo-Romans. So far as any pattern can be discerned in such a chaotic period, it was approximately this. South of the Loire, the Frankish element was greatly diluted: here Visigoths held sway at first, all the way to Andalusia, though outnumbered in Gaul by Gallo-Romans. Burgundians occupied the valleys of the Rhône and the Saône. In the north, the Franks were established in large numbers, the main concentration being of Salian Franks around Cambrai and the Somme, while to the east were the Ripuarian Franks, around Cologne and the upper Moselle.

In these circumstances it is astonishing, though none the less a fact, that the Church not only survived the collapse of the Roman Empire, but even inherited from it much of its mission of law and order. The Gallo-Roman bishops sought alliances with the barbarian kings, and were on the whole more successful with the Franks, who were heathen, than with the Visigoths and Burgundians who, though nominally Christian, were infected with the Arian heresy. It must be emphasised that the Franks, though heathen, were not total barbarians: they had after all had considerable contact with the Roman way of life before they invaded Gaul. A very important date in the history of the Franks in Gaul was the conversion to Christianity, in A.D. 496, of the Frankish king Clovis (Hlodovech). Church and king combined to curb the power of rival leaders who were still pagan, and also to drive back the Visigoths and to hold the Burgundians in check. During the Merovingian period, which begins with the death of Clovis in 511 and continues until the accession of Charles Martel in 719, the degree of unity—and certainly of 'national awareness'— was extremely limited. Yet for all that there gradually emerged the concept and even the reality of something which the chroniclers called *regnum Francorum* and later *Francia*, though it must be emphasised that both these terms embraced a good deal of what is now Germany as well as what is now France. In the north, it could be said that the administration was based on Germanic folk-custom slightly Romanised and increasingly Christianised; while in the south and centre, counts and bishops applied what was largely Roman law. In the south in particular, Germanic influence was more thinly spread, and civilisation there was predominantly of a Mediterranean and Byzantine type. Aquitaine and Provence came under Frankish sway when in 732 Charles Martel, having repelled a Saracen invasion, took control of an area which had hitherto been largely independent. There ensued a short period of comparative unity under Frankish rule.

The circumstances in which Franks and Gallo-Romans lived side by side in 'Francia' are by no means clear: these were extremely troubled and confused times, and there are few written records. It is certain that in the north, German peoples outnumbered Gallo-

Romans, while in the south the opposite obtained. There seems to be no doubt that many Gallo-Romans were at first simply dispossessed of their lands by the Franks, and that the law was for a long time different according to whether one was a Gallo-Roman or a Frank. Yet gradually, through intermarriage and alliances of interest, the distinctions between Gallo-Romans and Franks were broken down.

At first, few Franks could speak Latin, and yet they failed to impose their language in the long run, except in Flanders and on the left bank of the Rhine, areas which were or had been technically a part of Gaul. The fact is that Latin still enjoyed considerable prestige, and even at the height of Frankish domination it was extremely rare for any other language to be used in writing. Roman coins were still in use, new ones being minted on the model of the old, and a good deal of Roman law remained intact or was adapted to Germanic folk-custom. Even the famous Salic Law, the orally transmitted tribal code of the Salian Franks, was soon written down for the first time in Latin.

It is time to take stock of the linguistic situation. What was the nature of the Latin of 'Francia', in what ways did it differ from that of an earlier period, and, much to our purpose, in what ways does it point the way to French?

A weakening, through ignorance, through loss of tradition, and through chaotic conditions, of the norms of Classical Latin, and the increasing influence of the spoken language, led to a written Latin which is conspicuously non-classical and which reflects some, but by no means all, of the facts of pronunciation. Certain earlier tendencies occur with greater regularity. Among these may be mentioned: the placing of a prothetic [ɛ] before an initial [s] followed by a consonant: *isperare* (*espérer*); *ispo(n)sa* (*épouse*); *iscola* (*école*); syncope— reduction of syllables, particularly in words where a stressed syllable is followed by two unstressed ones (the type known as 'proparoxytons'): *postus* for *positus, domnus* for *dominus*; the reduction of the perfect ending *-avit* to *-aut*; the change of [k] and [t] + yod to [ts] (assibilation by palatalisation), implied by such spellings as *tercia* for *tertia, stacio* for *statio, observacione* for *observatione* and by 'reverse spellings' such as *Frantia* for *Francia*; the palatalisation of [d] + yod implied by the spelling *iusu* for *deorsum*; frequent misapplication of *h*, implying that it had no phonetic value (except in Germanic loanwords, to which I shall return); or its omission, as in *corte(m)* from *cohortem*; the spelling *-nn-* or even *-n-* for the consonant group [-mn-], implying assimilation; loss of final [-m] (already elided in Classical Latin prosody); omission of final [-k], whence *ho* or even *o* for *hoc*. *Ad* is often written *a* before a consonant; *non* is often weakened to *no*; *qu* tends to become *c* before *o* and *u*, hence *comodo*, for *quomodo*, *cotidianus* for *quotidianus*. In the final position, *e* and *i*, *o* and *u* are hopelessly confused, a fact which obviously has serious implications for the case-system.

A great many analogical changes are also attested: fifth-declension feminine substantives in -*es* behave like first-declension substantives in -*a* (*materies* > *materia*; *rabies* > *rabia*); the common-gender genitive plurals in -*um* or -*ium*, and the feminine genitive plurals in -*arum*, all tend to give way before the analogical extension of -*orum* (*fratrum* > *fratrorum* > O.F. *fraror*; *candelarum* > *candelorum* > O.F. *chandelor* > Mod. *chandeleur*); fourth-declension nouns in -*us*, helped by the phonetic identity of final -*o* and -*u*, behave more and more like second-declension nouns in -*us*; neuter and masculine are hopelessly confused; also, as mentioned before, neuter plural and feminine singular. Prepositions are used where they were not called for in Classical Latin. Furthermore, they often appear to take the wrong case. Yet, if when reading a Latin text of, say, the seventh century, we come across phrases like *cum dom(i)num, ad officio, pro caritatem*, we are over-simplifying the question if we say that the scribe did not know which case to use after the prepositions *cum, ad*, and *pro*. We must remember that final -*m* was not pronounced, and that -*u* and -*o* were not distinguished in the final unstressed position. Phonetically speaking, it would have made no difference whether the scribe used the accusative case or the ablative; with luck he might even have written 'correctly' *cum domino, ad officium, pro caritate!* The preposition *de* is used more and more in senses approximating to French *de*—as an indication of possession and, instead of the traditional *ex*, to express 'movement away from'. With feminine plural substantives, we often find the accusative form -*as* used where the construction calls for the nominative -*ae*: this anticipates the state of affairs in O. and Mod.F. As for that extremely important part of speech, the relative pronoun, we find *qui* often used for both genders in the nominative, and *que(m)* in the accusative. In the verbal system, there is considerable extension of the fourth conjugation in -*ire* at the expense of the second and third (-*ére* and -*'ere*). The passive is little used and wrongly used. The future simple of Cl.L. is extremely rare: instead, we find periphrases with auxiliaries like *debere* and *volere* combined with the infinitive. *Volere*, it is to be noted, replaces the classical *velle*, just as *donare* replaces *dare*. The new compound tenses with *habere* + perfect participle, are well attested. In vocabulary, many changes of form are phonetic in origin: *ancessor* for *antecessor*, *drictum* for *directum*, etc. Certain numerals, perhaps exposed to excessive wear and tear in rapid counting, appear in a contracted form which points the way to French: *viginti* > *vinti* (O.F. *vint*); *quadraginta* > *quarranta* (O.F. *carante*). There are also many changes of meaning and function, even where the word already existed in Classical Latin; thus *quantus*, in the plural, is used for *quot*: *quantae lacrimae* (O.F. *quantes lermes*); *rogare* 'to ask' is used in the sense of 'to command' (cf. O.F. *rover*); *inde* 'thence' is used like the French prefix *en* which derives from it: *inde minare* > O.F. *en mener* > Mod. *emmener*. *Mittere* 'to send' is used in the sense of F. *mettre* 'to place', 'to put'. Among adjectival suffixes, the analogical extension of *-osus*, *-osa* to many new words should be mentioned, giving rise eventually to O.F. adjectives in *-os*, *-ose*, Mod. *-eux*, *-euse*.

In the domain of syntax there are a great many changes, of which I shall single out a small number for mention here: a great extension in the possibilities of the infinitive, replacing among other things the supine and the gerund + *ad* after verbs of motion; and at the same time a decline in the accusative and infinitive construction (which had never been truly popular) in favour of clauses introduced by *quod* or *quia*. The distinction between direct and indirect speech is in full decay.

Characterising the language of Bishop Gregory of Tours, the French scholar M. Bonnet wrote 'Hardly a line of it could have been written in the classical age', and it must be added that Gregory's late sixth-century Latin is far superior, not only to that of many of his contemporaries, but even more to that of his seventh-century successors.

We saw that at an earlier date the vocabulary of the Latin of Gaul was modified under the influence both of Gaulish and to a lesser extent of Greek, though strictly speaking the Greek words were part and parcel of the Latin brought to Gaul in the later Empire and kept up to date by contact with Rome. This already modified vocabulary understandably underwent further modifications under Germanic influence during the fifth, sixth, seventh and eighth centuries, and later too. The words which the Franks brought with them and which were important, topical or inescapable enough to be adapted into Latin, referred to their way of life, to their conception of society, and to their equipment, and served to fill certain gaps, real or imagined, in the existing Gallo-Roman vocabulary. For practical purposes I shall confine myself here to examples which have survived to the present day in French: the reader may take on trust the assurance that there were many others which are found in O.F. but which have not survived. Such French outdoor terms as *jardin*, *haie*, *gerbe*, *gazon*, *loge* (O.F. *loge* = 'leafy bower'), *guède* 'woad', *hêtre* 'beech-tree' (rivalling but at first not replacing Lat. *fagus* > O.F. *fou*); *saule* 'willow' (rivalling *saus* < Lat. *salicem*); *houx* 'holly'; *mousse* 'moss'; and *roseau* 'reed', date from this period. Important Mod.F. verbs such as *blesser*, *choisir*, *gagner*, *garder*, *guérir* (O.F. *garir*), *guetter*, *haïr* are likewise of Germanic origin. The domain of warfare, of weapons, armour and equipment provided the ancestors of *guerre*, *bannière*, *écharpe*, *éperon*, *épieu*, *étrier*, *fourreau*, *hache*, *haubert*. *Rauba*, originally 'booty', later passed through the stages 'stolen clothing' > 'clothing' > 'dress/gown' (Mod.F. *robe*). *Le loquet* 'latch' is Germanic; so are *le banc* 'bench', *le fauteuil* 'armchair' (originally *faldistoel* 'folding-chair'); *le canif* 'knife', now 'pen-knife'; *l'échine* 'spine' (now used only of animals); and *la hanche* 'hip' (Lat. *coxa* 'hip' had come to mean 'thigh', now *cuisse*). Some common adjectives too are Germanic loan-words: *frais* 'fresh', 'cool'; *hardi* 'bold'; *laid* 'ugly', 'nasty'; *morne* 'gloomy', 'dreary'; *riche* 'rich'; *sale* 'dirty', and several adjectives of colour, supplementing the rather limited Latin range: *blafard* 'pale', 'wan'; *blême* 'pale', 'pallid'; *bleu* 'blue'; *blond* 'blond', 'fair'; and *brun* 'brown'. Like Gaulish, Germanic does not seem to have had much to add to Latin as regards abstract nouns, but there are two notable exceptions, the antonyms *orgueil* 'pride' and *honte* 'shame'.

Germanic suffixes, originally borrowed together with the words of which they formed the termination, subsequently became available for the formation of new words, whether from Germanic roots or from Latin ones: thus *-hart* and *-alt* gave rise to O.F. *-art* (Mod. *-ard*) and *-aut* (Mod. *-aud*), as in the modern *vieillard*, *veinard*, *clochard* and *lourdaud*, *badaud*, *nigaud*, *penaud*.

Some of the Germanic loan-words contained sounds which had no even approximate counterpart in the Latin of Gaul. The scribes, with only the letters of the Latin alphabet at their disposal, were faced with the problem of representing these new sounds to the best of their ability. A strongly aspirated initial [x] was represented by the letter *h*, which in words of Latin origin had ceased to have any value save a somewhat confused orthographic one. Though this Germanic *h* is no longer aspirated, it to this day prevents the elision of a preceding vowel, or liaison with a preceding consonant, and so still serves as an almost (but not quite) infallible guide to etymology. An initial [w] was written *uu* by the scribes, to show that it was different from a Latin initial *v* pronounced [β] in Gallo-Romance: hence *uuardare*, *uuadius*. This sound subsequently became [gw] before becoming a simple 'hard' [g], which is the value it has by the twelfth century in O.F. (*garder*, *gage*). In a few cases there was contamination of Germanic words beginning with [x] or [w], with cognate Latin words beginning with a vowel or with *v*: thus *altus* 'tall', 'high' became *haltus* > O.F. *haut*; and *vastare* 'to lay waste', *vadum* 'ford' and *viscum* 'mistletoe', developed as though they began with [w], giving respectively *gaster*, *gué* and *gui* in O.F., instead of **vaster*, **vé* and **vi*.

These were by no means the only ways in which Germanic speech-habits are believed to have affected the pronunciation of the Latin of 'Francia': they are simply the ones which are best attested in the writing of the time. There is in fact every reason to believe that Germanic influence went much deeper and led to very profound modifications, changes which eventually had the effect of distinguishing the speech of northern France very sharply from the speech of any other Romance area, even distinguishing it appreciably from the speech of the south of France, where Germanic influence on the language was less far-reaching. It must be emphasised that with few exceptions, these phonetic modifications of spoken Latin are *not* reflected in the Latin texts of the period, and have to be deduced or reconstructed from the evidence of the earliest French texts, when these finally appear from the ninth century onwards. If for convenience I deal with these changes in this chapter, it must be understood that I am anticipating as regards evidence, but not as regards the chronology or the detail of the changes themselves.

Three major phonological developments which precede the appearance of the earliest O.F. texts, and which are believed to have taken place gradually from the fifth to the early ninth century, are the reduction of proparoxytons, the loss of final unstressed syllables, and extensive diphthongisation in stressed syllables. These three changes are closely interrelated. Let us examine in detail what this means.

Syllabically speaking, V.L. words were of three types: oxytons, paroxytons and proparoxytons. An oxyton is strictly a word bearing the stress on the last syllable. In V.L., however, this could only apply to monosyllables. In other words, so far as V.L. is concerned, oxytons are monosyllables, but it should be noted for future reference that in Mod.F. *any* word with a 'masculine' ending (i.e. a word *not* ending in a syllable containing or consisting of 'feminine *e*' i.e. [ə] or [–]) is an oxyton, no matter how many syllables it has. Paroxytons, in V.L., were all words stressed on the penult (i.e. the last syllable but one): that is to say, all words in which the penult was long. If the penult was short, then the stress fell on the antepenult (the last syllable but two): this type is known as a proparoxyton. For example:

Oxytons:	*non, hoc, et, ac, me*
Paroxytons:	*múri, pórta, máre, hábet*
Proparoxytons:	*véndere, cúmulus, cámera*[1]

In speaking Latin, first as a foreign language and eventually as their native language, it seems that the Franks carried over into it the

1. The acute accent in the above and subsequent Latin examples merely indicates *stress* and has nothing to do with the quality of the vowels thus marked.

strong expiratory stress of Germanic. We may assume, from later developments, that they applied the stresses in the right places, but made them so heavy that some syllables preceding the stress were 'swallowed' (syncopation), while the syllables which followed it were reduced drastically. Furthermore, where the vowel in the stressed syllable was 'free', that is to say, where it ended the syllable and was not 'blocked' by a consonant,[1] it underwent considerable lengthening or drawling with the result that it tended to split by differentiation into a diphthong. Where it was blocked, it did not diphthongise. The particular phonetic changes which I am describing were not sporadic, but regular. It is an absolute rule that in the development of the Latin of northern France to early O.F., final unstressed syllables *all* disappeared with the following exceptions (which, by the way, are themselves rules!):

(1) If the final syllable contained [a], this vowel did not disappear, but weakened to a neutral sound [ə], represented by *a, o* or *e* in the *spelling* of the earliest O.F. texts, and thereafter normally by *e*; still syllabic in O.F. and *potentially* syllabic in Mod.F.

(2) Whatever its original quality, the vowel in a final unstressed syllable survived as a neutral [ə] if it was needed to support a group of consonants which could not otherwise be articulated.

(3) A final unstressed vowel survived if it was in hiatus with a preceding stressed vowel.

(1) and (2) resolve themselves into this: the only kind of final *unstressed* vowel possible in O.F. and Mod.F. is [-ə]. Final syllables containing any other vowel are by definition stressed, and the words concerned are consequently, by definition, oxytons. Final unstressed [i, e, o, u] all disappeared without trace by the ninth century. Now, since the paroxytons of V.L. might contain any vowel, including [a], in their final syllable, it follows that paroxytons *either* continued to be paroxytons in O.F. *or* became oxytons in O.F., according to whether final [a] survived in its weakened form [ə], or final [i, e, o, u] disappeared without trace. Thus, for example, *pórta* > *pórte* remains a paroxyton, but *múri* (or *múro*, or *múrum*) > *mur, hábet* > *a, máre* > *mer* become oxytons. As for proparoxytons, a common development was for the vowel in the unstressed penult to be 'swallowed'. The result of this was that consonants which had previously been separated by this vowel, came into contact and constituted a group which necessitated the preservation of the vowel in the *final* syllable

1. Thus the stressed vowel in *má/re* is free, while in *pár/tem* it is blocked. Note however that the consonantal groups [tr], [dr], [pr], [br] do *not* constitute a 'block'. Thus *pátrem, cápra* are to be syllabically divided *pá/trem, cá/pra*, and the tonic vowel is free.

to facilitate pronunciation. As has been said, whatever the original quality of the final vowel, it survived exclusively as [ə]: e.g. *véndere* > *vendre*; *cámera* > [*kamra*], later *cambre, chambre; cúmulum* > [*kumlu*] > *comble*. Some proparoxytons, however, reduced to oxytons: *dígitum* > O.F. *doi; frígidum* > *froid; víridem* > *vert*.

Of the seven cardinal vowels of V.L. ([a] [ɛ] [e] [i] [ɔ] [o] [u]), five diphthongised eventually, in the appropriate phonetic circumstances, that is to say, when they were tonic and free, i.e. stressed and not blocked by a group of consonants other than [tr] [dr] [pr] [br]. The vowels [i] and [u] did not diphthongise,[1] but the other five behaved as follows:

[ɛ] > [ɛɛ] > [iɛ]   as in *pédem* > O.F. *pié(t)* (*t* = [θ])
[e] > [ee] > [ei]   as in *fédem* (< Cl. *fidem*) > O.F. *fei(t)* > *foi*
[ɔ] > [ɔɔ] > [uɔ]   as in *bóvem* > O.F. *buof* > *buef*
[o] > [oo] > [ou]   as in *dolórem* > O.F. *dolour*
[a] > [aa] > [aɛ?]   as in (*máre* > O.F. *mer*)

The problem of [a] > [ɛ], exemplified by *máre* > *mer*, is a difficult one. It is generally supposed that there was an early diphthong [aɛ], soon reduced. At all events, the reduced form of this diphthong is certainly not written as a digraph (i.e. with two letters) in O.F., but simply as *e*, though it seems that the sound was for a long time distinct from *e* deriving from other sources: thus, for instance, *la mer* (< *máre*) does not rhyme or assonate at first with *l'enfer* (< *inférnum*).

There were other important changes. Initial consonants were well preserved, but between vowels some consonants were modified while others disappeared: [-t-] > [-d-] > [-ð-] as in *víta* > [βida] > [viðə] (O.F. *vide*, later *vie*); [-b-] > [-v-] as in *debére* > [devérə] > O.F. *devoir*; [-p-] > [-v-] as in *sapére* > [savérə] > O.F. *savoir*; but in [-b] + [o] and in [-p] + [o], the consonant disappeared altogether; [-s-] > [-z-], but [-k-] (written *c*) and [-g-] disappeared altogether, as in *secúrum* > O.F. *seür*, *a(u)gústum* > O.F. *aost*. Voiced consonants coming into the final position through loss of a final unstressed syllable (see above) were unvoiced, e.g., *grándem* > O.F. *grant*; *bóvem* > *buof, buef*; *vívum, vívo* > *vif*; *pédem* > *piét*.

These changes, nearly all common to the dialects of northern France, are fundamental to the subsequent development of French. The dialects of the south, for convenience collectively known as Occitan,[2]

---

1. [u], however, underwent an extremely important change. Over nearly the whole of France, north and south alike, it was fronted to [y].
2. From the Medieval Latin *lingua occitana*, itself a translation of *langue d'oc*. The terms *langue d'oïl, langue d'oc*, relating to the expression of the affirmative in north and south respectively, are first found at the end of the thirteenth century, but the linguistic division which they presuppose is very much older.

are not our concern: suffice it to say here that the changes which took place in the south were much less far-reaching and the general picture more conservative: the Latin diphthong [au] was preserved, there was little diphthongisation, tonic free [a] was maintained intact, intervocalic consonants were on the whole well preserved, or at all events did not disappear, e.g. *vidére > vezer securum > segur, maturum > madur*; final consonants tended to drop. To judge from a somewhat later linguistic situation, the boundary-line between north and south must for linguistic purposes be drawn from the mouth of the Garonne north-eastwards to Mont-luçon and then south-eastwards to the north of the modern *département* Hautes–Alpes. A third division must be made for the sake of completeness, again with reference to a somewhat later period (see map on p. 48). A roughly triangular area, with its apex pointing westwards towards Puy-de-Dôme, spreads out eastwards fan-wise, taking in the modern *départements* of Loire, Rhône, Ain, Isère and Savoie. This is the area in which Franco-Provençal dialects evolved, partaking of some characteristics of the north, and some of the south. However, the history of the French language is the history of the emergence and standardisation of a particular variety of northern French and its spread to the whole of what is now France. Though I shall allude later to the continued existence of Occitan and Franco-Provençal, my concern will not be with their characteristics or with their later evolution.

By the late eighth century, then, the spoken language of northern France had changed so drastically that it could hardly be called Latin any more. Latin, after all, is characterised by a certain grammatical system which relies heavily on flexional endings. How could this system be maintained if the preservation of final unstressed syllables depended, not on grammar, but on mere accidents of phonetic distribution, and if the final unstressed syllable could contain no vowel other than [ə]? The written language of the period reflects very few of the changes I have just mentioned, and what is more, precisely at this time, tends to reflect the spoken language less and less. The written language of the sixth, seventh and early eighth centuries, thoroughly unclassical as we have seen, reflected *some* features of spoken Latin, but certainly did not keep abreast with phonological developments or with successive *de facto* phonetic situations. What is more, as I have hinted, precisely at the period when the French language was beginning to emerge, the Latin texts begin to tell us even less, except as regards vocabulary. The reason for this will be given later.

Particularly valuable from the point of view of the transformations which the vocabulary had undergone are the *Reichenau Glosses*, compiled at the end of the eighth century. This text consists of over 3000 items, Latin words and phrases which by that time it had been found necessary to explain for the benefit of people who, though literate, could no longer understand that kind of Latin. The glosses are the more interesting because many of the words and phrases listed and explained are themselves not classical, or are only incidentally classical, since they are taken from St Jerome's Vulgate of the end of the fourth century.[1] Usually a Latin word is explained in terms of another Latin word deemed to be more familiar to the reader, but we also quite often find Latin words explained by Latinised Germanic ones.

Here are some examples of the first kind, followed by F. or O.F. derivatives in parentheses: *semel* 'once', *una vice* (*une fois*); *binas* 'in twos', *duas et duas* (*deux à deux*); *opilio* 'shepherd', *custos ovium vel berbicarius* (*berger*); *in ore* 'in the mouth', *in bucca* (*bouche*); *caseum* 'cheese', *formaticum* (O.F. *formage*, Mod.F. *fromage*); *optimos* 'best', *meliores* (*meilleurs*); *uvas* 'grapes', *racemos* (*raisins*); *iecore* 'liver', *ficato* (*foie*); *novacula* 'razor', *rasorium* (*rasoir*); *hiems* 'winter', *ibernus* (*hiver*); *cecinit* 'he sang', *cantavit* (*il chanta*); *ostendit* 'he showed', *monstravit* (O.F. *mostra*, Mod.F. *il montra*).

The following are typical of the second category, where a Latin word or phrase is explained by a Germanic loan-word: *pignus* 'pledge', *wadius* (*gage*); *manipulos* 'sheaves': *garbas* (O.F. *jarbes*, Mod.F. *gerbes*); *turmas* 'bands', 'troops', *fulcos* (O.F. *folc*); *coturnices* 'quails', *quacoles* (*cailles*); *papilionis* 'tent', *travis* (O.F. *tref*); *ocreas* 'boots', 'leggings', *husas* (O.F. *huese*); *t[h]orax* 'breastplate', *brunia* (O.F. *broigne*); *artemon* 'mast of ship', *mastus navis* (*mât*); *castro* 'camp', *heribergo* (O.F. *herberge*); *galea* 'helmet', *helmus* (O.F. *heaume*); *non pepercit* 'did not spare', *non sparniavit* (O.F. *espargner*, Mod.Fr. *épargner*); *pincerna* 'butler', *scantio* (*échanson*); *ruga* 'wrinkle', *fruncetura* (O.F. *fronceüre*).

A form like *anoget*, glossing *tedet* (Cl.L. *taedet*) and deriving from *inodiare*, is of phonetic interest because *g* appears to be an attempt to render the palatalisation of [d] + [j] (cf. *iusu* from *deorsum* in the same text).

To explain why the written Latin of the end of the eighth century and early ninth was singularly unsuited to throw light on the major changes discussed earlier, it is necessary to mention the Carolingian reforms of the late eighth century. Charlemagne, by far the greatest and most enlightened of the later Carolingian kings, decreed that

1. It is obvious that many terms used in the fourth century merely continued classical usage, for there was nothing approaching a total divorce between the vocabulary of Classical Latin and that of Vulgar Latin. If there had been, it would be pointless to call them both Latin!

there should be schools of young clerks (*lectores*) in every monastery and in every bishop's house. As a result, the number of trained and literate priests increased very considerably. Great cathedral schools came into being in Rheims, Orleans and Metz, and the new Benedictine abbeys also became centres of scholarship and instruction. But Charles did not aim only to recruit better parish priests: he also wished to train administrators and civil servants, for the old anarchy was disappearing, society was being organised on a more stable basis, and the need for documents and records had become urgent. This, by the way, is the reason why we have much more evidence about the reign of Charlemagne and his successors than about the earlier period: more records were being kept, and fewer were being destroyed by fire and acts of violence. In his concern to make more widely known the heritage of the Ancient World, Charles also had classical works systematically copied and duplicated on vellum—a medium far more indestructible than papyrus. Indeed, many of the works of classical antiquity survived *only* on Carolingian vellum: the originals have since been lost, and we would not have known these works at all if it had not been for Charles' initiative in having them copied. Scholars specially invited from Ireland and England, where the classical tradition had been better preserved, also helped to raise the standard of Latinity. The reforms of Charlemagne had the effect of restoring much of the purity of Classical Latin in such matters as spelling and grammar, and this, from the point of view of anyone who seeks information about the spoken language of the day, is a doubtful blessing, for it means that the written documents tell us *even less* about the realities of everyday speech than they did before. The much purer Latin which followed upon the reforms was quite remote from the spoken language. That is why, in the early ninth century, matters came to a head: it was no longer possible to pretend that Latin was anyone's native language, and the existence of a vernacular which was truly different was officially recognised for the first time.

At the Council of Tours in 813—the year before Charlemagne's death—it was agreed by the French bishops that priests were to preach in the Romance or Germanic vernacular, called respectively the *rustica romana lingua* and the *theotisca lingua* 'so that all may understand what is said'. No compromise is possible henceforward: on the one hand we have a greatly improved and chastened Latin, written and spoken by a tiny literate minority, and on the other hand the new Romance vernacular spoken by the masses and understood— and probably spoken too—by the literate, and now at last given recognition as a fact of life, though enjoying little or no prestige. That, incidentally, is why there is still no written French for this early period. Those who could write at all had been trained to write in Latin, the language of tradition and prestige. The language they heard spoken around them and which they spoke themselves when appropriate, was the *rustica romana lingua* just referred to, at first not considered suitable for writing and, even after it was first written down, destined to be for centuries overshadowed by Latin. The very name *romana lingua* suggests that the learned men of the day were well aware that the spoken language was Latin of a sort, a kind of 'poor relation'—but it was at least a relation whose existence had to be recognised. By 813, the year when the term was used, we are certainly entitled to identify the *rustica romana lingua* with early O.F.

In the next chapter, which will take us to the end of the eleventh century, we shall examine the nature of this language in the light of the earliest vernacular texts.

2

THE LANGUAGE OF THE EARLIEST
FRENCH TEXTS

In 814, Louis the Pious succeeded Charlemagne as Emperor of the Franks. When Louis died in 840, his three sons, Charles the Bald, Louis the German and Lothair disputed the inheritance. Charles and Louis soon found it necessary to form an alliance against their brother Lothair, who actually had the strongest claim to the Empire as a whole. It was to cement this alliance that the two brothers and their followers took solemn oaths in Strasbourg on 14 February 842. The texts of these oaths have come down to us, for they are quoted, in the original *romana lingua* and *theotisca lingua*, in the middle of a Latin chronicle by Nithardus entitled *The History of the sons of Louis the Pious*. Nithardus was a contemporary of the events, but the manuscript (Bibliothèque nationale lat. 9768, fol. 13) belongs to the end of the tenth century. As it was important that each army should hear the form of words pronounced by the leader of the other in a language they could understand, Louis the German took the oath in Romance, while Charles the Bald, normally Romance-speaking, pronounced the German version of the oath. After the leaders had each taken the oath, their followers also took a different oath, each in his own language, and we are given the text of this too, in Romance and in German.

The Romance text of the Strasbourg Oaths is the earliest document in the French language. If it comes as a surprise, being so conspicuously different from any kind of Latin which preceded it, this is essentially because the writers of even the most corrupt Latin texts were, to the best of their ability, *resisting* the vernacular. In setting down the text of the Oaths, Nithardus was, as it were, consciously surrendering to the vernacular, for a particular purpose: he was quite deliberately *not* writing Latin. Even so, it must be said that the text is in some ways disappointing. It is very short; it is also formulaic, i.e. repetitive, with the result that its vocabulary is very limited; it is visibly influenced by Latin spelling and even vocabulary and, though it reflects adequately some of the phonetic changes which had taken place, it fails completely to reflect many others. Its brevity at least allows me to quote it in full, with a translation. I have marked the stresses with an acute accent.

(*Louis*) 'Pro Déo amúr et pro christián póblo et nóstro commún salvamént, d'ist di in avánt, in quant Déus savír et podír me dúnat, si salvarái éo cist méon frádre Kárlo et in ajúdha et in cadhúna cósa, si cum om per dreit son frádra salvár dift, in o quid il mi altresí fázet, et ab Ludhér nul plaid númquam prindrái qui, méon vol, cist méon frádre Kárle in dámno sit.'

(*Followers of Charles the Bald*) 'Si Lodhuvígs sagramént, que son frádre Kárlo jurát, consérvat, et Kárlus méos séndra de súo part non lo·s tánit, si ió returnár non l'int pois, ne ió ne neúls cui éo returnár int pois, in núlla ajúdha cóntra Lodhuwíg nun li iv er.'

['For the love of God, and for the salvation of the Christian people and for our common salvation, from this day forward, in so far as God gives me knowledge and power, I will help this my brother Charles both in aid and in every thing, as one ought by right to help one's brother, on condition that he does the same for me, and I will never undertake any agreement with Lothair which, by my consent, might be of harm to this my brother Charles.'

'If Louis keeps the oath which he swore to his brother Charles, and Charles my lord, for his part, does not keep it, if I cannot deter him from it, neither I nor anyone whom I can deter from it, will be of any assistance to him against Louis.']

For all its inadequacies, this text can be demonstrated to be far closer to O.F. as it subsequently manifested itself, than to any sort of Latin. Even the apparently Latin words *pro*, *Déus*, *quid*, *númquam*, *consérvat*, *in dámno sit* are reconcilable with a truly vernacular pronunciation. An important feature to note is the regular loss of Latin final unstressed syllables in *amúr*, *christián*, *commún*, *salvamént*, *ist*, *di*, *avánt*, *quant*, *savír*, *podír*, *om*, *dreit*, etc. The—equally regular—preservation of final unstressed syllables is however to be noted in the following cases:

(1) Continuing Latin [-a] as neutral [ə] (normally written -*a* in this text, but note *súo* < *súa*): *ajúdha*, *cadhúna*, *cósa*, *consérvat*, *dúnat*, *númquam*.

(2) Supporting a group of consonants which could not otherwise be articulated: *nóstro*, *frádra*, *frádre*, *séndra* (< *sénior*), *Kárle*, *Kárlo*, *póblo* (note hesitation as between *a*, *o*, *e*, to represent the *same* neutral vowel [ə]). *Kárlo* (< *Cárolum*), *póblo* (< *pópuli*) also represent the typical reduction of a proparoxyton to a paroxyton.

(3) In hiatus with preceding stressed vowel: *Déo*, *Déus*.

Disappointingly, diphthongs are only sporadically noted as such: *dreit, plait, pois*; and there is much confusion in the scribe's application of the letters *e, i*. Etymologically, he is of course right to use *i* in *ist, in, cist* (< *isto, in, ecce-istum*), but phonetically the words were certainly [ɛst] [ɛn] [tsɛst]. As for *prindrái, savír* and *podír*, we must read them as *prendrái, savér* and *podér*, with the letter *é* in the last two standing for the diphthong [ei]. The change of intervocalic [-p-] to [-v-] is clearly indicated in *savír* (< **sapére*); but the change of intervocalic [-t-] to the voiced dental fricative [ð] is not so clearly indicated by the spelling *podír* (< **potére*), though the same sound is ingeniously noted as *dh* in *cadhúna, ajúdha, Lodhuvígs*.

As for *dúnat, jurát* and *consérvat*, we have here another imperfection of the system, since the letter *a* in a final syllable could represent either a stressed [a] or the neutral [ə]. The interpretation of *jurat* as *jurát* (preterite, from *juravit*) is based on the evidence of the German version of the oath. The subjunctive form *fázet* [fatsət] < *faciat* represents a quite successful attempt to reflect in writing the change of [kj] to [ts].

The more synthetic nature of Latin is still apparent in the use of vestigial 'cases' without prepositions. Phonetic changes had made it impossible to distinguish *formally* more than two cases in substantives: on the one hand a nominative or subject-case, and on the other an oblique case which, with or without prepositions, did duty for the other cases of Cl.L.

Nominative: Only masculine forms are attested: *Déus; om* (< *hómo*); *Lodhuvígs* (< *Hlodovícus*); *Kárlus* (< *Cárolus*); *méos* (< *méus*); *séndra* (< *sénior*); *neúls* (< *nec-úllus*).

Oblique: *Déo* (m.); *amúr* (f.); *póblo* (m.); *salvamént* (m.); *di* (m.); *ajúdha* (f.); *cósa* (f.); *dreit* (m.); *frádra* (m.); *Ludhér; plaid* (m.); *vol* (m.); *dámno* (m.); *sagramént* (m.); *Kárlo; part* (f.); *Lodhuwíg*. The various functions of the oblique form can be clearly seen:

(1) After prepositions: *pro . . . amúr; d'ist di; in ajúdha; per dreit; ab Ludhér; de súo part*.

(2) Absolute: *méon vol* 'by my will', 'by my consent'.

(3) Possessive: *(pro) Déo (amúr); (pro) christián póblo (salvamént)*.

(4) Dative: *(que) son frádre Kárlo (jurát)* '(which he swore) *to* his brother Charles.'

The word-order shows a strong tendency to throw the verb to the end of the clause; this had been a Latin tendency too, but it is strikingly confirmed by the word-order of the German text. The order *pro Déo amúr* is also paralleled in both Latin and Germanic. Another feature worth noting is the wide use made of subject pronouns. This is certainly not a characteristic of Cl.L., but it is attested in Late Latin. Curiously enough, even in later O.F., subject pronouns are used somewhat more sparingly than they are in this particular text. The impersonal use of *om* 'a man' in the sense of 'one' appears to be a 'native' development of a spontaneous Late Latin use of *homo* in a general sense: the influence of Germanic here has been postulated but is impossible to prove. At all events *om* anticipates the medieval and modern uses of the indefinite pronoun *on* which, true to its origins, can be used only as a *subject* pronoun. A new synthetic future tense, formed from the infinitive plus the contracted forms of *habere* (found in Late Latin, though without the contractions) is attested by the forms *salvarái* and *prindrái*, though *er* (< *ero*) continues the traditional Latin future.

The text of the Strasbourg Oaths, and the circumstances in which the oaths were sworn, will serve to remind us of the troubled state of France at the time. Before we look at the other, later vernacular texts, we should briefly survey the major political events and changes in the social structure from the ninth to the end of the eleventh century, taking note as we go along of their relevance to the cultural life of the period.

Around the time of the Strasbourg Oaths, unrest in France was due not only to conflict between the three rulers of the former Frankish Empire; it was due also to private wars between rival local rulers, to widespread brigandage and to the increasing threat from the Norsemen. It was in fact precisely because there was so much internal unrest in France that the Norsemen, who had begun by merely attacking shipping in the English Channel, were soon able to raid the northern and north-eastern coasts in depth, with comparative impunity. Their first raids began in 838, but from about 850 onwards they set up, at the mouths of the Seine, the Loire and the Somme, more or less permanent camps which enabled them to go far into the interior by sailing up the rivers, and Paris itself was thus several times threatened by Viking raiders; indeed, the island city was besieged by them from November 885 to September 886, and this only four years after their defeat at the hands of Louis III, whose victory over them at Saucourt was commemorated in 881 in a German poem, the *Ludwigslied* and, much later, in the O.F. epic *Gormont et Isembart*. In the north of France, the normal processes of agriculture and harvest were often grievously interrupted, and severe famine was by no means rare. The area of north-west France (then known as Neustria) which suffered most and which was occupied by Vikings in large numbers was eventually ceded to them in 911 by Charles the Simple and took, from the Norsemen, its present name Normandy. Rollo, the first Duke, became a Christian and the Normans, within a few generations, had forgotten their Norse and learned French, though not without carrying over into French a number of terms of Norse origin, terms which for the most part reflected their skill and experience as a sea-faring people.

The remainder of the tenth century is the story of a series of weak kings who had no firm territorial basis for their power, but who, though often—even normally—at loggerheads with powerful vassals, at least usually had the support of the Church. The feudal system, essentially a Carolingian phenomenon, did not make for political unity, nor for a common culture. France was split up into local spheres of jurisdiction. If there was any bond which was generally recognised, it was the bond between vassal and overlord. This made for some measure of stability, it is true, but only within a narrow domain, for there was no corresponding bond between vassal and vassal, or overlord and overlord. The great flaw in the system, as the historian C. H. Haskins has shown, was that the feudal ties were only vertical and not lateral. Vassals had certain obligations to their overlord, as he had to them (though the late Carolingian kings were seldom able to fulfil them), but vassals had no obligations to each other, and they both could and did carry on private wars, or open brigandage, to the exclusion of any wider feeling of unity, let alone national awareness. Communities tended to be purely local in orientation, largely or even wholly self-sufficient in their economy. Communications were extremely poor; the Roman roads had fallen into decay and were infested with bandits. There was no real capital: the Carolingian kings were peripatetic and resided in different places according to the time of year or the strategic needs of the moment. Natural boundaries like mountains and rivers counted for a great deal, and the regions formed by them had centres of their own, but there was no general centre or focal point in France as a whole. In these conditions it is not surprising that different dialects of early Romance should have developed, sometimes shading off into each other quite gradually, sometimes changing quite abruptly where there was a major natural barrier. The major dialect division, however, as has already been said, was between the northern dialects and the southern ones. We may use the convenient terms *langue d'oïl* and *langue d'oc* to distinguish these groups of dialects, so long as it is understood that though the broad distinction existed from an early date, the terms themselves are not attested until the end of the thirteenth century. They are in any case 'blanket' terms, for there was considerable variety within each group, and they also imply a division which was by no means absolute.[1]

1. Poitevin, which shows close affinity with Occitan up to and including the tenth century, can by the twelfth century be considered essentially a dialect of the *langue d'oïl*.

The political situation changed for the better in 987 when the Assembly of Senlis, eliminating the rightful Carolingian heir, elected Hugh Capet, hitherto Duke of Île-de-France, as King of France (987–96). The early Capetian kings were not much stronger as kings than Hugh Capet had been as Duke: many of their vassals, men like the Duke of Normandy, or the Counts of Blois, of Artois, of Flanders, or of Champagne, were more powerful than the kings were. The kings ruled *directly* only in their own lands, that is to say, only in a very small part of the total territory of France. They had no effective authority in remote regions such as Brittany, Gascony, Toulouse, or Aquitaine. They enjoyed however the support of one extremely powerful institution, the only stable one in France—the Church. The Church had elected Hugh Capet and his successors, and, having the strength of its convictions, maintained them in power and even protected them from their more powerful and unruly vassals. They would not have been able to administer justice outside their own lands—obviously a serious handicap—if the Church had not enabled them to do so. The Church did all it could to stress the sacrosanct nature of kingship, and helped to establish law and order by declarations and manifestations which it was able, at least to some extent, to enforce, if not by threat of anathema, then by the use of its own militia, which it levied from time to time and could place at the king's disposal in a just cause. Such measures as the *Pax Dei* ('Peace of God', 989) and the *Treuga Dei* ('Truce of God', 1027) helped to curb violence and private wars. King and clergy supported each other mutually and gained considerably in strength and prestige. Through undertaking the protection of the oppressed, the king gained the reputation of a righter of wrongs who could be appealed to as to a higher court of justice. Economically, too, the Church was not without its importance, because such commerce as there was, was largely organised by the great monasteries of the age, which were responsible for a good deal of the movement of commodities from one region to another. The monasteries were patronised by the king, who was titular abbot of St-Denis, St Martin de Tours, and St-Germain-des-Prés. Indeed, St-Denis soon became the spiritual centre of the kingdom. Even so, by the end of the eleventh century, France was far from being united under direct rule from Paris. All that can be said is that by this time Paris was definitely the capital. Conditions were at least somewhat more stable than they had been, and learning began to flourish in the great monasteries and in such cities as Chartres, Rheims and Orleans. The careful cultivation of Latin letters was firmly established well before the twelfth century. Finer churches were built, of stone instead of timber. Trade and travel increased. The Normans, in particular, opened up new possibilities outside France, in England (1066–), in the south of Italy, in Sicily, and even in the Levant. There was a vigorous western reaction to the capture of Jerusalem by the Seljuk Turks: in response to the appeal of Pope Urban II, himself of French descent, at Clermont on 26 November 1095, the French embarked upon the first Crusade and captured first Antioch (1098), then Jerusalem (1099).

Now it is time to give some attention to those few vernacular texts which have survived from the time of the Strasbourg Oaths to the end of the eleventh century. It is possible that others were written but did not survive: it is not likely that they were numerous. In the context of the other vernacular texts, the Oaths are exceptional in that they are secular, and in prose. The others are religious in inspiration and, with one minor exception, in verse. Like the Strasbourg Oaths, however, they are closely associated with Latin, not only in the readiness with which they reproduce Latin words virtually unchanged, but also physically, in that they tend to occur in manuscripts which *also* contain Latin texts. We are reminded that French was considered a suitable *written* medium only for works of popular edification and instruction: anyone who could read, could read Latin, and the French texts were composed to be read aloud to the illiterate, or to be learned by heart and subsequently recited to them.

Apart from the Strasbourg Oaths, the only other text to survive from the ninth century is the *Sequence of Saint Eulalia*, a poem of 29 lines relating the martyrdom of a fourth-century saint. It was composed *c.* 880 in Saint-Amand-les-Eaux, to the north of Valenciennes. It is sandwiched between a Latin poem on the same subject and a German one (see above, p. 32) about the victory of Louis III over the Vikings at Saucourt in 881. Though short, the French Sequence is linguistically more illuminating than the Oaths. It has greater syntactical variety, and though some words still appear in a completely Latin form (e.g. *anima, rex, Christus, clementia*) its spelling in general throws a good deal of light on the phonetic state of the language. If it still hesitates over the notation of neutral [ə] (written indifferently with *a* or with *e*, as in *anima, pulcella* but *figure, cose, polle, domnizelle*), on the other hand it clearly and consistently indicates diphthongisation, thereby marking a considerable advance on the crude system of notation used in this respect by the scribe of the Strasbourg Oaths; hence: *buona* < *bóna*; *ruovet* < *rógat*; *bellezour* < *bellatiórem*; *soure* < *súpra*; *ciel* < *célum* (Cl. *caelum*); *maent* < *mánet*; *tuit* < * *totti*.

The two-case system is better illustrated than in the earlier text, which contained no examples of the nominative masculine plural (Eulalia: *inimi* 'enemies'); the oblique masc.pl. (Eulalia: *pagiens* 'heathen'; *dis* 'days'; *empedemenz* 'torture(s)'); the nominative feminine singular (Eulalia: *pulcella* 'maiden'; *cose* 'thing'; *polle* 'girl'), or the oblique feminine plural (Eulalia: *colpes* 'guilt'). The scribe shows some ingenuity in his phonetic notation. Thus, although he somewhat economically attributes the same phonetic value [ts] to *c* before [e] or [i], to *z* in some positions and to *tc* before [ə] (as in *cels, ciel, pulcella, mercit, enz,* and *manatce* < *minacia*), he realises that the word which he pronounced [tso] could not properly be rendered by *co*, because in his system *c* before *o* has the value [k] (as in *cose*). He therefore combines *c* and *z* to form a digraph *cz*, and writes *czo* for the sounds [ts] + [o] (< *ecce-hoc*). Where the sound [k] was followed by [i] or [e], he realised that *c* would not do, because in that position, according to his system, *c* had the value [ts]: he therefore 'blocks' *c* by placing an *h* after it, thus *chi* [ki], *chieef* [kieef], *chielt* [kiɛlt].

A conspicuous feature of the morphology and syntax of this text is the occurrence of no fewer than six verb-forms which derive from the Latin synthetic pluperfect indicative. The forms are used, however, as simple preterites: *auret* (< *habuerat*); *furet* (< *fuerat*); *pouret* (< *potuerat*), etc. The *function* of the pluperfect had been taken over by a new Romance compound tense, and since the Latin preterite had been maintained in the vernacular, the use of the synthetic pluperfect as a preterite was something of a luxury, and it is not altogether surprising that we seldom find it after the Eulalia Sequence, and for the last time in the middle of the eleventh century (*firet* < *fecerat* in the *Life of Saint Alexis*). The moment has not yet come for a general discussion of the question of dialect versus standard O.F.—or of whether there was such a thing as standard O.F.—but it may be noted here that such forms as *diaule* ('devil'), *seule* ('world') and *raneiet* ('denies', 'abjures') are characteristic of the Picard-Walloon area. The conditional *sostendreiet* and the preterite (or pluperfect) *voldret, voldrent,* on the other hand, with their glide-consonant [-d-], are not.

Three texts are available from the tenth century, The *Jonah Fragment*, like the *Eulalia Sequence*, was composed in Saint-Amand-les-Eaux. It consists of notes, partly in Latin and partly in French, of a sermon based on Jonah, chapters i and iv. It provides some scraps of evidence about the verbal system: it attests, for instance, the 'eastern' imperfect ending of the first conjugation, *-evet* from *-abat*. Apart from that, it is chiefly important for extremely rare verbs, e.g. *entelgir* 'to understand' (< *intellegere*), found only in this context; *pentir* 'to repent', used as an impersonal verb; and the uncommon verbs *delir* 'to destroy' (< *delere*) and *comburir* 'to burn'.

The other two texts, the *Clermont Passion* of 516 octosyllables and the *Life of St Leger* of 240 octosyllables, were copied into the spaces left in a tenth-century Latin glossary preserved in Clermont-Ferrand. Both are at first sight a disconcerting mixture of French and Occitan. On closer inspection it is clear that they were originally composed in French but subsequently copied by a Provençal scribe who substituted southern forms for northern ones, though by no means consistently. The result is that some lines read exactly like the O.F. of a slightly later period, some have so marked a southern flavour that they could almost be read as Occitan (except for the assonances, which could not be Occitan) while a few lines could be read as either French or Occitan. In both texts, the style is somewhat abrupt and jerky. Once again we find imperfects in *-eve(n)t* (Passion: *aeswardevet*; St Leger: *regnevet*), suggesting the Picard-Walloon area, yet we also find the 'western' imperfect in *-ouet* which is incompatible with the other forms, and *vindrent* which with its glide-consonant, is alien to Picard-Walloon. There is hesitation between initial *ca-* and initial *che-* or *cha-*: *cadegrent*, but *chedent* (both from *cadere*); *cab* and *caritad* but *chamise*. If *ch* 'means what it says' (which is not certain) then it corresponds to a pronunciation which is neither that of the south nor that of the Picard-Walloon area, where [k] + [a] remained intact as in Occitan. It is interesting to see the Romance word *jorn* (< *diurnum*) used side by side with the older *di*: in the earlier texts only *di* is found. *Don* 'lord' (< *dóminus*) used as a noun in its own right, is at variance with later recorded French usage, where this word could be used only as a title to be followed by a person's name or by his rank. Once again we find pluperfect forms used with the function of preterites; Passion: *vidra* (< *viderat*), St Leger: *auuret* (< *habuerat*).

There remain only two texts which it is convenient to regard as 'early O.F.'. The first is *The Life of Saint Alexis*, a poem of 625 deca-syllables arranged in five-line stanzas having a common assonance. It was composed c. 1040–50, probably in Normandy, but the best and oldest manuscript, the Hildesheim MS, was copied about a hundred years later, and copied moreover in England by an Anglo-Norman scribe, with the result that one has quite frequently to seek for continental forms behind insular graphies. Its theme of a single-minded, not to say self-centred asceticism which causes considerable suffering to others, is not to our taste today, but we are at least free from the limping laconism of the earlier texts: the pace is leisurely, there is a wealth of detail, and the range of construction and vocabu-lary, and the large sections of direct speech, are invaluable for an assessment of the achievements of the French language by the middle of the eleventh century. French is now fully formed and rich in potential: it has largely broken away from Latin, though ever ready to fill gaps in its vocabulary—particularly the more abstract vocabulary—by recourse to the learned tongue. Germanic roots have been completely assimilated to the system: verbs like *enhadir* 'to conceive hatred for', *esguarder* 'to look at'; or a participle like *esmariz* 'distressed', combine Germanic roots with Romance prefixes and Romance terminations; just as a substantive like *marrement* 'grief' or an adjective like *besuinos* 'needy' combine a Germanic root with French terminations which had evolved spontaneously from Latin *-mentum* and *-osus* respectively. Here is a short extract from the text. Alexis, who had many years before left his wife and his parents behind in Rome, was on his way from Laodicia to Tarsus when to his dismay contrary winds forced him to land near Rome:

> 'E! Deus', dist il, 'bels reis qui tot governes,
> se tei plöust, ici ne volsisse estre.
> s'or me conoissent mi parent d'este terre,
> il me prendront par pri o par podéste:
> se jo.s en creit, il me trairont a perte.
>
> E neporuec mes pedre me desidret,
> si fait ma medre plus que femme qui vivet,
> avuec ma spouse que jo lour ai guerpide.
> or ne lairai, ne.m mete en lor baillie:
> ne.m conoistront, tanz jorz at que ne.m vidrent!'

['Oh God!' he said, 'good King who reignest over all things, if it were pleasing to Thee, I would not wish to be here. If now my kinsfolk in this land recognise me, they will seize me, by prayer or by force: if I believe them (i.e. allow myself to be persuaded), they will lead me to perdition. And yet my father misses me, so does my mother, more than any woman alive, together with my wife whom I left with them. Now I shall not fail to place myself in their keeping. They will not recognise me, it is so long since they saw me!']

Two phonetic features call for comment. Intervocalic [-d-] (sometimes written *th* by the Anglo-Norman scribe) had reached the phonetic stage [ð] prior to disappearing altogether. When followed by [r] too, as in *vidrent, fredre, pedre, medre,* [ð] < d, t was but weakly articulated, and was soon to fall. Other phonetic features will be discussed in retrospect, in connection with the *Song of Roland*. With the latter text, we come to a literary masterpiece which at the same time, as a linguistic document, carries us another fifty years further forward in the evolution of the French language, for, though it cannot be *proved* to have been inspired by the First Crusade, the preoccupations it reveals, and the spirit it breathes, are compatible with the supposition that it was. The poem shows both Norman and Central features, and is best preserved in an Anglo-Norman manuscript copied *c.* 1150 (Bodleian, MS Digby 23). It consists of 4002

decasyllables grouped in 298 *laisses* or stanzas of varying length, each
stanza having a uniform assonance. Though it certainly has many
points of contact with both the Latin and the vernacular hagiographic
texts which preceded it, it is essentially a national epic, a stirring tale
of heroism and treachery, of human strength and weakness, of the
terrible struggle between Christianity, represented by France, and
Heathendom. Although France was anything but politically united
at the end of the eleventh century, the anonymous poet idealistically
takes for granted a considerable measure of unity, and seems to
argue for a sinking of differences in the fulfilment of a national and
religious ideal. Significantly, contingents and heroes from all over
France, including Brittany, Aquitaine, Auvergne and Provence, are
referred to collectively as *Franceis*. As we shall see, this use of
François is reflected, in later texts, in the equally idealistic use of
françois with reference to the *language*—well in advance of anything
resembling 'standard French'.

A short extract will give some idea of the nature of the language
of the poem: it should however be borne in mind that the spelling
is Anglo-Norman, hence *u* for *o* in *mult, sunt, gunfanuns, dublez, tuz,
-um* for *-ons* (*purum*), and *e* for *ie* in *acer, destrers*, etc.

> Paien s'adubent des osbercs sarazineis,
> Tuit li plusur en sunt dublez en treis,
> Lacent lor elmes mult bons sarraguzeis,
> Ceignent espees de l'acer vianeis,
> Escuz unt genz, espiez valentineis
> E gunfanuns blancs e blois e vermeilz;
> Laissent les muls e tuz les palefreiz,
> Es destrers muntent, si chevalchent estreiz.
> Clers fut li jurz e bels fut li soleilz,
> N'unt guarnement que tut ne reflambeit,
> Sunent mil grailles por ço que plus bel seit;
> Granz est la noise, si l'oïrent Franceis.
> Dist Oliver: 'Sire cumpainz, ce crei,
> De Sarrazins purum bataille aveir.'
> Respont Rollant: 'E Deus la nus otreit!
> Ben devuns ci estre pur nostre rei:
> Pur sun seignor deit hom susfrir destreiz
> E endurer e granz chalz e granz freiz,
> Si.n deit hom perdre e del quir e del peil.
> Or guart chascuns que granz colps i empleit,
> Que malvaise cançun de nus chantét ne seit!
> Paien unt tort e chrestïens unt dreit;
> Malvaise essample n'en serat ja de mei.' (ll. 994–1016)

[The heathen equip themselves with Saracen hauberks: / Most of these
are lined with triple mail; / They lace on their stout Sarragossan helmets, /

They gird on swords of steel from Viana; / They have fine shields, and spears from Valence, / And pennons white and blue and red; / They abandon their mules and their palfreys; / They mount their war-horses, and ride in serried ranks. / Bright was the day and fair was the sun, / They have no equipment that is not ablaze with light, / They sound a thousand bugles, to make a finer show. / Great is the noise, and the French heard it. / Oliver said: 'Sir companion, this I believe, / We may do battle with the Saracens.' / Roland answers: 'May God grant it to us! / Here we must stand for our king: / For his lord's sake, a man must suffer hardship / And bear both great heat and great cold, / And also lose both skin and hair. / Now let each man look to laying on great blows, / Let no shameful song be sung about us! / The heathen are wrong and the Christians are right; / No bad example shall ever come from me.']

The extract contains several Germanic loan-words: *s'aduber*; *osbercs; elmes*; *espiez*; *gunfanuns*; *blancs*; *blois*; *guarnement*; *guarder*. Subject pronouns are omitted. Note the borderline use of the indefinite *hom*, as well as its etymological spelling. Both the definite and the partitive articles are used, but it will be noticed that they can also be omitted, particularly before plural substantives. The lines tend to be syntactically self-sufficient: coordination of clauses is left largely to the imagination, and subordinate clauses tend to be minimally brief, so that they do not transcend the line. *Que malvaise cançun* etc may be an independent clause, or it may continue and complete the subordinate clause in the previous line. Some other points may be noted. The two-case system is in the main well observed, but shows some signs of its early decline in Anglo-Norman (*Oliver*, nominative singular, has no flexional *s*; and *chrestïens*, nominative plural, has a superfluous *s*, while *cumpainz* should have no flexion). For practical purposes, *sire* (< **séior*), nominative and vocative, is the subject form of *seignor* (< *seniórem*). The possessive *lor*, in *lor elmes*, derives from *illorum*: only later did it take *s* before a plural complement. *La nus otreit*, with the direct object pronoun occurring before the indirect, already emerges as normal O. and Mid.F. usage. To judge from *guarnement* and *guarder*, the development of Germanic initial [w] to [g] was not yet complete: the scribe of the *Roland*, like the scribe of the *Life of Saint Alexis*, seems to be representing the stage [gw].

Elsewhere in the poem, we find that the weak fricative [ð] so well preserved in the *Life of Saint Alexis* in words like *pedre, fredre, medre, emperedre*, has been dropped from the spelling, while the occasional suggestion of intervocalic [-ð-] (l. 272 *sedeir*, 2829 *sedant*, 270 & 1992 *vedeir*, 98 *cadables*) is a mere orthographic relic, as is shown by a predominance of forms without *d*. It is interesting to note that up to and including the *Life of Saint Alexis*, the prothetic [ɛ] before [s] + consonant, attested in V.L. in forms like *isperare* (< *sperare*), is not yet a fixture, but is used only when the preceding word ends in a consonant, e.g., Eulalia: *une spede* 'a sword'; Alexis: *sa spede, ta spouse*, but *ad escole*. By the time of the *Song of Roland*, however, *e-* occurs regularly, irrespective of phonetic circumstances, and the final vowel of a preceding word (normally [-ə], but [-a] in the feminine definite article and possessive) is simply elided, as before any other vowel.

An interesting morphological and semantic feature of the *Roland* is that it contains survivals of the Latin neuter plural, still with plural meaning. The normal development was for neuter plurals in *-a* to become feminine singular in form and singular in meaning, but in *la brace* (< *bracchia*) 'both arms', 'two arms', we have a feminine singular, and in *milie* 'thousands' (< *milia*), *carre* 'carts' (< *carra*), and *deie* 'fingers' (< *digita*) we have invariable forms, plural in meaning, and apparently masculine.

In general, we may observe that since the Strasbourg Oaths, the syntax of the early vernacular texts has moved progressively away from Latin. Latin letters continue to loom large as inspiration and as background, and Latin continues to have a considerable influence on the vocabulary, though less and less on the spelling. Syntactically, however, the texts go their own way.

A by no means uncommon feature of all these early texts is the adaptation of learned Latin words to the minimal requirements of the vernacular, e.g., *virginitét, figure, clementia* (probably pronounced [klementsə] in the *Eulalia Sequence*; *custodes* 'guards', *caritad* 'charity' in the *Passion*; *gladies* 'swords' and *exercite* 'army' in *Saint Leger*; *unanime, encredulitét* and *duretie* (< *duritia*: the later, popular, O.F. form is *durté*) in the *Jonah Fragment*; *nobilitét* and *umilitét* in the *Life of Saint Alexis*; and *antiquitét, sinagoge, tenebres, humilitét* (note the *h*!) in the *Song of Roland*. Sometimes the learned adaptation of a word into French proved unacceptable in the long run, and further modifications had to be made. This is particularly conspicuous in the treatment of words which in Latin were pro-paroxytons, e.g. *imáginem, vírginem, ángelus*. This phonetic pattern was regularly reduced in words of popular origin, e.g., *póblo* (< *pópuli*) in the *Strasbourg Oaths* and *veintre* (< *víncere*) in the *Eulalia Sequence*. Nevertheless *ánima*, occurring in the latter poem, is confirmed by the metre as having three syllables. Later, however, in the *Life of Saint Alexis*, we find the words *imágine, ángele, vírgene* occurring in consecutive lines (ll. 87–9) in metrical circumstances which make it clear that there was only *one* syllable after the stress, and the same applies to the word *áneme* in l. 332. Thereafter, we normally find these words in the form *image, ange, vi(e)rge, anme, ame.*[1]

Other words reveal by their form an uneasy compromise between the popular and the learned. We have seen that *schola* became *escole*, that is to say, was affected by two regular phonetic changes, the development of prothetic [ε] before initial [s] + consonant, and the weakening of final unstressed [a] to [ə]. Yet this word resisted, through learned pronunciation, the normal diphthongisation of tonic free [ɔ] to [uə], later [uε]: it was, after all, *the* learned word *par excellence. Siecle,* attested in the *Life of Saint Alexis,* is another case in point. It looks superficially like a 'normal' reduction of a Latin proparoxyton [sεk(u)lu] (< Cl.L. *saeculum*), to a paroxyton, but actually, the regular development for this word would have been **sieil* (cf. *vieil* < [*vεk(u)lu]). The diphthongisation of [ε] to [iε] took place, but in other respects the word was influenced by and, as it were, restrained by the continued existence of the Latin word, much used in religious contexts. Latin *male* (adv.) and *malum* (adj. and subst.) should both have given *mel* in O.F. The form *mel* is in fact well attested, but it is from the beginning much less common than *mal*—again, one supposes, because of the association with *malum* in ecclesiastical writings.

On the surface, the texts we have examined so far suggest a startling lack of standardisation. To take a particularly glaring example, the V.L. word *capum* (Cl.L. *caput* 'head') appears in the *Eulalia Sequence* as *chieef* (*ch* = [k]); in the *Jonah Fragment* as *cheve*; in the *Passion* as *cab* (almost, but not quite, an Occitan form); in *Saint Leger* as *quev* and *cap*, the latter an Occitan form; and in *Saint Alexis* and *Roland* as *chef,* an Anglo-Norman spelling for *chief.* One could believe that such differences spring from a number of quite independent and unconnected attempts to write down the vernacular, using the limited resources of the only alphabet available, the Latin one. Yet the reflexes of *capum* constitute an extreme case, and behind the vagaries of southern scribes we can discern important features which confirm and are confirmed by those early texts which were *not* copied by southern scribes, and even more by later texts, when evidence becomes more plentiful. The language of the Strasbourg Oaths

1. In *Roland* 1. 3268, *ymágine* has only three syllables, and in 11. 2619, 3664, *ýdeles* has only two. It should be added that the pronunciation of Latin later came to be modelled on that of the vernacular, which had no proparoxytons. That is why learned words borrowed in the thirteenth and fourteenth centuries from what had once been proparoxytons, presuppose a paroxytonic source. It is not *frágilis, sólidus, útilis,* but *fragílis, solídus, utílis* which account for *fragile, solide, utile.* O.F. *fraile* (Mod. *frêle*), however, goes back to the original proparoxyton *frágilis.* Note also early O.F. *útele,* later replaced by *utile,* and *áb(e)le,* later replaced by *(h)abile.*

is northern, but it cannot be more precisely localised than that.[1] With that exception, however, the ninth and tenth century texts suggest as their place of composition the north-east of France, the Picard-Walloon area, close to the linguistic frontier between 'Romania' and 'Germania'. Even so, we find in them features which appear to be incompatible with that area: thus, in the *Eulalia Sequence*, *sosten-dreiet* and *voldrent* with their glide-consonant [-d-] are not Picard-Walloon forms, and if the *Passion* contains the typical north-eastern first conjugation imperfect in *-evet*, it also contains the corresponding western form *-ouet*, while all the texts contain 'neutral' forms which, to judge from later evidence, were common to more than one area of northern France. With the *Life of Saint Alexis* and the *Song of Roland*, there is a significant shift of emphasis away from the north-east. Both texts, it is true, were copied by Anglo-Norman scribes, but the first seems to have been originally composed in Normandy, and the second either in Normandy or in Île-de-France. The one is more archaic than the other, and there are Norman features in both, but neither is consistently written in a Norman dialect. In so far as the language is *not* Norman, and in so far as the language of the earlier texts is *not* Picard-Walloon, what are we to call it? What do the complex linguistic facts suggest? It is not too soon to ask these questions, but a little premature to attempt an answer to them until we have seen more evidence, of a kind to be found in the next chapter.

In the meantime, we may also note the clear emergence, in the south, of Occitan texts which pose the same sort of problem for the south as the texts we have just been considering pose for the north—the problem of variety versus common features. The earliest Occitan texts at least deserve a brief mention here: *Boecis* ('Boethius'), a poem of 257 decasyllables, belonging to the early eleventh century, and the *Life of Saint Foi of Agen*, which probably belongs to the middle of the same century. Occitan, both as a spoken and as a written language, was a potential rival to French. On the other hand, French had by this time survived the demise of two other rivals, German, which had virtually ceased to be spoken on French terri-tory by the end of the tenth century (Hugh Capet was the first French king who did not understand it), and Norse, which had ceased to be spoken in Normandy by the early eleventh century. In the extreme north-west, west of a line running roughly from Mont-Saint-Michel to the mouth of the Loire, Breton was universal in the tenth century. In that same century, however, the Breton kingdom fell and there-after the region was to be subjected to a strong Norman and Anglo-

1. The fact that the Oaths were sworn in Strasbourg is, of course, immaterial. Strasbourg lay in a German-speaking area at the time.

Norman (i.e. French) influence. Within two hundred years, the border between French and Breton had been pushed appreciably further west (see map, p. 48).

The principal additions to the French vocabulary during the period 842–1100 derived from Latin, whether they were learned words minimally adapted to French while remaining the same part of speech, or new formations from Latin roots, created by affixation. Frankish words already in the language, like Latin ones, were liable to give rise to new derivatives, and there were also some late borrowings from Frankish. The Norse element in French has not yet been dealt with: it is limited in range, but none the less important. By no means all the original borrowings from Norse have survived, and some were from the beginning confined to the dialect of Normandy, where such place-names as Bec ('stream'), Caudebec ('cold stream') and Trouville (< *Torolf-villa*), as well as such family names as Anquetil (< *Ansketell*) and Burnouf (< *Bjoernwulf*) recall Scandinavian settlements and settlers. Most of the words which passed into the standard language concern seafaring: *la vague* 'wave'; *la crique* 'creek'; *le tillac* 'deck'; *la hune* 'top'; *le hauban* 'shroud'; *la carlingue* 'keelson'; *l'étrave* 'stem-post'; *l'étambot* 'stern-post'; *le tolet* 'thole-pin'; *le guindas* 'windlass'; *les agrès* 'tackle', 'rigging'; *le turbot* 'turbot'; *le marsouin* 'porpoise'; the verbs *équiper*, originally 'to embark', then 'to make the ship ready'; *guinder* 'to hoist'; *cingler* 'to sail before the wind'. *Le havre* 'haven' (also a place-name) and *la girouette* 'weather-vane' are also of relevance to the fisherman and to the sailor. Other terms of Scandinavian origin include *le duvet* 'down'; *le but* 'aim', 'goal'—originally the block of wood at which one shot arrows; *le harnais* 'harness', 'trappings'; the verbs *nantir* 'to give security'; *hanter* 'to haunt', 'to frequent'; *regretter*, cognate with a Scandinavian word meaning 'to weep' (the prefix is Latin); and the adjectives *rogue* 'arrogant' and possibly *joli*, originally 'gay'.

Contacts between France and England during the ninth and tenth centuries, and in the first half of the eleventh, were peaceful: a certain amount of trading was interrupted from time to time by piracy, or by unfavourable conditions prevailing for a time inside the one country or the other. Charlemagne had been on friendly terms with Offa of Mercia, and letters from the one to the other have come down to us. Relations between Normandy and England had been particularly close in the years leading up to the Conquest. Like the Norsemen, the Anglo-Saxons contributed something to the language of sea-faring, for the points of the compass, *nord*, *sud*, *est*, and *ouest* appear to be of Anglo-Saxon origin: so do the words *varec* 'sea-wrack'; *flotte* 'fleet'; *rade* 'harbour road'; *bouline* 'bowline'; and the root of the word *bateau* 'boat'. A few other early borrowings have not survived, e.g., *utlage, ullage* 'outlaw', more particularly 'pirate'; *gotelef* 'honeysuckle'; and *videcoc* 'woodcock'. *Estrelin* 'penny', was an early borrowing which died out, to be borrowed again at the end of the seventeenth century as *sterling*.

The events leading up to the First Crusade, and Norman ventures in eastern Europe and in the Mediterranean, led to the introduction of a small number of loan-words from Arabic, from Persian, and from Byzantine Greek. There is already a sprinkling of these in the *Song of Roland*; from Arabic: *algalife* 'caliph', *almaçor* 'high dignitary', *amirail* and *amirafle* 'emir', *ciclaton* 'long silken garment', *jazerenc* (adj.) 'made of (Algerian) chain mail', *muserat* 'throwing-spear'; from Persian: *azur* 'bright blue', *eschecs* 'chess', and possibly *tabor* 'drum'; and from Byzantine Greek *drodmund* 'large galley', *galée* 'galley', *calant* 'flat-bottomed boat' (Mod. *chaland* 'barge'), and *ca(d)ables* 'catapults'.

The prominence given here to such exotic words must not blind us to the fact that the most obvious and prolific source for neologism in the eleventh century, and indeed at all times in the history of the French language, was Latin. Though there had been loss of many classical words, the vocabulary of Late Latin had widened considerably in response to new contacts and new needs, and it already included, for example, a great many Greek words over and above those particularly associated with the Church, as well as a host of words associated with the feudal organisation of society.

3

OLD FRENCH: LANGUAGE OR DIALECT?

The twelfth and thirteenth centuries saw the widespread acceptance of the vernacular as a literary medium, side by side with Latin. From the beginning of the thirteenth century, we also find the vernacular being used to some extent in local documents in Picardy. Indeed, from the year 1254 onwards, French is used as well as Latin even in documents emanating from the royal chancellery in Paris.

The literature of the period is extraordinarily rich: the Renaissance of the twelfth century concerned the vernacular as much as it concerned Latin. The *Song of Roland* was followed by a host of other epics, feudal or politico-religious in theme, and having the same formal pattern as that early masterpiece, though as a general rule far longer and less well constructed. A new verse form, the octosyllabic rhyming couplet, arose early in the twelfth century and was used above all for what were known as *romans*, a word which at first suggested no more than a (verse) text written in the vernacular, and not necessarily—or at all—a work of fiction.[1] Thus *Le Roman de Brut* and *Le Roman de Rou* turn out to be respectively verse chronicles about the early history of Britain and the early history of Normandy, while the 'romances' of antiquity, *Thèbes*, *Enéas*, and *Troie* are in reality metric versions of classical and post-classical sources which were certainly regarded as serious history. Even the Arthurian romances of the *matière de Bretagne*, as it was called, were carefully related to a king whose historicity was not in doubt. The same verse form was also used for didactic and moralising works, for shorter narrative poems such as the so-called Breton *lais* and the later *fabliaux*, for drama, to judge from the anonymous *Mystère*

1. In a work of high seriousness, the *Vie de Saint Thomas Becket* (1174), the author Garnier de Pont-Sainte-Maxence declares 'never was so good a *roman* made or composed. . . . There is not a word in it that is not the truth' (Ed. Walberg, ll. 6161–3). Exceptionally, this particular *roman* is in 12-syllable lines.

d'Adam and from Jean Bodel's *Jeu de S. Nicolas,* and occasionally for lyric poetry, though in this last domain, which was strongly influenced by Provençal love-poems and political satires, various more complicated verse-forms, with or without refrains, were often preferred. As for prose, there is little of it before the end of the twelfth century, after which it comes to be used side by side with verse for romances (inheriting the name *romans*), for chronicles, and for some types of didactic literature.

In the thirteenth century, though the first rapture and freshness are lost and vernacular literature becomes less original, more imitative and derivative, it still bears witness to the ever higher regard in which French was being held as a serious medium of expression.

It is during these two hundred years that the language of Île-de-France in general, and of Paris in particular, came to be accepted as the desirable norm of speech, and consequently as at least the basis for the desirable norm in writing (see map on p. 48). There were many reasons why the language of this region should have gained in prestige. At first, there was no obvious reason for regarding the speech of Île-de-France, roughly the region bounded by the Seine, the Marne and the Oise, as anything more than one of the many Romance dialects spoken in northern France. Normandy, Picardy, Wallonia, Champagne, Lorraine, Anjou, Maine and Touraine, and Anglo-Norman England too, all had their own dialect, and no doubt local sub-dialects too; but by the end of the eleventh century, these spoken dialects had not yet diverged as much as they were to do later, and they shared a great deal of common ground. Incidentally Poitou, earlier strongly under Occitan influence, was by now strongly under the influence of northern French.

Unlike their Carolingian predecessors, the Capetian kings were firmly established in a fixed capital, and that capital was Paris. Not only was the royal Court there, the law-courts were there also, and so were those schools which were soon to constitute themselves into a university. St-Denis, close by, was the spiritual centre of the kingdom. Not for nothing do the heathen in the *Song of Roland* say that when they conquer France they will be able to 'lie in the town of St-Denis' (l. 973), for that would have symbolised the total defeat of the French and of Christendom. Geographically and linguistically, Paris occupied a central position with regard to northern France and Anglo-Norman England: other dialects converged on the capital, and its language did not diverge markedly from any of the immediately neighbouring dialects. There were, then, good *a priori* reasons why the language of Paris and the surrounding region should have enjoyed prestige and encouraged imitation. The name given to the dialect of Île-de-France is Francien: is, not was, for the term was invented

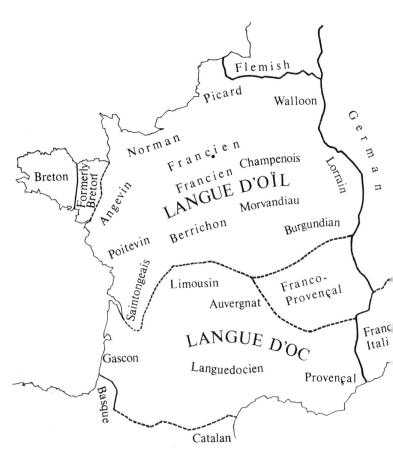

Dialect map of France, c. A.D. 1200

for convenience in the last century, and certainly never occurs in a medieval context. The texts, when they have occasion to refer to the language of northern France, call it simply *franceis*, *françois* or *roman(z)*, and make no further distinction. Both terms are somewhat vague. *Roman(z)* could mean any Romance vernacular, and therefore did not exclude Occitan. *François* is sometimes used in a way which suggests Île-de-France, but it may occasionally have a wider meaning, just as *France* itself, somewhat in advance of political events, could have an idealistic wider connotation. In explaining the meaning of an unfamiliar or exotic word, an author might say: 'this is what it means *en françois* . . . '. Now, even if we interpret *en françois* as meaning 'in the language of Île-de-France', we are still entitled to wonder at this exclusivity, and to ask why the language of Île-de-France should thus be singled out for special mention by, for instance, an author who was himself writing in Normandy. The fact is that, whatever the form of French being discussed at the time, and, for that matter, whatever the form of French used in discussing it, it is quite exceptionally rare to find any term more precise than *françois* used to describe it. In 1174, at the end of his *Vie de Saint Thomas Becket*, Garnier de Pont-Sainte-Maxence remarks 'Mis languages est bons, car en France fui nez' (l. 6165: 'My language is good, for I was born in *France*'). Garnier came in fact from Pont-Sainte-Maxence, which is near Senlis in the royal domain, and it is probable that *France* means 'Île-de-France'. He has just told his readers that he wrote the poem in Canterbury, and he may have wished to reassure them that he was for all that no Anglo-Norman—a fact of which the reader has already had more than 6000 lines to assure himself. Either the narrower or the wider sense of *France* would, of course, have made his point in that case, and it is really only the evidence of other texts which entitles us to take it in the narrower sense. In 1182, a *trouvère* from Artois, Conon de Béthune, complained in a poem that the Queen Regent, Alix de Champagne, and her son King Philippe-Auguste, had criticised his language, and he goes on to say:

> 'encore ne soit ma parole françoise,
> si la puet on bien entendre en françois.
> ne cil ne sont bien apris ne cortois,
> s'il m'ont repris, se j'ai dit mos d'Artois,
> car je ne fui pas norriz a Pontoise.'

['although my speech is not *françois*, yet it can be clearly understood by speakers of *françois*; and those who reproached me for uttering Artesian words, are neither polite nor courteous, for I was not brought up in Pontoise.']

As the Artesian dialect can hardly have been 'not French' in the broader sense of the word *françois*, it is likely that Conon meant indeed the language of Île-de-France. Pontoise, only twenty-six kilometres north-west of Paris, lies fairly and squarely in the domain of Francien.

In the thirteenth century, further testimonies reinforce the view that the language of Paris constituted a desirable standard, at least in speech. In his translation of Boethius' *Consolatio Philosophiae* (1298 ?), an anonymous poet from Meun apologises for his 'wretched, rough and uncouth language', on the grounds that he was not born in Paris. Philippe de Beaumanoir, a Picard poet, says of the French-speaking English heroine of his romance *Jehan et Blonde* (*c.* 1275): 'you could tell from her speech that she was not born at Pontoise', and at about the same time Adenet le Roi, from Brabant, wishing to indicate how well his heroine *Berthe aus grans piés* and her parents, who are somewhat vaguely described as German or Hungarian, spoke French, says that they spoke it so well that they might have been born at St-Denis.

It seems clear that in the twelfth and even more in the thirteenth century, the poets who speak of Paris, of St-Denis and of Pontoise as representing a linguistic ideal have the *spoken* language in mind. How far is this reflected in the written usage of the day?

The texts must be approached with caution. Many, in fact most, twelfth-century texts survive in copies, or copies of copies, made fifty, or eighty, or even a hundred years after the original date of composition. A scribe might transfer to the text he was copying some features of his own dialect, or the dialect of the person dictating to him. Yet, when due allowance has been made for this factor, and when one examines a text known to have been composed in, say, Bayeux on the one hand, and Troyes or Artois on the other, one is far more struck by the resemblances than by the points of divergence. And how is one to explain that fundamental *inconsistency* which characterises O.F. texts, for they seem to be torn between regionalism and supra-regionalism? There is really no such thing as an O.F. text written in 'pure dialect'—even if the 'dialect' in question is that of the Île-de-France. What we find instead is a collection of apparently incompatible ways of writing the same word. It must be said at once that different ways of writing the same word are incompatible only if one associates them too closely with regional pronunciations. A text composed in Normandy or Picardy may contain Norman or Picard forms side by side with Parisian forms which are 'incompatible' with them, or would be if one carried literalism to the length of reading the words aloud and giving to each the pronunciation suggested by the face value of the spelling. One would then be implying that people living in northern France in the twelfth and thirteenth centuries were in the habit of saying indifferently [tʃastɛl] or [kastɛl]; [tʃãmbrə] or [tʃetif] or [ketif]; [tʃãntsõn] or [kãntʃõn]; [dʒãmbə] or [gãmbə]; [garder] or [warder]; [tʃəvaus] or [kəvaus]—and of readily substituting [lə] for [la]. This is so wildly improbable that we must seek the explanation in a different and more plausible hypothesis, after asking and trying to answer certain questions. Was the text written originally in a pure, unadulterated and consistent dialect, and are the inconsistencies due to subsequent recopying? There is no doubt that subsequent recopying could change, for instance, the proportions of Parisian and non-Parisian forms—but it is also not only possible but extremely probable that the texts were not written down in a consistent way in the first place.

Here the case of Jean Bodel from Arras in Artois is instructive. There is little doubt that his own dialect was the Artesian variety of Picard. Around the year 1200 he wrote one of the most famous of all medieval French plays, *Le Jeu de S. Nicolas*. It has come down to us in a unique manuscript containing this and several other Picard works, and copied nearly a hundred years later. The language is mixed. There are many Picard forms in it, but it can hardly be said to be written consistently in the Picard dialect. Scribes may have either eliminated some of the Picard features which were present in the original, or added new ones, or both. Yet it is reasonable to suppose that Jean Bodel did not write his text consistently in Picard in the first place, since some of his rhymes would not have been rhymes in that dialect. Why did he not write consistently in Picard? The case of Jean Bodel is far from unique. Several substantial twelfth-century texts known to have originated from Normandy have come down to us in forms which are never consistently Norman and are, not infrequently, only superficially Norman.[1] Now, either they were not written consistently in Norman in the first place, or they were subsequently altered in a particular direction, with a particular bias—and in either case we would like to know why. Here again, the evidence of rhyme shows that some of the rhymes would not have been rhymes in Norman. We are surely forced to conclude that the linguistic awareness of the authors concerned, and quite possibly their linguistic ideal, transcended the boundaries of their own dialect. Of what did they have a wider linguistic awareness? There are only two possibilities, and they are not mutually exclusive. One is the 'pre-dialectal unity of the *langue d'oïl*', as it has been called; the other is that written form of French which most closely approximated to the speech of Île-de-France. The first means in effect 'that which the

1. An early attempt to solve this problem was to suggest that because the forms were mixed, the text must have been composed originally in the borderland between two different dialects. This view, which inevitably led to the 'discovery' that *all* O.F. texts must have been written in borderlands, is now discredited.

dialects of northern French had in common': the second is self-explanatory. The dialect of Île-de-France was *par excellence* what the other dialects had in common. So far as it was cultivated in regions to which it was not native, it ceased in effect to be a dialect and began to become a national language. 'A language', Auguste Brun once wrote, 'is a dialect which has risen in society: other dialects are its poor relations'. The phrase 'the pre-dialectal unity of the *langue d'oïl*', however, can perhaps still usefully be invoked to explain why the earliest texts of all contain forms which are not typical of their region of origin, at a time when the language of Paris had not yet become the obvious norm. To put it another way, it does not really matter whether what all the dialects had in common was Parisian French or not, at first, but it seems a remarkable coincidence, to say the least, that so much that is common to all the dialects happens to be characteristic of the language of Paris too, as it later manifested itself.

A further point remains to be made. Those authors who were apologetic about their language might well have escaped censure, even in the most fastidious court circles, if their works had been read aloud by a Parisian, for, faced with having to read aloud from a common *scripta*, the reader, once he had identified the word, would give it his own pronunciation—exactly as we do today when we are reading aloud. Even the highly standardised French and English spelling systems of today do not *prevent* a reader from pronouncing words according to his own idiolect. A Norman reading a Parisian text aloud in Normandy, and a Picard reading the same text aloud in Picardy, might pronounce the words as they pleased: they might even, eventually, come to substitute Parisian sounds for their own.

We may sum up the situation in these terms. The earliest texts were written down in regionally marked northern French. We have no records of Parisian French from the same period, with which to compare them. In any case, there was at that time no particular reason why the language of Paris *as such* should have been regarded as a norm and accordingly imitated in writing. We must bear in mind that at such an early stage there was no very wide gulf between the speech of one area of northern France and another, and in writing down the vernacular at all, a good deal of the notation (making due allowance for the inadequacies of the Latin alphabet) would serve as well for the speech of one region as for that of another. By the end of the twelfth century, however, the situation had changed, for by that time the language of Île-de-France was regarded as a desirable spoken norm. A written language which approximated to it would therefore command prestige, even before Paris itself became an important centre for literary activity, as it did in the thirteenth century. Indeed, already in the second half of the twelfth century, the written language in fact suggests Francien more strongly than it suggests anything else. Even when, as was often the case in this period, texts were composed in Normandy, the Norman element emerges as superficial and could nearly always be read as Francien.

In 1204, Normandy, which had been since 1066 an apanage of the English kings, was annexed by Philippe-Auguste, and thereafter the language of Norman texts tends to approximate even more to the language of Paris, subject to a further complication, which is that in general, in the thirteenth century, if there is a regional element which tends to colour texts which are basically Francien, it is no longer Norman, but Picard. Thus in that century we find that, so far as there is a standard language used for literary composition, it is Francien coloured by Picard. Naturally this Picard element might be more marked in texts actually composed in Picardy, but even texts known to have been composed in Île-de-France—and copied there—are by no means exempt from it. To this somewhat composite written language the name *scripta franco-picarde* has been aptly applied. What it amounts to is that some Picard forms, and many Picard spellings, were acceptable as alternatives in the written language of Paris, though they may not have corresponded exactly to spontaneous Parisian speech. After all, there is a measure of artificiality in *any* written language.

As for the language of vernacular *documents*, found from the beginning of the thirteenth century onwards, at first above all in Picardy, here the regional element was more pronounced, since the documents were far more likely to be of purely local interest or importance. Even so, from the beginning, a strong common French element was present, and this element becomes more and more plainly identifiable with Francien. The regional element gradually recedes, even from texts which can have been intended only for local consumption; but it has not entirely disappeared even at the end of the Middle Ages.

We must of course assume that there was appreciably more difference between geographically widely separate spoken dialects of northern France than appears in the texts of the period.

In England, Anglo-Norman continued to be spoken by the ruling classes throughout this period, and was the medium of an extremely rich literature. As a spoken language, however, it had little prestige in France. The dialect of Champagne differed very little from the language of Île-de-France, though it shared a few features with Picard. The court of the Counts of Champagne was for a time an important literary centre, reaching its peak with the romances of Chrétien de Troyes (fl. 1165–85); but towards the end of the thirteenth century the dynasty of the Counts of Champagne died out, and Champagne came under direct rule from Paris. At about the same time, the hitherto prosperous Picard towns began a period of economic decline, and ceased to be serious rivals to Paris as centres of literary activity, although the Picard dialect continued to leave traces in the 'standard' literary language until the end of the fifteenth century. In the south, the prestige of Occitan (called at the time *lemosi* or *proensal*) suffered a severe set-back as a result of the Albigensian Crusade (1209–13), launched by Pope Innocent III. The campaign, led by Simon de Montfort, led to the fall of the Toulousain dynasty, and thus indirectly to the political subjection of the south to the royal authority. Though this made very little difference to the use of Occitan as the *de facto* everyday language of the south, it delivered a crippling blow to the literary form of it, and put an end to its influence on the language and literature of the north.

To attempt a description of O.F. as a system of communication inevitably involves some measure of arbitrariness, since it means 'stopping the clock' at a particular moment in time, while the language never ceased to evolve. It also means seeking out the common Francien element although this never appears in an absolutely pure and unadulterated form in any one text. For practical purposes, however, it is usual to take the language of the later twelfth century as a norm, although this means that very little prose is available for study, the texts of the period being overwhelmingly in verse. It also involves stating, as rules, features which in practice do not lack exceptions, and implying a fixity which is constantly being belied by analogical and other changes. There was, incidentally, no contemporary grammar of O.F.: the language was used, it was not described or analysed.

A host of regular sound changes of the type selectively illustrated at the end of Chapter 1, together with many sporadic changes, had given rise to a wide range of vowel sounds, which included several diphthongs and two triphthongs Mod.F. has neither diphthongs nor triphthongs. The O.F. vocalic system consisted of the following twenty-eight sounds:

Oral vowels: [a] [ɛ] [e] [i] [ɔ] [u] [y] [ə]. At this time the vowel [o] was absent from the system: it had existed earlier but had recently closed to [u]. Soon a new [o] was to arise when [ɔ] closed in some positions.

Nasal vowels: [ã] [ẽ] [ĩ] [õ] [ỹ]

Oral diphthongs: [áu] [ié] [ói] [óu] [óu] [yí] [uó]

Nasal diphthongs: [ẽi] [iẽ] [ói] [uẽ] [yí]

Triphthongs: [eáu] [iéu] [uéu]

An earlier diphthong [éi] had become [ói] in the course of the twelfth century, and an earlier [ái] had reduced to [ɛ] and [e] by the end of the eleventh century. It is to be noted that the nasals, whether diphthongal or not, were not pure: that is to say, they did not involve complete assimilation of the following nasal consonant, which was still articulated.

There were twenty-one consonantal sounds, bringing the total of sounds to forty-nine: [b] [d] [dz] [dʒ] [f] [g] [h] [k] [l] [lj] [m] [n] [ɲ] [p] [r] [s] [t] [ts] [tʃ] [v] [z]. [h] occurred only in words of Germanic origin (see p. 21). [r] was the trilled variety: the uvular [R] so characteristic of Mod.F. did not arise until centuries later (see p. 112). [dz], [dʒ], [ts] and [tʃ] were soon to lose their dental element, becoming in the thirteenth century [z], [ʒ], [s] and [ʃ].

The sounds of O.F. have just been indicated *phonetically*: the way they are represented in O.F. *spelling* is rather a different matter. The spelling of the twelfth century has its inadequacies, but at least it has the merit of attempting to suggest the pronunciation, rather than the real or imagined etymology of words, or their real or imagined relationship to each other. In principle, every letter was pronounced, though *how* it was pronounced could not always be ideally indicated by the Latin alphabet. No distinction was made in writing between *i* = [i] and *i* = [dʒ]; and none was made between *u* representing the sound [y], and *u* representing the sound [v]. The letter *e* was used for four different sounds: [e], [ɛ], [ə] and long [e] deriving from Latin tonic-free [a] (see p. 24). On the other hand, the scribes represented diphthongs and triphthongs reasonably well, and can be forgiven for not indicating whether the diphthongs were of the rising or falling variety, e.g. *ui* which could represent [ýi] or [yí]. (Actually, [ýi] became [yí] in the course of the twelfth century.) *C* before *i* or *e* was pronounced [ts]; before *o* or *u*, [k], and before *a* sometimes [k] and sometimes [tʃ], but this last sound is more often written *ch*. *G* before *i* or *e* was [dʒ]; before *o* or *u*, [g], and before *a*, [g] or [dʒ] (this last sound more often written *i*). Between vowels, -*ss*- was normally [-s-]; while in the same intervocalic position, a single *s* was normally pronounced [z] (as in Mod.F.). The sounds [lj] and [ɲ] were written in a variety of ways: the former (*i*)*ll*(*i*) and the latter (*i*)(*n*)*gn*(*i*). Recent changes were not always reflected in the spelling: on the one hand the change of the diphthong [ei] to [oi] is well represented, but the reduction of [ai] to [ɛ] and [e] only sporadically so (*faire* and *fere*).

We must not, then, idealise the phonetic nature of O.F. spelling.

Etymological letters were liable to intrude, even during this most realistic period of spelling. Thus Latin *h*'s, which had no phonetic value, are occasionally found in words like (*h*)*ome*, (*h*)*ore*, while *grand* for *grant* is by no means uncommon. Association with related forms explains non-phonetic spellings such as *vifs* (*vis* + *vif*); *osbercs* (*osbers* + *osberc*); and *chiefs* (*chiés* + *chief*) (see below, pp. 57-8).

The phonology of a language and its morphology are not separable from each other in practice. We have already seen how the early sound changes which took place in northern France between the fifth century and the end of the eighth were not compatible with the continuation of the flexional system of Latin. A new system, on much simpler lines, had constituted itself in early O.F. We have already seen it in operation in the earliest texts, but we have yet to analyse it more closely. Of all the Romance vernaculars, French and Occitan (Provençal) were the only ones to preserve the Latin nominative case systematically, at least for a time. This conservatism is usually attributed to stronger scholastic influences in the region concerned. At all events, the forms of O.F. substantives can often be related to attested V.L. forms, but where these are lacking, analogical creations have to be postulated. The most important masculine declension is well represented by the word *mur* 'wall' < *múrus*.

	Sing.	Pl.
Nom.	*murs* < *múrus*	*mur* < *múri*
Obl.	*mur* < *múrum*	*murs* < *múros*

The final unstressed vowels are regularly lost, and so is -*m* in a final unstressed syllable, but the flexional -*s* of *múrus* remains. Learning O.F. involves *un*learning Mod.F., in which in most substantives *s* is indissolubly linked with the plural notion, and the absence of *s* with the singular. O.F. words of which the oblique form ends in *s* or *z* are indeclinable, e.g. *vis* 'face', *cors* 'body', *voiz* (f.) 'voice'.

The second masculine declension has no nominative *s* in the singular, because there was none present in Latin, e.g. *frere*:

	Sing.	Pl.
Nom.	*frere* < *fráter*	*frere* < **frátri*
Obl.	*frere* < *frátrem*	*freres* < *frátres*

We can, of course, postulate an oblique plural form **frátros* corresponding to the nominative plural **fratri*: the phonetic result would be exactly the same as that arising from *frátres*, but it is better not to postulate more than is absolutely necessary.

The third masculine declension is the most difficult and irregular, since it shows the greatest discrepancy between forms. Here it is the nominative singular which, for good phonological reasons, is 'odd man out': the other forms have an extra syllable in Latin, attracting a later stress.

Sing.	Pl.
ber < *báro* ('warrior', 'hero')	*baron* < **baróni*
baron < *barónem*	*barons* < *barónes*

Similarly, *présbyter/presbýterum* gave rise to *prestre/provoire*, *infa(n)s/infántem* to *enfes/enfant*, *népos/nepótem* to *niés/nevou(t)*, and *imperátor/imperatórem* to *emperere/empereour*. Occasionally, an extra syllable in Latin did not involve a shift of stress, hence:

Sing.	Pl.
uem, om, on < *hómo*	*ome* < **hómini*
ome < *hóminem*	*omes* < *hómines*

and

cuens, quens, cons < *cómes*	*conte* < **cómiti*
conte < *cómitem*	*contes* < *cómites*

Feminine substantives offer less difficulty. A very high proportion, ending in *-a* in Latin, end in *-e* in O.F. and are invariable, since *-a* and *-am* gave the same result in the singular, while in the plural *-as* replaced *-ae* as the nominative form. Hence

fille < *fília*	*filles* < *fílias*
fille < *fíliam*	*filles* < *fílias*

O.F. feminine substantives *not* ending in *-e* are similarly invariable, with the reservation that from an early date this type tends to take an *-s* in the nominative singular—probably by analogy with the first masculine declension: hence *fin(s)*, *amor(s)*, etc. A third feminine type, very thinly represented, is characterised by a shift of stress and an extra syllable:

ante ('aunt') < *ámita*	*antains* < **amitánes*
antain < **amitánem*	*antains* < **amitánes*

The commonest substantive in this category is *suer* 'sister':

suer < *sóror*	*serors* < *soróres*
seror < *sorórem*	*serors* < *soróres*

Particularly in the first masculine declension, where oblique singular (and nominative plural) forms have a consonantal ending, certain final consonants drop when they come into contact with flexional *-s*. This phonetic fact is confirmed, though not consistently, by scribal usage (see p. 56 above). Thus the nominative singular and oblique plural forms of *chief* 'head', *banc* 'bench', *buef* 'ox' and *nom* 'name' are phonetically, and often orthographically *chiés*, *bans*, *bués*, and *nons*; but one is quite likely to find them written sporadically *chiefs*, *bancs*, *buefs*, *noms*.

Some final consonants give rise to -*z* [ts] and not -*s* in the nominative singular and oblique plural; but since from an early date final -*z* and final -*s* appear to be interchangeable, there is no need to record here particulars of these cases.

With regard to adjectives, here again phonetic principles explain the forms.

Masc.sing.	Masc.pl.	Fem.sing.	Fem.pl.
lars < *lárgus*	*larc* < *lárgi*	*large* < *lárga*	*larges* < *lárgas*
larc < *lárgum*	*lars* < *lárgos*	*large* < *lárgam*	*larges* < *lárgas*

An important class of O.F. adjective continues Latin adjectives of the *tristis*, *grandis* type, which had no distinctive feminine forms. Nevertheless, there is a partial distinction in O.F. in the nominative singular, e.g.

Masc.sing.	Masc.pl.	Fem.sing.	Fem.pl.
forz granz	*fort grant*	*fort grant*	*forz granz*
fort grant	*forz granz*	*fort grant*	*forz granz*

Analogically, one finds also the nominative singular feminine forms *forz, granz*. The modern analogical feminine forms *grande, forte*, etc., are attested quite early, but are rare in the O.F. period.

An adjectival type corresponding phonetically to the masculine third declension imparisyllabics is represented by some O.F. survivals of Latin comparative forms:

Masc. & fem.sing.	Masc.pl.	Fem.pl.
mieldre < *mélior*	*meillor* < **melióri*	*meillors* < *melióres*
meillor < *meliórem*	*meillors* < *melióres*	*meillors* < *melióres*

The definite article is declined as follows:

	Masc.sing.	Masc.pl.	Fem.sing.	Fem.pl.
Nom.	*li* or *l'*	*li*	*la* or *l'*	*les*
Obl.	*le, lo, l'*	*les*	*la* or *l'*	*les*

The indefinite article *un(s)*, *une* is declined and has plural forms, signifying 'some', 'a pair of', 'a set of'.

The Latin pronouns *me te se* undergo a twofold development according to stress, which in practice means according to position and function: hence on the one hand [mə] [tə] [sə] (written *me*, *te*, *se*), and on the other the stressed forms written *moi toi soi*. The possessives *meus tuus suus* also undergo a twofold development according to stress and function. The unstressed forms give rise to the O.F. possessive adjectives (type *mis, mon; mi, mes*; fem. *ma, m', mes*; similarly *tis* and *sis*), and the stressed forms give rise to the pronouns *miens, mien,* fem. *meie, meies,* which were however occasionally used adjectivally. Latin *suus,* originally indicating possession by the subject, was extended to cover possession by any third person singular. True to its etymology, *lor* (< *(il)lorum*) is invariable and is not affected by the number of its complement. The O.F. demonstratives derive from *ecce ille, illa* etc and *ecce iste, ista* etc. originally applied respectively to that which was remote from the speaker and that which was near. This semantic opposition, however, soon became blurred. The modern distinction of function between adjectival *ce, cet, cette, ces* and pronominal *celui, celle, ceux, celles* had not yet emerged as such in O.F. From an early date, however, *cels* (> *ceux*) virtually ceased to be used as an adjective and was replaced in this function by *cez* > *ces,* which also largely replaced the forms *cestes, celes* used adjectivally. In the end, *cestes* did not survive at all, while *celes* survived only as a pronoun. In O.F., *celui* and *cestui* were available as emphatic forms of the oblique singular masculine demonstratives *cel* and *cest,* in both functions. Only *celui* survived, and is restricted to pronominal use.

Much might be said about the conjugation of verbs. Phonetic laws, as we have seen, are no respecters of parts of speech, and they account, together with sporadic changes and a good deal of analogy, for the O.F. verb-forms. To take one example among many of the interrelation of sound-change and analogy, the final *-o* of the first person singular of the Latin first conjugation present indicative is preserved in O.F. (as *-ə*) only if it follows a group of consonants which could not be articulated without this supporting vowel. Otherwise it has disappeared without trace. Hence on the one hand *jo, je chant* < *cánto, j(o) aim* < *ámo,* and on the other *j(o) entre* < *íntro, jo, je semble* < *símulo.* However, already in the twelfth century, on the analogy, partly of forms like *j(o) entre, jo semble,* and partly of second and third person forms in *-es, -e* (< *-as,* < *-at*), we occasionally find *jo chante, j(o) aime.*

Some extremely important irregularities in verbal stems deserve mention here, since they well illustrate the relationship between regular sound-change and the consequent inevitable creation of irregular morphological patterns.

We have already seen that when the vowels [a ɛ e ɔ o] occurred in tonic free syllables, they regularly diphthongised at an early date (and, in the case of the diphthong arising from [a], reduced early to a simple vowel). If we apply this to the development of, for example, first conjugation verbs with a monosyllabic radical, we shall see that in the present indicative and present subjunctive the relevant diphthongisation took place whenever the appropriate conditions were present, that is to say, in the stem-stressed forms when the relevant vowel was free; which means in effect in the three persons of the singular and the third person plural. In the first and second persons plural, however, the stress shifted from the stem to the termination, with the result that there was no diphthongisation of the vowel in the stem. Hence, in the present indicative, the following patterns:

(*trover* < *tropáre	*amer* < *amáre*)
truef < *trópo	*aim*[1] < *ámo*
trueves < *trópas	*aimes* < *ámas*
trueve < *trópat	*aime* < *ámat*
trovons < *tropámus	*amons* < *amámus*
trovez < *tropátis	*amez* < *amátis*
truevent < *trópant	*aiment* < *ámant*

Similarly with *laver* (*lef* < *lávo, lavons* < *lavámus*); *lever* (*lief* < *lévo, levons* < *levámus*); *plorer* (*plour* < *plóro, plorons* < *plorámus*); *peser* (*pois* < *pé(n)so, pesons* < *pe(n)sámus*); *esperer* (*espoir* < *spéro, esperons* < *sperámus*), and many more otherwise regular verbs. There were similar alternations in some irregular verbs: e.g. (*il*) *muert* but (*nos*) *morons*; (*jo*) *vien* but (*nos*) *venons*—to quote examples which, though the earlier diphthongs have since been reduced, preserve to the present day an alternation in the stem. It is true to say, however, that most of these alternations, and particularly those affecting first-conjugation verbs, have subsequently been levelled, usually on the model of the type represented by the infinitive, a form which in the first conjugation was (and is) never stressed on the stem.

Another type of irregularity affecting the present indicative and present subjunctive of first conjugation verbs was *syllabic alternation*. What it amounts to is this. A syllable which in certain forms of the V.L. verb was tonic, survives in O.F., whereas when, owing to a shift of stress, the same syllable became pretonic (as it was in most of the forms of the verb), it was reduced by syncopation, and is lost to O.F. Hence the following kind of 'anomaly' in the paradigm of the present indicative[2] of certain first conjugation verbs. Let us take V.L. *parábolo*, becoming *paraulo, as typical:

(*jo*) *parol* < *paráulo
(*tu*) *paroles* < *paráulas
(*il*) *parole* < *paráulat
(*nos*) *parlons* < *paraulámus
(*vos*) *parlez* < *paraulátis
(*il*) *parolent* < *paráulant

1. Tonic free [a]+nasal gave first the nasal diphthong [ãi]. By the end of the twelfth century this sound had developed to [ẽi].

2. There was a similar anomaly in the present subjunctive.

Similarly with *disnier* < *disjejunare (*jo desjun* but *nos disnons*); *aidier* < *adjutare* (*j(o) ajut* but *nos aidons*); *mangier* < *manducare* (*jo manju(e)* but *nos manjons*) and other verbs.

Since the verbal endings were more distinctive then than they are today (though obviously far less distinctive than they had been in Latin), subject pronouns were used sparingly, and moreover admitted of considerable emphasis and contrastive force. *Il*, it should be noted, was masculine plural as well as singular: both derive from V.L. *ellī. The dominant syntactical features of O.F. may be summarised as follows:

Word-order. Though not fool-proof (since most feminine substantives were invariable), the two-case system permitted great flexibility in the arrangement of the principal elements of a sentence. Ambiguity could usually be eliminated by the latent probabilities of the context. Any of the six permutations of subject, verb and object were possible, though some were more common than others, and one of the most common was already the modern order subject, verb, object. Inversion of verb and subject, however, was particularly frequent, being normal whenever an adverb or adverbial expression, or a grammatical object, opened the sentence or the clause. The order subject–object–verb (known as *rejet*) was extremely common in relative clauses. The substantival object of an infinitive normally preceded the infinitive. In compound tenses the substantival object frequently comes between the auxiliary and the past participle. Pronoun objects of an infinitive precede the modal verb, when there is one, and not the infinitive. Unstressed pronoun objects are avoided in the first position in the sentence: to judge from the written language, one said, for example *Molt me poise* ('I am very sorry'), *Or me poise* ('(Now) I am sorry'), *Ço poise moi* ('I regret this') or *Moi poise* ('I am sorry'), but not *Me poise*. In combinations of object pronouns, the accusative comes before the dative, an order which survives today only when both pronouns are of the third person. It was normal (probably for reasons of euphony) to omit *le*, *la*, *les* before *li* (= *lui*) and *leur*, since the presence of a transitive verb and of the dative pronoun allowed the sense to be deduced, e.g. *cil li aportet, receit les Alexis* ('He brings [them] to him [and] Alexis takes them'). *En* comes before *i*—the reverse of the modern order. The position of adjectives is very unsettled: suffice it to say that even ethnic adjectives, adjectives of colour, and adjectives of technical category could precede the substantive.

The infinitive. Any infinitive could become a substantive of the first masculine declension. Although various modal verbs could take a direct infinitive, and although accusative and infinitive, and dative and infinitive constructions existed, subordinate clauses with finite verbs were used instead of the 'prepositional infinitive' common today in the type *prier quelqu'un, ordonner, conseiller à quelqu'un, de faire quelque chose*.

Negation. Used with verbs, *ne* constituted sufficient negation in itself. *Pas, point, mie, gote* could be added for emphasis, but were often dispensed with. It is to be noted that the words *onc, onques, aucun,* and *rien*, although often used with *ne*, were *positive* when used without it, and meant respectively 'ever', 'some/any', and '(some)thing'. *Rien* was even a feminine substantive in its own right (< *rem*). The phrase *du tout* ('completely', 'utterly') had as yet no negative associations.

The article. The definite article is often omitted before abstract nouns, and before plural nouns whether abstract or not. The partitive, which incorporates the definite article, is not usual before the names of substances, hence *boire vin, mangier pain*, etc., unless the substance is very precisely identified and specified; thus *mangier del pain, boire del vin* mean 'to eat some of the bread, drink some of the wine *already referred to*'. This is understandable, since the definite article, which derived from a demonstrative (< *ille, illa*), still possessed considerable particularising force in O.F. It is for the same reason that a phrase like *toz les jorz* could not be used with reference to unspecified days: it meant 'for the whole of *those* days—the days in question'. The indefinite 'every day' was rendered by *chascun jor(n)*.

Coordination and subordination of clauses. In O.F., subordination is often only implicit: clauses may be stated without formal connexion and it is up to the reader (or hearer) to supply the logical or semantic links. Relative pronouns and subordinating conjunctions could often be omitted, or, if given, did not need to be repeated. There seems to have been no aesthetic objection to coordinating a long series of statements or actions by means of *et* or *si* (< *sic*) instead of subordinating some to others in a temporal or other relationship. Nevertheless, quite elaborate and intricate subordination is well attested, even in verse—indeed, at this early period, above all in verse. We must not assume that *parataxis* (simple juxtaposition of clauses, without formal links) was inescapable in O.F. syntax: to a considerable extent it was a matter of style and genre. A conjunction such as *que* could fulfil a variety of different functions, though the mood used after it helped to reduce the number of possible interpretations.

Mood. There is already in O.F. morphology some measure of formal *rapprochement* between indicative and subjunctive. The imperfect subjunctive was used in speech, and was common in both the protasis and the apodosis of conditional sentences. The subjunctive was normal after verbs of thinking and believing used affirmatively.

Tense. The past definite was normal in conversation with reference to the remote past, and sometimes even with reference to events of the same day, although in this last function and to some extent in the first, it overlapped with the perfect tense. Idiomatically, the past definite was also used, particularly in verse, in descriptive passages where Mod.F. would require the imperfect.

Comparison. The comparative and the superlative degree are not always formally distinguished.

Vocabulary and word-formation. The basically Latin vocabulary is of two kinds: popular words with a continuous history in the language since V.L., and learned words coined at various periods direct from Latin and minimally assimilated to the phonetic and morphological requirements of French. Words borrowed after a particular sound change is complete will in theory escape the operation of that change: they may nevertheless in practice be affected by analogy, and thus sometimes look as if they have undergone the sound change. The non-Latin element in the vocabulary of O.F. consists, in diminishing order of importance, of German, Celtic, Scandinavian, Oriental languages, and Anglo-Saxon. There is much hesitation as to suffixes, thus *tristece* (< *tristitia*) is rivalled by *tristor* and *tristance*; *folie* by *folage*, *folor* and *foleté*; and *avueglece* 'blindness' by *avuegleüre*, *avuegleté* and *avueglement.* Learned and popular forms of the same word sometimes correspond to a substantial difference of meaning (e.g. *cherté* 'dearth', 'dearness': *charité* 'charity') and sometimes not (e.g. *verté, verité*; *entente, entencion, intention*; *soisté, societé*). Some O.F. words suggest that, so long as a basic 'motivation' was inherent, the context could be left to indicate which of two antonymous meanings was relevant, e.g. *deteor* 'debtor' or 'creditor'; *chartrier* 'jailor' or 'prisoner'.

There is a strong Germanic quality about O.F. Quite apart from the earlier influences of Germanic speech-habits on the sounds of the Latin of Gaul, giving O.F. its phonetic characteristics, and quite apart from easily identifiable loan-words, Germanic influence can be seen—or divined—in various other ways. It can be seen in those dominant features of O.F. word-order—inversion and *rejet*; it can probably be seen in the frequent anteposition of the adjective; it can be seen in idioms like *soi tiers, soi quart* ('oneself and two others', 'oneself and three others'); in the absolute use of *devoir* (*ço que deit?* = 'what does this mean?', 'what is this for?') and *pooir* (*il ne puet hors* 'he cannot get out'); and in the readiness with which verbs are combined with adverbs indicating the direction of the action: *aler fors/hors* 'to go out'; *aler en voie(s)* 'to go away'; *geter en voie(s)* 'to throw away'; *venir ens* 'to come in'; *metre jus* 'to put down'. Indeed, this last feature is so strongly rooted in O.F. that it is by no means uncommon to find tautological uses of the adverb, which thus merely indicates, or reinforces, an idea already implicit in the verb itself, e.g. *lever sus* 'to get up' or (transitive) 'to lift up'; *avaler aval* 'to go down'; *monter amont* or *monter sus* 'to climb up', 'to rise up'; *entrer ens* 'to go or come in'; *issir fors* 'to go out'; and (*s'*)*aprochier prés* 'to draw near'.

Compared with Mod.F., O.F. seems loosely structured, content to leave a great deal to the imagination as regards grammatical relationships, content to rely rather heavily on context. Faced with a twelfth-century text, the reader with a knowledge of Mod.F. will experience considerable difficulty. Mod.F. spoils one for the task, firstly because it indicates grammatical relationships very clearly and indeed rigorously by means of a word-order which is largely fixed, and by a series of unequivocal grammatical 'markers'; and secondly because it uses a spelling system which, being based far more on etymology than on pronunciation, enables one to identify at once words which in speech may not be differentiated at all. O.F., on the other hand, is very free as to word-order; it often omits—or does not repeat—its limited grammatical markers, and its spelling tends not to distinguish between words which were pronounced alike or nearly alike.

To conclude this brief survey of O.F., let us look at some short specimens of the language, admittedly torn from their context.

> Totes autres pierres passoient
> Celes del graal sanz dotance.
> (Chrétien de Troyes, *Perceval*, Ed. Roach, ll. 3238–9)

Here the two-case system does not help: subject and object are both feminine plurals in -*es*. Only the context tells us that the first element is the direct object and not the subject of the sentence. The meaning is 'Those (sc. precious stones) of the Grail certainly surpassed all other stones.'

> Erec de son oste depart,
> Que merveilles li estoit tart
> Que a la cort le roi venist.
> (Chrétien de Troyes, *Erec et Enide*, Ed. Foerster, ll. 1479–81)

Merveilles is adverbial, and modifies *tart* or *estoit tart*, which is impersonal. The first *que* expresses causality; the second introduces a subordinate clause dependent on the impersonal expression in the previous line. *Le roi*, being the oblique form of *li rois*, cannot be the subject of the clause: it is in fact dependent on *la cort* and is the equivalent of *del roi*. *Venist* (imperfect subjunctive) is used without a subject pronoun, because it is perfectly clear by O.F. standards that *Erec*, though invariable, is the subject. The meaning is 'Erec takes leave of his host, for he greatly longed to reach the king's court.'

Mult s'acorderent li Venisien que les eschieles fussent drecies es nés et que toz li assaus fust par devers la mer. Li François disoient que il ne se savoient mie si bien aidier sor mer com il savoient, mais quant il aroient lor chevaus et lor armes, il se savroient miels aidier par terre (Geoffroi de Villehardouin, *La Conquête de Constantinople*, Ed. Faral, para. 162).

[The Venetians were unanimously of the opinion that the scaling-ladders should be set up on the ships and that the whole attack should take place from the sea. The French said that they could not operate nearly so well at sea as they (sc. the Venetians) could, but (that) when they had their horses and their weapons, they would be able to operate better on land.]

Com il savoient is particularly striking, because in Mod.F. *il(s)* cannot be used emphatically or alone in contrast with another pronoun, least of all another pronoun of the third person. In O.F. this was not only possible, but normal. Note also that the *que* of *disoient que* is not repeated, and that *lor* is invariable.

Sachiez que la renomee de cel saint homme alla tant qu'ele vint a l'apostoille de Rome Innocent; et l'apostoille envoia en France, et manda al prodome qu'il preechast des croix par s'autorité (ibid., para. 2).

[Know that the fame of that holy man went so far that it reached Pope Innocent in Rome; and the Pope sent (messengers) to France, and conveyed to the good man that he was to preach the Crusade with his authority.]

Apostoille (sometimes *apostolie*) is a learned word. The second occurrence of the word lacks flexional -*s*, although it is the subject of the clause. *Autorité* is also learned. The feminine possessives *ma ta sa* were regularly elided to *m' t' s'* before a vowel, until in the fourteenth century the masculine forms *mon ton son* were extended in use to feminine substantives and adjectives beginning with a vowel.

By the end of this period (*c.* 1300), the position of Francien is strong. It is the accepted basis for the written language, and the 'common ground' of the northern dialects. Its influence in Poitou, a region earlier within the orbit of Occitan, is considerable, and it is gaining ground in the Franco-Provençal area, centred upon Lyons.

Outside France, and outside Anglo-Norman England, where French was still the language of the ruling classes, Crusades and political and military activity had carried the language to southern

Italy and Sicily, to Greece, to the Levant, and to Palestine. Naples and Sicily were ruled first by the Normans and later by the Angevins. Although Sicily was lost to Aragon in 1282, the Angevin dynasty continued to rule in southern Italy until the fifteenth century. Cyprus was ruled by the Lusignans, a Poitevin dynasty which was to last until the late fifteenth century.

The prestige of French did not depend entirely on political influence, however. In northern Italy, the language was widely cultivated as a literary medium. Not only did copies of French epics and romances circulate in Italy, Italians themselves composed in French, hence Brunetto Latini's symposium of medieval lore entitled *Le Livre du Tresor* (1262–6), Martino da Canale's *Chroniques des Venitiens* (*c*. 1275), and the account of Marco Polo's travels in the East, written down in French by Rustichello da Pisa (1298), who is known also for his activity in the domain of Arthurian romance. Both Brunetto Latini and Martino da Canale justify their use of French by saying that it is the most pleasing form of speech and the most widely used; while far away in Norway the author of the *Speculum Regale* urges the particular study of Latin and French 'because they are the most widely known'.

4

MIDDLE FRENCH DEVELOPMENTS

The dates and duration of the Mid.F. period are as arbitrary as the term 'Middle French' itself. A consensus makes it begin in the first half of the fourteenth century and end in the first half of the seventeenth, on the grounds that by the early fourteenth century significant changes were beginning to manifest themselves while others, already complete, were seriously undermining the system as it had operated previously, and on the grounds that by the early seventeenth century we are already beginning to find French which, in all its essentials, is strikingly modern.

For convenience, the main emphasis in this chapter will be on the internal development of the language, particularly as regards phonology, morphology and syntax, in the fourteenth, fifteenth and sixteenth centuries; but since the sixteenth century is important also for the rise of conscious attitudes towards the language question, conscious attempts to formulate linguistic norms, and in general for an intense and active preoccupation with linguistic matters, the discussion of these themes will be deferred until the next chapter.

The historical and political background to the period may be briefly summarised. The successive French kings were engaged in complicated struggles both with the English kings and with their own powerful vassals. It must be remembered that Guyenne and Gascony, a substantial area of France, were English territory, while other parts of France too were claimed and sometimes overrun. In the middle of the so-called Hundred Years War (1337–1453), the assassination of the Duke of Orleans (1407) at the instigation of Jean sans Peur, Duke of Burgundy, led to a full-scale war between the Armagnacs (partisans of Orleans) and the Burgundians, in which the whole country took sides. In 1419 the Burgundians allied themselves with the English, thus heightening an already grave threat to the survival of France as a nation. The king, Charles VII, was forced to leave the capital for Bourges, and it was only after his return in 1436 that the Treaty of Arras brought about some measure of national unity against the English menace. A series of successful campaigns led in 1450 to the dislodging of the English from Normandy, where they had been in occupation since 1415; and in 1453 to their expulsion from Guyenne and Gascony, where they had held sway since the middle of the twelfth century. Only Calais remained in English hands. Subsequently, Louis XI (1461–83) met with a large measure of success in his efforts to unite France under the Crown. By subtle diplomacy he was able to disarm both England and Burgundy, and to gain control of both Provence and Anjou, bequeathed to the crown in 1481 by their last rulers. Local parliaments, set up in Toulouse (1444), Grenoble (1453) and Bordeaux (1462), only served to emphasise the royal authority in the regions concerned. Brittany was united with the French crown when Anne de Bretagne married Charles VIII of France in 1491. Feudalism was almost extinct, and a new national consciousness had taken its place.

The literature of this period is plentiful, yet except for a few masterpieces it does not equal what had gone before or what was to follow. At all events, against the background of a considerable Latin literature, French was by this time a common enough medium in the domain of *belles-lettres*, though it was still largely excluded from science and, except for works of popular piety, from theology. The accepted norm throughout this period is the language of Paris, slightly coloured by the spelling conventions and to some extent the forms current in Picardy. The last northern French author to write in a strongly marked dialect was the Picard chronicler and poet Jean Froissart (1337–*c*. 1404). In the south, although dialects of Occitan were universally spoken, the written language tended overwhelmingly to be, for literary purposes, either Latin or French, the deciding factor being essentially the one which prevailed in the north too, namely genre and subject matter. For official purposes, however, more use was made of Latin, and for a time of local languages, than of French.

With the advent of printing (the first press was set up in Paris in 1470), the output was for a long time predominantly Latin, for the most urgent need was for Latin texts and commentaries; but, insofar as it was *not* Latin, it was essentially in the language of Paris *and in no other French dialect*. By the end of the fifteenth century, there were some sixty presses in Paris, and about forty in Lyons. Throughout the period, there is a steady increase in the use of French for official purposes, in legal documents and in public records, not only in the royal chancelleries but also, regionally, in the chancelleries of dukes and counts. The local colouring of regional archives gradually fades and the language of Paris predominates. By the end of the fourteenth century, French was the language normally used in the official documents of Marche, Auvergne, Forez, Lyonnais and Bas-Dauphiné. During the second half of the fifteenth century, it was making slow but steady progress southwards, to east and west of the Massif Central.

Outside France, during the same period, the French language recedes. By the end of the fifteenth century, it had ceased to be an influential language in the south of Italy, in Sicily and in Cyprus. In England, it was learned purely as a foreign language. Some *manieres de langage* or 'conversational grammars', composed in England, have come down to us, but they are very inaccurate and of little value for the study of continental French.

Several important phonological developments took place during this period. Of these the first in order of importance (because of its drastic effect on the two-case system) was the muting of final consonants. This process had begun as early as the thirteenth century when the following word began with a consonant. By the sixteenth century, the process was complete, although, to judge from the would-be phonetic spelling of certain sixteenth-century grammarians, final consonants were still heard not only in liaison (which then was not confined to groups closely related in sense), but also before a pause. Final [-r] was no exception to the rule, and by the end of the fourteenth century infinitives in *-er*, *-ir* and *-oir* ended phonetically in [-e], [-i], and [-we] respectively. The [r] was still pronounced in liaison, however, and before a pause, and was later restored to the *-ir*, *-oir* classes, but not to *-er*. Loss of final [-r] also led to some confusion between names of agents in *-eur* and the common adjectival suffix *-eux*, since they were both pronounced alike. A result of this which still makes itself felt in Mod.F. is that the feminine forms of agents, and of adjectives in *-eur* (the [r] was soon restored) tend to end in *-euse*.

Final *e* [ə] was at first syllabic, though very weak after a vowel (as in *aimée, hardie, fondue*); but around the beginning of the sixteenth century it ceased to have any syllabic value in this position, except in verse and in song. Until well into the nineteenth century, however, it had the effect of lengthening the preceding vowel. After a consonant, final *e* [ə] was still pronounced until about the middle of the sixteenth century. Internally, it had become mute after a vowel as early as the fourteenth century, hence *pri(e)ra* confirmed by scansion; and from the same period dates its disappearance between two consonants: *car(re)four*; *char(re)tier*; *guer(re)don*; *lar(re)cin*; *ser(e)ment* —a pronunciation sometimes, though by no means regularly, reflected in contemporary spelling. [a] + [s] + consonant early moved back to [ɑ]. In a final position + [s], [a] did not reach this stage until the sixteenth century (*pas*: [pa(s)] > [pɑ]). Pretonic vowels in hiatus ceased to be syllabic early in the period, being absorbed by the tonic vowel immediately following. This is amply confirmed by the metre of verse texts, although the spelling of words like *meur* [myr], *seur* [syr], *beu* [by], *veoir* [vwɛr], *seoir* [swɛr] is slow to adjust itself to the new pronunciation. The early reduction of [dʒ], [tʃ], to [ʒ], [ʃ], led to the absorption of the first element of the diphthong [ie] in words like *mang(i)er*, *ch(i)ef*, *ch(i)er*, but here too the spelling proved conservative. The numerous diphthongs, and the three triphthongs, of O.F. all tended towards reduction during this period, and few of them even reached the sixteenth century. One of these, written *au*, was still pronounced [ao] for at least some sixteenth-century grammarians, before becoming [o] later in the century. The triphthong [eáu] had become the diphthong [eo], before also reducing to [o] for most speakers by the end of the sixteenth century. When final or before a vowel, [wɛ] was still a diphthong for some as late as the sixteenth century; but there had been, and continued to be, much hesitation as to the pronunciation of this sound, generally represented in spelling by *oi*. The popular tendency was to reduce it to [ɛ], but learned influence preserved or restored the diphthongal pronunciation. Hence on the one hand the (modern) pronunciation of such words as *tonnerre, verre, Anglais, Français, faible, craie* and the imperfect and conditional endings *-ais, -ait, -aient* (earlier written *tonnoirre, voirre, Anglois, François, foible, croie, -ois, -oit, -oient*); and on the other hand the pronunciation which prevailed in most words, [wɛ], later [wa], as in *moi, toi, soi, soif, loi, paroi, effroi, émoi*. The 'learned' pronunciation [wɛ] is sometimes unequivocally written *oue* in Mid.F. texts before [r]: thus spellings like *mirouer, espouer, rasouer, montouer, pressouer* are by no means uncommon for *miroir, espoir, rasoir, montoir, pressoir*.

There was much hesitation between [ɛ] and [a] before [r]. The popular tendency in the fourteenth century was to open [ɛ] yet further (it is merely a matter of lowering the tongue a little) to [a] before [r], and this pronunciation has prevailed in some words, e.g. O.F. *lerme > larme*; *sercelle > sarcelle*. Learned influence opposed this change, however, with the result that not only did [ɛr] prevail in many words, it was even over-zealously introduced into words where [ar] was historically correct, e.g. O.F. *asparge, jarbe, sarcou, garir* becoming *asperge, gerbe, cercueil, guérir*.

Pretonic [ɔ] tended popularly towards [u] (written *ou*), as in *pourter, vouler* for *porter, voler*, but in cultivated speech [ɔ] was maintained, supported by Latin etymons, by related substantives (*la porte, le vol*), and by the tonic forms of certain verbs (*je porte*, *je vole*). The popular tendency prevailed in some words, however, hence *douleur, moulin, vouloir*; but it is to be noted that in these cases related stem-stressed forms did not support a pronunciation with [ɔ], e.g. (*il*) *duelt, la meule, il veu*(*l*)*t*. In tonic syllables there was much hesitation, e.g. *chose/chouse*, with [o] emerging triumphant in the end (see p. 113).

[s] before consonant disappeared from the pronunciation in the thirteenth century, lengthening the preceding vowel in tonic syllables (*te*(*s*)*te, be*(*s*)*te*). It is to be noted, however, that in words introduced into the language in the Mid.F. period this change did not necessarily, or usually, take place; hence *fe*(*s*)*te* but *festin*. Furthermore, the V.L. and early O.F. inhibition about initial [s] + consonant was overcome in Mid.F.; hence the learned *scolastique* side by side with older *e*(*s*)*cole*, and the substantive *e*(*s*)*table* < *stabulum* side by side with the learned adjective *stable* < *stabilis*. *Esprit*, by the way, owes the preservation of its [s] to learned influence (cf. Lat. *spiritus, spiritualis*).

The nasal vowels opened during the period up to the end of the sixteenth century: [ĩ] > [ẽ] > [ɛ̃]; [ỹ] > [ø̃] > [œ̃]; [ẽ] > [ɛ̃]; [õ] > [ɔ̃]. The nasal diphthongs [iẽ], [yĩ] became [jẽ] (pop. [jẽ] > [jã]) and [ɥĩ]. [ẽi,], [õi] generally became [ẽ], [wẽ] by the sixteenth century. By this time the assimilation of the nasal consonant was complete. Denasalisation before intervocalic [m], [n], [ɲ] makes considerable progress during this period.

Some of the changes mentioned are reflected in contemporary spelling, but not consistently. Indeed, Mid.F. spelling is in general extremely unsatisfactory as a representation of the spoken word. The fact is that by now, spelling was largely in the hands of the lawyers' clerks, the minor civil servants of the age, men of small learning employed to compile and copy the ever-growing mass of documents which an increasingly centralised administration called for. The *praticiens*, as these clerks were called, had organised themselves into a powerful corporation as early as 1303. They were to some extent aided and abetted by the availability of cheap rag-paper, replacing the more expensive parchment and vellum which invited careful lettering.

It must be admitted that even if the conventions of spelling had remained unchanged, the phonetic changes which we have just noted would inevitably have led in the long run to a gulf between spelling and pronunciation. As a matter of fact, spelling conventions changed very considerably during the fourteenth and fifteenth centuries, but, unfortunately, they changed in a direction which was largely irrelevant to phonetic change. Hasty and ill-formed letters made certain visual safeguards desirable, if not essential. *Un*, the indefinite article, looked like a cluster of up-and-down strokes. To make it more readily identifiable, a *g* was added, hence *vng*, *ung*. Since a final unpointed *i* could easily be mistaken for the last stroke of such letters as *u*, *v*, *n*, *m* (thus *m*, for instance, could be misread as *iu*, *in*, *ni*, *ui*, and vice versa), final *y* was preferred, hence *amy*, *cry*, *midy*, *party*. Because an initial *u* could be read as *u* or *v*, it was found convenient to place an *h* in front of the sign *u* to indicate that it must be read as a vowel, hence a written distinction between *uile* = *vile* = mod.F. *ville*, and *huile* 'oil'; *uit* = *vit* 'he lives' and *huit* 'eight'. *Seu* < *savoir* could be read as *sen* or *s'en* (there were no apostrophes), so the form *sceu* helped to indicate the pronunciation and thus to identify the word as the past participle of *savoir* (which was often written *scauoir* or even *scapuoir*). In the absence of an acute accent, some scribes tried to overcome the problem of indicating the sound of final stressed [e] by writing *-et*, and wrote *-ez* for the equivalent of the modern *-és*. Unfortunately other scribes—and indeed sometimes the same ones—also wrote *-ez* for the final unstressed *e* [ə] plus *s*.

In general, the scribes were guided by two principles, both ultimately connected with Latin: namely differentiation and *rapprochement*. Differentiation meant that words which were different in meaning and believed to be unrelated were given a different spelling, even if they were homophones (i.e. identical in pronunciation): hence *pois* 'peas', *poids* 'weight', and *poix* 'pitch' for earlier *pois*, which had been used for all three; hence also *doit* or *doibt* 'he owes', 'he must' versus *doigt* 'finger'; hence *mes* (possessive), *mais* ('but'), *mets* ('dish') for earlier *mes*; hence *seau* 'bucket' and *sceau* 'seal' for earlier *seau*. *Rapprochement*, on the other hand, involved spelling alike words which were believed to be semantically and morphologically related: hence *grand*, rather than *grant*, because of *grandeur* and *grande*, *il perd* for earlier *il pert*, because of *nous perdons*, *il(s) perdent*. The muting of final consonants made this last kind of substitution all the easier: it made no difference to the pronunciation.

Where a preconsonantal [l] had, as was regular, vocalised to [u], the earlier spelling had not always taken account of the fact (*autre*, but often *altre*). Mid.F. scribes indicated both the old and the new sound and wrote *aultre*. In contact with final *-s*, *-al*, *-el*, *-ol* had become *-aus*, *-eus*, *-ous*. Scribal practice used the graphy *ꭓ* as an abbreviation for *-us*, but a later generation of scribes thought that *-aꭓ*, *-eꭓ*, *-oꭓ*, were a poor reflexion of the sound, and added the *u* which they could hear, hence *-aux*, *-eux*, *-oux*. Unfortunately the principle of *rapprochement* led them to indicate the relationship with the original *-al*, *-el*, *-ol* and they added an *l*, so that in the Mid.F. spellings *chevaulx*, *cheveulx*, *genoulx*, the original [u] is represented three times over.

A preoccupation with etymology (*rapprochement* with Latin), with or without a concern for greater legibility, gave rise to such spellings as *febvre* 'smith' (*fevre* + *faber*); *doubte* (*dote, doute* + *dubium, dubitare*); *pauvre* (*povre* + *pauper*); *sept* (*set* + *septem*); *dictes* (*dites* + *dicitis, dicere*); *faictes, faict* (*faites, fait* + *facitis, facit, factum, facere*); and to the generalised use of Latin initial *h* (*ore, eure* > *heure*). Nor were the *praticiens* always right in their surmises about etymology—they assumed that *pois* (< *pensum*) derived from *pondus*, and accordingly wrote it *poids*; they supposed that *lais* (< *laisser*) derived from *legare, legatum*, and wrote *legs*; they believed that *forsené* (< *for* 'out of' *sen* 'sense' + *é*) had something to do with *force* and wrote *forcené*; and they fancied that *savoir* might have some connexion with *scire*, and therefore wrote it *scauoir*, when they did not try to have the best of both worlds by writing *scapuoir*. Double consonants (not a conspicuous feature of O.F. spelling) come into their own now under Latin influence (*ville* for earlier *vile*); or, with or without that influence, as an indication of nasalisation or (later) denasalisation: *bone* > *bonne*; *feme, fame* > *femme*; *ome* > (*h*)*omme*. Since *c* before *e* or *i* had become [s], there was much hesitation between initial *s* or *c* (*cengle/sangle* < *cingula*; *sercueil/cercueil* < *sarcophagus*); and intervocalic *-ss-* or *-c-* (*chac*(*i*)*er/chasser*; *muc*(*i*)*er/musser* 'to hide'). At this time, hesitation in spelling between *conter/compter* and *penser/panser* is merely eloquent of hesitation in spelling, and has nothing to do with the subsequent divergence of meaning later consecrated by separate spellings.

To be fair to the *praticiens*, many hesitations in spelling were due to hesitation in pronunciation—hesitation, in fact, as to the correct form of the word in question. *Soustance, sustance* and *substance* were all in use: so were *soutil* and *subtil, s'astenir* and *s'abstenir, assoudre* and *absoudre, oscur* and *obscur*. When at the end of the fifteenth century the humanists reformed the pronunciation of Latin, which had long been pronounced as if it were French, it became usual to pronounce every letter in Latin words, and the same principle was brought to bear, in French, on words recently coined and still being coined from Latin, as well as on words of older stock, whose spelling was being Latinised.

As regards morphology, the most important single transformation in this domain was the breakdown of the two-case system, brought about by the loss of flexional *s* from the pronunciation. Even in thirteenth-century French (and earlier still in Anglo-Norman) there had been signs of faltering: by the fourteenth century the system was in full retreat. Thus we find flexional *s* widely used where it is not called for, e.g. oblique singular *chevaus* or *chevals*; nominative singular *freres, bers, barons*; and sometimes even *le ber* as an oblique form. *S* ceases to have any relevance to the two-case system, and becomes a sign of the plural irrespective of case, or, to a diminishing degree, an orthographical survival, as in the (nominative) form *Dieus, Dieux* quite often found even in the fifteenth century. The poet François Villon, trying to write a ballad 'en vieil langage françoys' in 1461, clearly has no conception of the two-case system as such, and his 'Old French' amounts to no more than muddled orthographical reminiscences. As a rule, it was the oblique forms of substantives which were generalised; but in a few cases the nominative has survived, e.g. *soeur, peintre, prêtre, traître*, together with the very special case of *on*. There are even a few cases where both nominative and oblique have survived, though with a differentiation of meaning or at least of use: *sire, seigneur, sieur; copain* and *compagnon*; *gars* and *garçon*; *pâtre* and *pasteur*; *chantre* and *chanteur*. Some substantives owe their present form to back-formations from the plural: thus earlier *chapel/chapeaus, chastel/chasteaus, genoil/genous* give rise, after the breakdown of the two-case system and an ensuing period of hesitation, to the new singulars *chapeau, chasteau, genou*, in opposition to plural forms which were increasingly written *chapeau(l)x, chasteau(l)x, genou(l)x*. Even so, the forms *chastel, chapel, genouil*, are occasionally found as late as the sixteenth century. Needless to say, the definite article, more widely used than it had been before, since it came to be a grammatical marker, an indication of number and gender as well as of 'definition', also lost its case distinctions. Hesitation and uncertainty in the use of the article led to its agglutination to the substantive in a few cases; thus *l'endemain* 'the next day', *l'uette* 'uvula' and *l'ierre* (f.) 'ivy', became *(le) lendemain, (la) luette, (le) lierre. En + le* had in early O.F. become *el*, then *ou*, and *en + les* had become *es*. *Ou* (< *en + le*) came to be confused with *au*, which gradually replaced it, and *es* was gradually replaced by *aux* after a long period of coexistence, though *es* is by no means uncommon even in the sixteenth century. *Dans*, by the way (< *de intus*), is extremely rare until the sixteenth century, when it begins to assume some of the functions of *en*. Already by the end of the thirteenth century, the original demonstrative force of the definite article had weakened considerably,[1] and the article tended to be used more and more mechanically, though it could still be omitted before abstract nouns, and before plurals, whether abstract or not. The weakening of the definite article had implications for the partitive too. Thus, though *boire vin, mangier pain* are still found, on the other hand when we come across examples of *boire del* (= *du*) *vin, mangier del pain*, we can no longer assume

1. Note, however, the survival of demonstrative force in Mod.F. *de la sorte* and *du coup*.

that the wine or bread has already been referred to. When a plural substantive is preceded by an adjective, the combination may be introduced by *de*, by *des*, or indeed by nothing. The indefinite article continues to be used in the plural, but to an increasing extent only in the sense of 'a pair of', 'a set of', or with nouns which have no singular. Demonstrative forms such as *celui* and *celle* could still be used adjectivally as late as the sixteenth century, while *ceste* could still be used as a pronoun. *Cestui* (or *cettui*) had both functions, but was used less and less. The feminine plural adjective *cestes* was extremely rare by the fifteenth century. *Cil*, a formal survival of the O.F. nominative singular, is still found in the sixteenth century, but without distinction of case. The possessive shows considerable analogical development. The O.F. feminine stressed forms *moie, toie, soie* (earlier *meie, toe, soe*) were gradually replaced by the analogical forms *mienne, tienne, sienne* based on the masculine *mien, tien, sien* (earlier *mien, tuen, suen*). During the fourteenth century, the old elided feminine unstressed possessives *m', t', s'* were replaced by the masculine forms *mon, ton, son* before feminine nouns and adjectives beginning with a vowel. By the middle of the fifteenth century, only a few survivals are found, increasingly stereotyped, e.g. *m'amie, m'amour* and the exclamation *par m'ame*! By the fifteenth century, *leur* nearly always takes an analogical *s* before a plural complement. *Vo*, originally a Picard form of the unstressed singular possessive (a back-formation from the plural *vos*) continued to be used sporadically in Parisian texts. Subject pronouns are still frequently omitted and, when used, may be separated from the verb and given a full stress. The plural form *il* is now, however, generally replaced by *ils*, a form which is also sometimes used instead of *elles*. *Elle*, earlier nominative only, comes to be used as an oblique form as well, under the influence of the plural pronoun *elles*, which had traditionally had both functions. This new oblique use of *elle* leads to the elimination of the older stressed feminine object pronoun *li*. The *un*stressed *in*direct object pronoun *li*, used for both genders, is replaced by *lui*, formerly a stressed accusative and dative masculine form, but henceforward used for both genders as a dative, and occasionally also used for *elle* as a direct object pronoun, while still continuing its traditional use as a masculine accusative form. It might be pointed out here that stressed forms of pronouns were normal in Mid.F. before the infinitive and the present participle, though rare before finite verbs, e.g. *pour moy abandoner*; (*en*) *soy hastant*; but *il se hasta*. Even the sixteenth century maintained for a time the medieval possibility of substituting *eulx* (masculine *and* feminine) for reflexive *soy* or *se*. As regards the relative pronoun, the most noteworthy feature is the use of *que* for *qui* in the nominative, first as a singular, and later as a plural pronoun as well. The oblique *qui*, dependent on a preposition, was frequently used of things as well as persons.

There is a notable increase in the use of analogical feminine forms of adjectives of the *grant*, *fort* type, though it must be added that *grant* showed itself to be particularly conservative, the feminine *grande(s)* being in the main used predicatively rather than attributively, e.g. *la besoigne est grande*, but *ceste grant besoigne*. Present participles too only gradually adopt the termination *-ante* when feminine. This hesitation in adjectives and participles has its relevance to the formation of adverbs, since the important class ending in *-ment* owed its origin to the addition of *-mente*, the ablative case of the Latin *mens*, to the feminine form of the adjective. Thus we find hesitation between the older, phonetically regular *forment*, and the newer *fortement*, between *diligenment* and *diligentement*, between *granment* and *grandement*, and between *vaillanment* and *vaillantement*. It is, incidentally, not always the new form which prevailed in the end: *fortement* and *grandement* survived, it is true, but *diligentement* and *vaillantement* did not. Adjectives in *-al* and *-el* (the former is learned, the latter popular), and such words as *tel* and *quel*, are also slow to adopt analogical feminine forms. In the case of adjectives in *-al*, this meant that even as late as the sixteenth century we sometimes find feminine plurals in *-au(l)x* as well as in *-ales*, e.g. *royales*, but also *royaulx* in *ordonnances royaulx* and *lettres royaulx*. The feminine forms of a small number of adjectives came to be used for both genders: *large* (O.F. masc. *lars/larc*); *vuide* (O.F.masc. *vuis/vuit*); *roide* (O.F.masc. *rois/roit*); and *chauve* (O.F.masc. *chaus/chauf*). This phenomenon is due to various associative influences, e.g. the substantives *largesse*, *largeur* supporting *large*; the verbs *vuider*, *roidir* supporting *vuide*, *roide*, and, in the case of *chauve*, perhaps association with the feminine substantive *teste*.

In the verbal system a large number of analogical levellings take place during this period. The older imperfect (and conditional) endings *-oie*, *-oies*, *-oie(t)* give way gradually to the forms *-ois*, *-ois*, *-oit*. In the present indicative, the first person singular termination *-e* becomes universal in first conjugation verbs, except where the stem ends in a vowel (*je suppli, je pri*). In the present subjunctive of first conjugation verbs, the earlier distinction from the indicative in the singular is lost, except in rare stereotyped optative expressions such as *Dieu gart/gard . . .* and *se m'ait/m'aid Dieu*. In all conjugations, the first and second persons plural of the present subjunctive tend increasingly to end in *-ions*, *-iez*, but the older terminations *-ons*, *-ez* are still sometimes found, as late as the sixteenth century. In the imperfect subjunctive of first conjugation verbs, the older first and second persons plural in *-issions*, *-issiez* are gradually replaced by

-*assions*, -*assiez*. In the third person singular, the form -*asse* is often found, side by side with the 'historical' form -*ast*. In the past definite, there is much regularisation of alternating stems; thus *oi, eus, eut/ot* become *eus, eus, eut*; *feis, fesis, feist* become *f(e)is, f(e)is, f(e)ist*; and *foi, fus, fut* become *fus, fus, fut*; and, except in the first conjugation, an *s* is commonly added to the first person singular in the many cases where there was none before: on the one hand the traditional *je dis, je fis*, and on the other the innovations *je parti(s), je dormi(s)*. The third person plural of first conjugation verbs sometimes appears as -*arent*, a phenomenon which may be explained by the analogy of the other terminations -*as, -a, -ames, -astes*, though it is also in line with the popular tendency to open [ɛr] to [ar] (see p. 70). By the end of the sixteenth century, however, this termination was considered to be a 'Gasconism'. Analogical -*s* is frequently added to the first person singular of the present indicative of verbs other than the first conjugation: *je vien, vieng, viens*; *tien, tieng, tiens*; *je fai(s)*; *je sen(s)*; *je di(s)*; *je meur(s)*. *Je croy, je voy* held out somewhat longer, and indeed, *j'ai* has done so down to the present day. Vocalic alternation (see pp. 59–60) is substantially levelled in those verbs in which it is the only irregularity: nevertheless one still finds not infrequently in the fifteenth century, and occasionally even in the sixteenth, such alternations as *lieve/levons*; *poise/pesons*; *espoire/esperons*; *maine/menons*; *pleure/plourons*; *treuve/trouvons*. The regular futures of *venir* and *tenir*, *je vendrai* and *je tendrai*, were in O.F. in homonymic collision with the future of *vendre* and *tendre*. To remedy this, Mid.F. substituted the forms *je viendrai, je tiendrai*, based on the stem-stressed forms of the present indicative. As for syllabic alternation (see pp. 60–61), it is rare by the sixteenth century, though Palsgrave (1530) still notes *je desjune, je manjeue*, and *je parole*. The -*t*- of euphony in inverted forms of the third person singular, avoiding hiatus with a preceding -*e* or -*a*, appears to be a sixteenth-century development: it is extremely rare in the texts of the period, but is discussed by some of the grammarians.

Syntax. Early in the period, the two-case system ceased to function. Very slowly, the word-order adapted itself to the new situation. Sentences may still begin with a direct object, but they tend to do so only when there is a strong logical link with the previous sentence, e.g. *Telles paroles dist le bon roy*; *Autre chose fist Nostre Seigneur*. The device known as *reprise*, by means of which a word or phrase may be isolated at the beginning of a sentence, and 'taken up' later by means of a pronoun, comes into its own: it had existed in O.F., but had been little used. Now the type *Cest ome vi ier* comes to be rivalled by *Cest homme, (je) le vi hier*. The order subject–object–verb (*rejet*), though still not uncommon in relative clauses, where the subject is a pronoun, becomes rare where the subject is a substantive, e.g., in a certain type of prose style: *Le diable son ame gouvernoit*. Another important development in word-order is that inversion is no longer automatic after a preceding adverb or adverbial phrase. It is still quite frequently found in the fifteenth century, but the direct word-order is also common, and particularly so when the subject is a pronoun. The noun object of an infinitive still usually precedes the infinitive (or, where relevant, the finite verb on which the infinitive depends); and the noun object may still be intercalated between the auxiliary and the past participle. There is still much hesitation as to the position of the adjective, but at least there is a strong tendency to make such common monosyllabic adjectives as *grant, fort, bon* precede, and to avoid placing adjectives of colour before the substantive.[1] A common feature of Mid.F. is the separation of coordinated adjectives by the substantive they qualify, thus: *tres mauvai. homme et cruel; longs doys* ('fingers') *et gresles; ce bon vin et frais un beau chasteau et plaisant*.

Pronoun objects continue throughout the period to occur in the order: direct before indirect, as in O.F. (see p. 61), and to precede the finite verb rather than the dependent infinitive, e.g. *il le m'a donné; se vous me voulez courroucer*. Also, as in O.F., the object pronoun, whether direct or indirect, precedes the second of two coordinated imperatives, though it follows the first (*Apprenez-les a tous maulx, et les batez*) unless the first imperative is introduced by some other word (*Or t'en va* [*et me laisse*]). In the interrogative, the O.F. type with absolute inversion still frequently occurs: *Vient ton argent? Est ta puissance perdue?* The *reprise* construction *Ton argent vient-il? Ta puissance est-elle perdue?* is well attested in the fifteenth century, but the modern type *Est-ce que ta puissance es perdue?* is not found at all before the sixteenth, and is extremely rare even then.

With increased stereotyping, subject pronouns lose much of their autonomy, yet they can still be used emphatically and separated from the verb, e.g. *Il, par invention grande, mesla deux especes de animaus* compare, however, two contradictory examples from a poem of Charles d'Orléans (1394–1465): *Je qui suis Fortune nommée*, side by side with the modern type *Moy, Fortune, je parleray*. The O.F. type of identification *ce sui je, ce es tu, ce est il, ce somes nos, ce estes vos, ce sont il(s)* is still usual in Mid.F., until the very end of the period.

Mid.F. continues and even refines upon the laxity of O.F. sentence

---

1. In the sixteenth century, *rouge vin, blanc pain*, etc., were considered to be Picardisms.

structure. *Pour* and *sans* + infinitive may be used without reference to the subject of the main clause, e.g. *si vous en ay je batus/pour en estre chastiez* 'so that you might mend your ways'; *le guolfe de Cret qui dure ccclxxx milles/sans veoir terre* 'without any sight of land'. The relative clause may be remote from its antecedent: *et ce bien lui aprint adversité, qui n'est pas petit* 'and it was adversity which taught him this not inconsiderable benefit'. Participles and gerunds do not have to be related to the subject of the main clause: e.g. *L'artillerie . . . vint tuer un trompette en apportant un plat de viande,* and *Ceux de dedans tuerent un herault en les allant sommer,* both from Commynes. As in O.F., articles, demonstratives, possessives and adjectives do not have to be repeated, even when added substantives imply a change of gender or number, e.g. *la grant ayde et secours; sa vie, meurs et condicions; le prince sera ennuyé du service, gratuité et plaisance qu'il avoit prins en ceste proprieté.* Verbs tend to agree, as in O.F., with the nearest of two or more coordinated subjects. Object pronouns may be used without change or repetition, even when coordinated verbs are incompatible as to construction, e.g. *pour les festier et faire bonne chiere;* and the same auxiliary may be used for two coordinated verbs which in isolation call for different auxiliaries, e.g. *tout m'est failli et habandonné. Avoir* is sometimes used instead of *estre* as the auxiliary of the verb *aller.* The relative *que* is often used extremely loosely, as a grammatical *passe-partout: en toutes les manieres que on y peut faire et avoir prouffit; la cause que* (= *pour laquelle*) *l'un eschappe.* On the credit side, however, Mid.F. is meticulous—though pleonastic—in repeating a subordinating *que* when the construction has been interrupted, e.g. *Gardez que ceste dame que je vous baille que lui* (= *elle*) *et son enffant gectés dedans la mer.*

Parts of speech may overlap in function. Thus in *le regnant a tort* 'the usurper', *regnant* has the best of both worlds: it is substantivised by the definite article, but it nevertheless has a complement. In *au repasser celle eaue* 'in crossing that river once again' and *jusques au souffrir durs tourmens* 'to the point of enduring grievous hardships', we may see a similar phenomenon. As in O.F., *any* infinitive may be substantivised.

The adjectival and verbal functions of the present participle are not yet distinguished, and the participle agrees with its subject irrespective of function. It is to be noted, however, that the agreement is normally only in number (*-ans* or *-ens*), and not in gender. Forms in *-antes* functioning verbally occur, but they are rather rare, and this may help to explain that with the muting of final *-s* and final *-t*, participles in *-ans* could no longer be distinguished phonetically from (invariable) participles in *-ant*. There is no rule for the agreement of the past participle of verbs conjugated with *avoir*. On the one hand there is often no agreement with a preceding direct object (as is obligatory in Mod.F.), and on the other hand we not infrequently find agreement by anticipation when the participle precedes the direct object. The first statement of the modern rule was made by the poet Clément Marot in a poem published in 1538 (see pp. 115-16).

The O.F. possibility of expressing manner or instrumentality by using *par* with the infinitive is maintained in Mid.F., though we also see the beginnings of the Mod.F. construction with *en* + present participle, e.g. *par les maudire* = *en les maudissant*; *par toy reciter* = *en te récitant*, but on the other hand, in Guillaume Tardif's *Grammatica compendiosissima* (1475), *en amant*, and not *par amer*, is given as the equivalent of Lat. *amando*. As in O.F., *pour* + infinitive (not always, as we have seen, related to the subject of the main clause) was frequently used to express causality as well as finality, a possibility which sometimes gave rise to ambiguity. The so-called 'narrative infinitive', e.g. *et l'autre de crier*, where *de crier* = *cria*, is attested in the thirteenth century, but does not become at all common until the end of the fourteenth. In the third person, *aller* + infinitive may be used as the equivalent of a past definite (*va parler* = *parla*). This is to be distinguished carefully from the modern use of *aller* + infinitive to express imminent futurity. The latter construction, however, is clearly attested for the first time in the fifteenth century, and thus partly overlaps chronologically with the other. To the already existing means of expressing passivity—the *on* construction and the use of *estre* + past participle of transitive verb (only with the agent introduced far more often by *de* than by *par*)—Mid.F. adds the possibility of using the reflexive with a passive sense: *le vin se boit*; *tous voz faiz se delaissent*.[1] The dependent infinitive, whether 'pure' or introduced by a preposition, undergoes considerable extension, thus *le roy commanda au chevalier (de) aler a Bourges* begins to rival the O.F. type *le roy commanda au chevalier que (il) alast a Bourges* (see pp. 61-2).

On the whole, subordination is more explicit than it had been in O.F. Conjunctions are less readily omitted, there are more of them, and they indicate grammatical relationships more precisely. Compound conjunctival expressions are not yet so stereotyped, however, as to exclude the intercalation of adverbs and parentheses; hence for example *pour ce (seulement) que . . .* ; *puis (doncques) que . . .* ; *pour ce (vrayment) que . . ,* ; *pour ce, (comme dit est), que . . .* This is possible in Mod.F. only in the case of *lors (même) que*. Negation continues O.F. usage, but *pas, point* are more frequently added, with-

---

1. Note, however, that in Mid. and even Classical French, this construction was not restricted, as it is now, to inanimate subjects.

out undue emphasis. In absolute negation involving the use of partitive *de*, only *point* is used at first (*je n'ai point d'argent*): *pas* is not used in this way until the sixteenth century, and then only rarely. In contradiction of statements or in reply to questions, *non* is used with the appropriate tense and person of the auxiliaries *estre, avoir*, if either of those verbs has been used in the previous utterance. Otherwise *faire* is used, standing for any other verb. *Non* is rarely used alone in answer to questions: this function is normally borne by *nenny, nenil*.

The use of the imperfect subjunctive in hypothesis declines very noticeably during the Mid.F. period. Even in O.F., it was already rivalled by the modern type of hypothetical sentence characterised by the imperfect indicative in the if-clause and the conditional in the consequent.

The perfect is used more and more for the past definite, although the latter tense could be used in conversation up to and well beyond the end of the Mid.F. period, with reference to events having no connexion with the present; but even here it is seriously rivalled by the perfect. Thus Commynes could write *Aprés ceste journée est demouré le roy Edouard pacifique en Angleterre jusques a sa mort.* O.F. uses of the past definite such as *hui ne manjai* 'I haven't eaten today', become impossible in Mid.F., which eventually adopts a 'twenty-four hour rule' excluding the use of the past definite to narrate the events of the same day. Thus *hier ne manjai (pas)* was still possible, though rivalled by *hier n'ai (pas) mangé*. We not infrequently find the two tenses used side by side with the same function, e.g. *Je t'ai receu quand tu y vins*. In O. and Mid.F., the pluperfect and the past anterior were virtually interchangeable. In the fifteenth century we find the first uses of the *passé surcomposé*—the type *j'ai eu aimé*, later to be the subject of comment by sixteenth-century grammarians. Its use (confined to subordinate clauses) is certainly to be related to an increased use, in the spoken language, of the perfect in preference to the past definite in main clauses.

Rien and *quelque chose* show increasing signs of grammaticalisation, and consequently tend to lose their original feminine gender. Legalistic phrasing, plus Latin influence—the two often went together—leads to widespread use of such 'pointers' as *ledit, ladite, susdit*; and of *lequel, laquel(l)e*, considered more explicit than *qui* and *que*, which did not vary in number or gender.

Vocabulary. The vocabulary of O.F. undergoes a steady transformation. Many words disappear after being pushed into a subordinate position by the advent of neologisms coined from Latin and having more prestige and novelty value. The new Latinisms often have the same origin as the older word they eventually replace: *antif/antique*;

aver/avare; *batoier/baptis(i)er*; *beneiçon/benediction*; *cloufichier*[1]*/crucifier*; *enferm/infirme*; *excomengier/excommunier*; *esmer/estimer*; *grief/grave*; *leün/legume*; *mecine/medecine*; *mire, miege/medecin*; *orine/origine*; *rade/rapide*; *roelle* (*du genoil*)/*rotule*; *souef/suave*; *treü/tribut*. Other words, whether of Latin or Germanic origin, are rivalled or replaced for one reason or another: *baut* by *joyeux*; *broigne* by *cuirasse*; *certaineté* by *certitude*; *gehir* by *avouer*; *guerredon* by *recompense*; *heaume* by *salade*; *huese* by *botte(s)*; *ost* by *armée*. It must be emphasised, however, that in every case there was a considerable period of coexistence. Some words are not changed in form, but undergo a kind of internal re-evaluation. Thus *glaive* (a somewhat irregular development of Lat. *gladium*), which in O.F. regularly meant 'lance', is 'relatinised' in Mid.F. and comes to mean 'sword'—its only meaning today. *Chose publique* appears as a calque of *res publica*, and *sourcil*, in the sense of 'arrogance', as a calque of *supercilium*. There is much hesitation between more, and less, learned forms of the same neologism: *medecin/medicin*; *femenin/feminin*; *interroger/interroguer*; *subjuger/subjuguer*; and *naviger/naviguer*—but also *navier* (not to mention *nag(i)er* < *navigare*, used more and more in the sense of 'to swim' rather than 'to sail'). The gender of some not uncommon words, subsequently fixed, is still hesitant: *comté*; *duché*; *espace*; *evangile*; *evesché*; *honneur*; *miracle*; *ordre*, etc.

Latin is overwhelmingly the principal source for neologisms. Whether as a result of translation from Latin or not, large numbers of new learned words are attested for the first time in this period, e.g. *argonaute*, *bibliotheque*, *cadavre*, *chaos*, *chimere*, *confisquer*, *epithete*, *evidence*, *exsangue*, *faciliter*, *redempteur*, *regularité*. A few words are borrowed from Provençal: in the fourteenth century *abeille* (strictly a hybrid of northern *aveille* and southern *abelha*), *bastide*, *emparer*; in the fifteenth *banquette*, *cable*, *cadeau*, *cigale*. Flemish provided *brodequin*, *boulever* (> *boulevard*), *digue* and *biere* 'beer' in the fifteenth century. Commercial, diplomatic, military and nautical relations with Italy led to the introduction of a substantial number of Italian loan-words. Professor T. E. Hope has calculated that 59 were borrowed in the fourteenth century, and 91 in the fifteenth. Of these only a few need be mentioned here: *accort*, *ambassade*, *ambassadeur*, *banque*, *banqueroute*, *canon*, *cavalcade*, *courtisan*, *escadre*, *estropier*, *guider*, *perruque*, *plage*, *race*, *trafic*, and, transmitted via Italian from Arabic: *arsenal*, *douane*, *magasin*, *chiffre* and *zéro*, the last two deriving from the same Arabic word. Considering the Hundred Years War and the frequent presence of

---

1. There is an element of popular etymology (*clou+fichier*) in this word.

English soldiers on French soil, the English contribution during this period is very slight: *bigot, dogue,* and *milord,* all borrowed in the fifteenth century.

There were as yet no dictionaries of French, but there were glossaries of Latin and French, some of which were partial adaptations of the frequently copied thirteenth-century *Catholicon* of Giovanni Balbi of Genoa, in which Latin words were explained in Latin. A great many of the French equivalents given in these derivative glossaries are in fact minimal adaptations of the Latin words, while others are analytical explanations, e.g. *ablactare = sevrer enfant; exsanguis = senz sanc.*

The prestige of Latin, the view that French was inferior to it, and the activity of such translators as, in the fourteenth century, Nicolas de Vérone (Lucan), Pierre Bersuire (Livy), Raoul de Presles (St Augustine), and Nicolas Oresme (Aristotle in Latin), and in the fifteenth Jean de Rovroy (Frontinus), Jean le Bègue (Sallust), Vasque de Lucène (Quintus Curtius), Robert Gaguin (Julius Caesar), Laurent de Premierfait (Cicero), and Octovien de Saint Gelais (Virgil), led to an influence of Latin on French which went far beyond the mere renovation of vocabulary. Latin constructions, too, were imitated in French, though they were not all ideally suited to a language with a very different morphology. In the main they were intended to give the language greater dignity and brevity. Six constructions, in particular, are worthy of mention in this connexion.

(1) Absolute constructions, based on the Latin ablative absolute. This type had been rudimentary in O.F., and confined to *oïr* and *veoir,* e.g. *oïant tous, veant tous* 'publicly and heard by all'. It now came into its own, e.g. *Faiz les veux dessusdis . . . ; Laquelle chose entendue . . . ; Tout preambule presupposé . . . ; Ces deux multiplications adjostees ensemble . . .*

(2) The accusative and infinitive. This construction existed in O.F., but was limited to verbs of perception and factitive verbs. In Mid.F. it is widely used with verbs of cognition, declarative verbs, and even with *vouloir, regretter* and *souffrir* (= *permettre*), e.g. *On dit telles estre les Arpies; le Juif ne souffroit pas soy estre converti; cuiderent le plus lointain estre le plus seur.*

(3) The linking relative (*relatif de liaison*) used at the beginning of a sentence or clause in preference to a demonstrative, e.g. *Quoi faisant, s'esloigna; Pour lesquelles garder furent establis cinq chevaliers.*

(4) The use of a substantive linked with a past participle and dependent on a preposition (based on the Latin type *post pacem conclusam; ab urbe condita*), e.g. *après aulcuns jours trespassez; aprés la messe oÿe; non obstant maintes peines eues; par paour con-*

ceue; sur laquelle offre ainsi faicte; *depuis ceste exposicion fete, jetée et arrestée.*

(5) The use of the subjunctive in subordinate clauses dependent on the conjunction *comme*, which was wrongly assumed to derive from Latin *cum* (it derives in fact from *quo modo*), e.g. *comme il y ait ja long temps esté* (causal); *comme le prieur se pourmenast* (temporal).

(6) The use of *Que si . . .* ('but if', 'if however') as a calque of Latin *quod si*, e.g. *Que si je ne te l'ay rendu de mot a mot selon le latin, tu doibs entendre que cela a esté faict tout exprés*; *Que si on les escrivoit en une autre (sorte), on pourroit soubstenir l'orthographe estre raisonnable.*

The causal use of *comme celui/celle qui* (= 'because he/she') may or may not owe something to the Latin *quippe qui.* At all events this construction was common already in O.F.

One result of translation which eventually affected original composition as well was the use of doublets, or linked pairs of synonyms or near-synonyms. In translation this sprang from a fear or conviction that no single French word could possibly be the exact equivalent of a Latin one, so that, if one was to convey the sense of the original, one must provide two terms, hoping that the exact nuance or stylistic equivalent lay somewhere between the two, e.g. *dressa et institua*; *ars et bruslé.* Unfortunately, this became a mere trick of style in original compositions, hence in some authors the almost automatic use of two terms for one: *frequentoit et visitoit; le lieu et espace; venir et proceder de . . . ; perpetrez et commis*; *pechez et offences; visceres et entrailles.*

Latinism was at the time a basic need of the language, and though at its most undiscriminating it became a gratuitously regressive mania, it nevertheless helped on the whole to make grammatical relationships somewhat more explicit, to tighten up sentence structure, and to provide stylistic ornaments. Though Mid.F. presents a bewildering variety of forms and constructions, together with an increasingly unwieldy vocabulary, at least it shows great flexibility and adaptability. It already shows some of its stylistic potential, in the many different registers which, by the fifteenth century, are discernible according to subject matter and, in the case of dramatic works, according to character. Nor is the attitude to language a complacent one: there is at least a dawning awareness that the French language lacks rules, and that this is a major reason why it is inferior to Latin. Translators occasionally comment on the inadequacy of French in their eyes, or try to justify their approximations or their over-elaborate renderings. There are even, from the late fourteenth century onwards, several treatises on *la seconde rethoricque*, understood as versification, which show some preoccupation with certain phonetic, rhythmic and even semantic aspects of the vernacular. A glimmer of things to come is to be seen at last in Guillaume Tardif's *Grammatica compendiosissima*, printed in 1475. In the middle of this grammar of Latin, the author quite suddenly introduces French verb-forms corresponding to his Latin paradigms. It is not much, yet it shows some curiosity about the French language, and the suspicion that it too has a system, if only one could discover it.

To end this chapter, here is a short prose extract from the middle of the fifteenth century. It is from the anonymous *Cent Nouvelles Nouvelles*:

Quand l'yvroigne entendit que encores le failloit enterrer, ains qu'il montast en paradis, il fut tout content d'obeÿr. Si fut tantost troussé et mis dessus le chariot, ou gueres ne fut sans dormir. Le chariot estoit bien atelé; si furent tantost a Stevelinghes ou ce bon ivroigne fut descendu tout devant sa maison. Sa femme et ses gens furent appellez, et leur fut ce bon corps saint rendu, qui si tres fort dormoit que, pour le porter du chariot en sa maison et sur son lit le getter, jamais ne s'esveilla. Et la fut il ensevely entre deux linceux sans s'esveiller bien de deux jours aprés.

[When the drunkard heard that he still had to be buried before he could go up to heaven, he was content to do as he was told. So he was promptly lifted up and placed on the cart, where he soon fell asleep. The cart was well harnessed, and they were soon in Scheveningen, where that good drunkard was lifted down right in front of his house. His wife and his servants were called, and that precious holy relic was handed over to them, so soundly asleep that for all their carrying him from the cart into the house and throwing him on his bed, he never woke up. And there he was laid to rest between two sheets, and did not awaken for a full two days thereafter.]

Features calling for particular comment are the (optional) inversion after *et*, and the fact that the subject of *pour le porter . . . et . . . le getter* has to be guessed from the context.

5

PROGRESS AND PRESTIGE IN THE
SIXTEENTH CENTURY

The Mid.F. developments which were still taking place in the sixteenth century have for the most part been already dealt with in the
previous chapter. The main emphasis in the present chapter will be
not on internal changes but rather on attitudes towards language, for
the sixteenth is the first century in which the French language was
discussed as a possible rival and successor to Latin, and the first
century in which attempts were made to describe it, analyse it,
legislate for it, compare it in detail with other languages, and speculate
about its origins. Furthermore, although to an increasing extent
French had, since the thirteenth century, been *one* of the languages
used for official purposes, it was not until the sixteenth that it was
recognised as *the* official language to the exclusion of Latin and
provincial languages or dialects.

The political unification of France continued, a major step being
the confiscation to the crown of Auvergne, Bourbonnais and Marche
on the death of Charles III, Constable of Bourbon. Numerous
administrative measures consolidated the royal power even in the
remoter provinces, but a series of wars, at first with Italy and then
with the Holy Roman Empire, prevented that prosperity at home
which might otherwise have ensued, and ended with the loss of the
Italian territories won in earlier campaigns, a loss only partly offset
by the recovery of Calais from the English (Treaty of Cateau-
Cambrésis, 1559). In the meantime Protestantism had made considerable headway in France, and attempts to repress it led to eight
outbreaks of civil war spread over the period 1562–93. The Valois
dynasty came to an end with the assassination of Henri III in 1589,
and the Bourbon dynasty was founded when Henri de Navarre
abjured the reformed religion and became Henri IV of France in
February 1594. By the time of his assassination in 1610, Henri IV

had done much to conciliate and reassure the Protestant minority (Edict of Nantes, 1598) and to restore the central authority over the country as a whole.

Against such a troubled background as this, the gains and achievements of the French language, and the richness of its literature, are all the more remarkable.

Before we consider the polemics about the respective merits of French and Latin—or for that matter French and Italian—it will be convenient to deal first with the linguistic unification of France. The polemics, after all, concerned the language of literature and learning: no one seriously suggested that the nation as a whole should speak Latin or Italian.

At the end of the fifteenth century, French was already the only vernacular used for literary purposes in the north. The spoken language was to an increasing degree based on the language of Paris, Orleans, Tours, Chartres, etc., though regional pronunciations were certainly widespread and carried no particular social stigma as yet. There were numerous rustic dialects too, local variations of regional variations of Francien, spoken in parts of Normandy and in the north-east, but they were not used in writing. Breton was still widely spoken in Brittany, but the original linguistic boundary had moved a considerable distance westwards since the early Middle Ages, and in *la Bretagne bretonnante* itself, a minority could speak, and sometimes write, French. South of the Loire, Poitou and Saintonge had long been French-speaking, but the original boundary of the *langue d'oc* was still a major barrier as regards the spoken language, though the written language was already often French by this time in Auvergne, Marche and Dauphiné. Indeed, it can be said that in the areas where Gascon, Languedocien, Limousin and Provençal (known collectively as Occitan) were universally spoken, French was used more readily in literature than in official documents, for which Latin or local languages were often preferred. There was very little literature indeed in any vernacular other than French, and those few authors who wrote in local languages in nearly every case wrote also in French. The linguistic state of France in the early part of the sixteenth century was described by John Palsgrave in his *Esclarcissement de la langue françoyse* (London, 1530). Palsgrave makes it clear that the best French was *spoken* in Paris and in the region between the Seine and the Loire, and that, whatever part of France one came from, the only kind of *written* French to have prestige was that based on this spoken tongue. He adds that all over France people holding certain offices were able to speak that kind of French. There was, of course, still room for argument about what constituted the best kind of Parisian French. The humanist and grammarian Robert Estienne based his

grammar (1557) on an intellectual and social *élite* compounded of the
Court, the Parlement, the Chancellery and the Treasury. His son
Henri, however, while still accepting the language of Paris as the
norm, rejected on the one hand the artificialities of the courtiers, and
on the other some idiosyncrasies of the *menu peuple*, insisting on a
basic standard common to Paris and other major cities such as
Orleans, Vendôme, Chartres and even the more remote Bourges.
Throughout the sixteenth century, the written language, like the
spoken, was liable, whether through inadvertence or as a matter of
deliberate policy, to incorporate certain regional features. Insofar as
these were inadvertent, they steadily declined as the century wore
on, and insofar as they were deliberately cultivated, the vogue for
them passed. In the south of France, by this time politically united
with the north, and constantly reminded of the fact by regional Parle-
ments and by the ubiquitousness of the royal authority, French was
steadily gaining ground among the literate minority, though as a
language of administration and of written record it was still to some
extent rivalled by Latin and Occitan. A series of royal edicts, from
1490 onwards, had tended to oust Latin from legal proceedings, but
still permitted the use of regional vernaculars. At last, in August
1539, article 111 of the Ordonnances de Villers-Cotterets (a series of
edicts aimed at reforming the administration of justice) excluded
other vernaculars by insisting that all court proceedings, deeds,
judgements, etc., were to be set down *en langage maternel françois et
non aultrement*. Even before the Edicts, French was being used for
official purposes in many towns in the south. After the Edicts, in little
more than ten years, French was used everywhere, even in areas where
the French king had as yet no jurisdiction, such as Béarn, Savoy and
Comtat Venaissin—used, moreover, in ecclesiastical as well as civil
administration and archives. By the end of the sixteenth century, in
the south of France, French was virtually the only vernacular written
and printed. Men like Monluc, Du Bartas and Montaigne could have
written their works in Gascon, had they chosen to do so: significantly,
they did not. It is true to say that French was as yet spoken only by a
tiny minority in the south, but it was an influential minority, and one
which was steadily growing.

Outside France, there was no area in which French was widely
spoken, though it was zealously cultivated by a cultured minority
in England, in parts of Germany, in the Lowlands, and in Savoy.
There was a demand for teachers of French, for grammars and
dictionaries, and owing to the emigration of large numbers of
Huguenots of some education, the demand could be met. A number
of grammars of French were published abroad during the sixteenth
century, mostly in Latin it is true, but sometimes in the language of

the country concerned. Dictionaries of French and English, French and Flemish, French and German, began to appear. Such pedagogical works as these were of uneven value, but at their best they serve today to throw considerable light on the everyday spoken language of Paris. One of the most notable and successful refugee teachers of French was Claude de Sainliens, who settled in London and 'Englished' his name as Claudius Holyband. His conversational grammars *The French Schoolemaister* (1573) and *The French Littelton* (1576) are lively, accurate and instructive. Holyband also produced, in Latin, a treatise on French pronunciation (1580) and a valuable French–English dictionary (1593).

In the Levant, French had lost ground since the time of the Fourth Crusade. Nevertheless, in the reign of François I, the treaty concluded in 1535 with the Ottoman emperor Suleiman the Magnificent gave French a somewhat privileged position as a language of trade and diplomacy in the eastern Mediterranean. In the New World, French traders carried their language to Canada, but there was no permanent French settlement there until the early seventeenth century (Acadia 1604, Quebec 1608). Attempts to settle in South Carolina, in Florida and in Brazil proved abortive.

In France, while the French language was in fact steadily strengthening its position as the official language and as the everyday working medium of communication, scholars were arguing about the respective merits of French and Latin. Latin still enjoyed considerable prestige: it was the usual language of international diplomacy, the usual medium of instruction in schools and universities, and the language of the Church except for its popular sermons. Latin had fixity and rules; it had proved its worth in the domain of thought and literature, and it had been the language of a great empire which the men of the Middle Ages and of the Renaissance greatly admired, while deploring its paganism. On the other hand, the sheer weight of tradition, and its very fixity, counted against it when it came to attempts to adapt it to the inevitable new needs of a totally different society. Latin had in fact throughout the Middle Ages adapted itself, or, to put it another way, it had been corrupted from below by the vernacular. It was pronounced as if it were French, and many medieval Latin words, idioms and phrases were simply transpositions of French. The New Learning, first in Italy and then, some fifty years later, in France, had the effect of renovating Latin studies, of producing better versions of the old texts, and even of producing texts hitherto unknown. The pronunciation of Latin was reformed in the early sixteenth century by such humanists as Erasmus and Charles Estienne, who insisted on a scholarly, would-be ancient pronunciation quite distinct from modern vernaculars. As for the forms of Latin, its grammar and its idioms, these were critically studied in several works written specially for the purpose. Of these not the least interesting is the book entitled *De corrupti sermonis emendatione*, published in 1530 by Mathurin Cordier. In this the reader is warned to avoid in Latin various kinds of gallicism of which the author provides many examples. One might have supposed that this restoration of Latin letters, this quest for pristine purity, would by enhancing the prestige of Latin overshadow the rising vernacular, already looked at askance by men like Charles de Bouelles (*De differentia vulgarium linguarum et gallici sermonis varietate*, Paris 1533), who saw in French no more than corrupt Latin, and, in the multiplicity of its spoken dialects, a further argument against it. In reality, however, the humanist revival of pure Latinity had the opposite effect, for it showed very clearly that, however worth cultivating the Latin language was for aesthetic and scholarly purposes, it was not really suited to the modern age; it was, so to speak, too good for day to day concerns. Its very new-found purity rendered it unsuitable for everyday use. The easy-going adaptability of medieval Latin to the ever-changing needs of society now stood condemned. We must not suppose, however, that Latin was promptly abandoned in favour of French as the vehicle of learning and science; and if some humanists, such as Guillaume Budé, Jean Bodin and Henri Estienne paid the vernacular the compliment of writing some of their works in it, they nonetheless wrote far more in Latin.

In the main, the men of the Renaissance who were in favour of extending the range of French to include domains hitherto reserved for Latin were ready to concede that, as yet, French was not ideally equipped for the task, but that did not deter them from advocating its use: it could, after all, be enriched precisely 'by contact with the ancient tongues' (Claude de Seyssel, 1509); it could—and should—'borrow the garments and adornments of others' (Antoine Fouquelin, 1557). Indeed, in 1548 and 1550 respectively, Jacques de Beaune and Louis Meigret both claimed that French had already benefited from its close contact with Latin and Greek, and that it was precisely that contact which had enabled it to compete with those languages. The best-known plea for the use of French, however, was the work of the poet Joachim du Bellay. It appeared in 1549 under the title *Deffense et Illustration de la langue françoyse*. As a matter of fact, it was original only in its application to French: it owed much of its substance and most of its arguments to an Italian work, the *Dialogo delle lingue* (1542), whose author, Sperone Speroni, had argued for the use of the Tuscan dialect in Italy. Adapting this, Du Bellay argued that no subject is beyond the range of French, provided that it follows classical models. Translation is not enough:

original works are needed to 'illustrate' French (i.e. to give it distinction). French must clearly innovate if it is to equal the richness of the ancient languages. Just as Geoffroy Tory had done in 1529 in his *Champfleury*, Du Bellay pointed out that Latin and Greek too, in their early days, had lacked rules and dignity, and he made the further point that since no modern could hope to rival the ancients in their own languages, Frenchmen would be better employed striving to create masterpieces in a language in which they were not handicapped from the outset. A few humanists went further, and within two years of the appearance of the *Deffense et Illustration*, both Barthélemy Aneau and Guillaume des Autels were arguing that French did not need to imitate any other language. In academic life, too, French had its advocates. The great humanist Jean Bodin put up a plea in 1559 for the use of French as the medium of instruction in arts and sciences alike; while at about the same time Pierre de la Ramée struck a new note by lecturing in French at the Collège de France. To argue for French was of course not to argue that it was necessarily and in every respect the equal of Greek or Latin, but many felt that French was already revealing some of its potential and should be given its chance. In the domain of *belles-lettres*, the use of French was not in question. As for the various branches of science, although much was still being written in Latin, much was also being translated from that language and, more important, French was itself being used to an increasing extent in the composition of original works. It was in French that Ambroise Paré published his important treatises on surgery, and he was followed in this by Julien le Paulmier, Jacques Dalechamps and Laurent Joubert. Forcadel and Peletier du Mans published mathematical treatises in French. Important works on geography by André Thévet, and treatises of natural philosophy and astronomy by Pontus de Tyard, were so many further successes for the vernacular. Thanks to Pierre de la Ramée and Antoine Fouquelin, even dialectic, hitherto a stronghold of Latin, passed under the banner of French. History too was now often being written in French. The most jealously guarded bastion of Latin was theology, and here the Church and the Sorbonne combined to maintain an intolerant attitude, but had to yield in the end, since important manifestos of Protestantism, such as Calvin's *Institution chrétienne* (1541: originally published in Latin 1536) had begun to appear in French, and had to be countered. By the end of the century, the principal Catholic theologians were writing in French, and no longer necessarily or exclusively in Latin.

The rivalry of French and Italian was of a different kind. It was, in fact, far more theoretical. There was no great danger that Frenchmen would write their works, whether scientific or literary, in Italian rather than French or Latin, and even less danger that the nation as a whole, or even its cultured *élite*, would adopt Italian in preference to French as a spoken language. There were two aspects to the 'quarrel'. One was simply the comparison of French and Italian as two vernaculars considered to be worthy, but competing, vehicles of culture and learning. The other was the attack on Italian influence on the French language itself.

The fact that French was even in the running in comparison with Italian is a tribute to the progress it had made in the previous hundred years. Exhausted by wars, France had lagged far behind Italy both culturally and economically. The French campaigns in Italy between 1494 and 1525 had brought the French nobility into contact with a civilisation from which they could not withhold their admiration. Long before the marriage of Catherine de' Medici to the future Henri II in 1533, Italian culture was being enthusiastically imitated in France. François I personally patronised such men as Primaticcio, Leonardo da Vinci, Andrea del Sarto and Benvenuto Cellini. Lyons was almost an Italian city, as well as a staging-post for Italian artists, poets, architects and musicians on their way to Paris or Fontainebleau. French gentlemen spent years at Italian universities; French printers improved their craft in Italy. Italian actors performed plays in French cities; Italian masterpieces were read in the original and zealously translated. If, in the thirteenth century, there had been Italians who wrote in French, there were now not a few Frenchmen capable of writing in Italian.

Already in 1513, in a courteous though rather vague comparison of French and Italian, entitled *La Concorde des deux langaiges*, Jean Lemaire de Belges concluded that the two languages were strictly equal in merit. Enthusiasm for things Italian had not yet turned into bitterness and resentment at favours shown to Italians at Court and in other high places. Later, however, in the regency of Catherine de' Medici and in the reigns of Charles IX and Henri III, Italian influence in France had become much stronger, while on the other hand the cultural inequalities, thanks to her own admittedly later Renaissance, were levelling out; France was no longer so obviously eclipsed by Italy in literary, artistic and scientific matters, or even in classical studies for that matter; and the French language was, following Du Bellay's precept, 'illustrating itself' from day to day. If even Italian cultural superiority could be challenged, there was all the more reason for resenting the favoured position of Italians in France. Anti-Italian feeling ran particularly high in Protestant circles after the Massacre of St Bartholomew (24 August 1572), for Catherine de' Medici was generally held to have instigated it. The affectation of

Italianisms in speech, and to a lesser extent in writing, was merely a side-effect of Italian influence in general. Nevertheless it provoked no fewer than three detailed protests from the pen of the same man, the Protestant humanist Henri Estienne.

In 1565, in a work entitled *Traicté de la conformité du langage françois avec le Grec*, Estienne had already expressed his conviction that French is superior to Italian, on the grounds that it is 'demonstrably' nearer to Greek than any other language, and that Greek is 'as all men acknowledge' manifestly superior to all other languages. (Estienne was not alone, by the way, in discerning affinities between French and Greek.) His attack on the Italianising affectations of courtiers was comparatively mild in this first work. In 1578, however, he inveighed against them with considerable truculence in his *Deux dialogues du nouveau langage françois italianizé, et autrement desguizé, principalement entre les courtisans de ce temps*. 'Celtophile', in whom we may see Estienne himself, takes to task his courtier acquaintance 'Philausone' (the name means 'lover of Italy') for his Italianised jargon, for saying things like: *j'ay l'usance de spaceger par la strade aprés le past* ('I'm in the habit of taking a walk in the street after dinner'); *quelque volte* 'sometimes'; *in case* 'at home'; *Dieu soit ringratié* 'thank God'; *il m'incresce fort* 'I'm very sorry'; *sa maison est fort discoste* 'his house is a long way off'; *ragasch* 'boy', 'page'; *cattif* 'bad'; and for using *se fermer* in the sense of 'to stop', 'to come to a halt'. Celtophile clearly regards the pronunciation [ɛ] for [wɛ] as an Italianism too, for he attributes to Philausone forms which he spells *dret, endret, voudret, alet, francés*, while he is careful to attribute to himself the forms which he writes *droit, endroit, voudroit, aloit, françois*. [ɛ] for [wɛ] was certainly a common substitution, but it was not necessarily an Italianism for all that.

Estienne followed up this onslaught in the following year with his *De la precellence du langage françois*, in which he demonstrated to his own satisfaction that, judged by such subjective criteria as *gravité, gentillesse, bonne grâce, brièveté* and *richesse*, Italian is clearly inferior to French. It is of course not possible to prove the inferiority or superiority of one language to another in this way, or indeed in any other. Moreover, Estienne was at fault in making no distinction between affectations of the kind he attributes to Philausone, and quite unaffected loan-words of real practical value—technical terms associated with a host of new concepts, above all relating to military, nautical, financial, architectural and artistic matters. In fact it has been calculated that some 460 Italian words were borrowed in the course of the sixteenth century, the peak period being 1540–60. Of these, a very high proportion have proved their usefulness and are still current, having long since lost all association with Italy or with Italian: they are to all intents and purposes an integral part of the French vocabulary today. Even those common verbs *attaquer, briller, manquer,* and *réussir,* which one takes completely for granted today, were borrowed from Italian in the sixteenth century. Architectural terms borrowed during the same period are *antichambre, appartement, arcade, architrave, balcon, balustrade, corniche, façade, frise, médaillon, piédestal, pilastre, site, volute,* together with the words *architecte* and *architecture* themselves. Financial: *bilan, escompte, faillite* (*banqueroute* had been borrowed in the fifteenth century). Military: *bastion, bataillon, campagne, caporal, cartouche, casemate, cavalerie, cavalier, escorte, fantassin, infanterie, parapet, sentinelle, vedette.* Nautical terms include: *accoster, bourrasque, boussole, escale, fanal, frégate, gondole, mousse, remorquer.* Fine arts: *arabesque, artisan, cadre, damasquin, estampe, figurine, galbe, relief.* Textiles and clothing: *brocart, brocatelle, capuchon, peluche, soutane.* Music: *cantilène, concert, contrebasse, fugue, madrigal, sérénade, sourdine, théorbe, trio, trombone, villanelle.* Food: *artichaut* (transmitted from Arabic), *cervelas, marron, saucisson, semoule, vermicelle.* Literary: *sonnet, tercet.* Useful adjectives borrowed at this time include *altier, bizarre, brave, brusque, burlesque, fruste, grotesque, jovial* and *leste.* French also acquired a new suffix from Italian—*-esque,* albeit mainly with Italian words; while the superlative or hyperbolical ending *-issime,* already present in French as a Latinism, underwent a further slight extension under Italian influence. One minor later development is curious enough to be worth mentioning here. The Italian suffix *-one* was augmentative in force, but on becoming *-on* in French it came under the attraction of the French *diminutive* suffix *-on.* This explains why *vallon,* which originally, when borrowed, meant a *wide* valley, soon came to mean a *small* valley, a dell: it also explains why *carafon,* borrowed somewhat later, meant for a time 'large carafe' and 'small carafe' (it now means only the latter), and why, to this day, *médaillon* may mean either a large or a small medallion!

Compared with Italian, the influence of other languages was slight. From Spain, a major power at the time, with which France was intermittently at war, came a few military and nautical terms such as: *caboteur, cabotier, camarade, casque, caracole, escouade, parade,* the words *cédille* and *parangon,* and, from Spain's far-off colonies, *cannibale, maïs, patate, savane. Abricot,* transmitted by Spanish from Arabic, was originally the Late Latin *prae-coquum: nègre* and *mélasse,* borrowed at this time, both have Latin roots. The presence of German mercenaries in France during the wars of religion are responsible for the transmission of *chenapan, fifre, Huguenot* (< *Eidgenosse*), *reître* and the verb *trinquer*; while mainly commercial contacts with Flanders and the Lowlands led to the borrowing of *bélître* (originally = 'beggar'), *frelater*, (*la*) *vase*, and the nautical terms *bâbord* and *tribord*.

It is a pity that the most comprehensive description of the French language to appear in the sixteenth century, John Palsgrave's *Esclarcissement de la langue françoyse* (1530) had no effect whatsoever in France, being written in English (in spite of its French title) to teach French to English-speakers. There were several other grammars of French, however, some in French and some in Latin, and all of them, in spite of mutual influences, offering different things. Their interest is of three kinds. Firstly, they throw some light on the history of linguistic theory. This is no primary concern of ours, save insofar as their inadequacies and the limitations of their achievement may be excused in relation to the background of linguistic ideas against which they were composed. Secondly, they throw some light (though not enough) on the living language of the day, considered as a system, and on recent innovations in it. Thirdly, they are of interest because of their possible effect, by prescription or proscription, on the subsequent development of the language.

Let it be said at once that the grammars of the age were overwhelmingly descriptive rather than prescriptive, and, if only for that reason, can hardly have been expected by their authors to have much influence. It must be added that, for reasons closely connected with the linguistic ideas of the day, they were lamentably incomplete, even when considered as purely descriptive grammars. The reason why they were written is to be sought in the statements often made in the early (and even in the later) decades of the century, about the lack of rules for French, about the elusiveness and shapelessness of French as compared with Latin. It was to determine what the basic rules and characteristics of French were, that the early grammarians attempted their analyses of the language spoken and written around them. Unfortunately, their only training in linguistic analysis as the term was then understood was Latin grammar, plus, in some cases, some knowledge of Greek or Hebrew. Whether or not they believed that French derived from Latin (and that derivation was by no means to be taken for granted in sixteenth-century thought), it was the method used for analysing Latin grammar which they applied to the analysis of French. Obviously it was only with considerable strain and a good deal of stretching and lopping that French could be made to fit the Procrustean bed of Latin. Renaissance French was already a highly analytic language, and Latin a highly synthetic one. Not unnaturally, the Renaissance grammarians got into difficulties when they tried to account for the French definite article, a grammatical feature which had no counterpart in Latin; and when they tried to discern cases in noun declension. They seem to have regarded the article, and forms like *au, du* (in which they do not appear to have recognised the presence of *le*) as indicating case. Thus a typical declension would be: (*le*) *pere* (nominative and accusative); *du pere* (genitive and ablative[1], instrumental); *au pere* (dative); *ô pere* (vocative); plural (*les*) *peres des peres, aux peres, ô peres*. The partitive article seemed baffling, and the indefinite article was regarded simply as a numeral. Latin had three genders, and the grammarians were somewhat uneasy at being able to discover only two in French, though some thought that they could see a neuter in certain forms of the masculine. The typical sixteenth-century grammar consisted first of all of sounds and spelling (with widespread confusion as between sounds and the letters used to represent them, thus digraphs are liable to be described as diphthongs), and then of a survey of the parts of speech: noun (including adjectives), pronoun, verb, participle, adverb, preposition, conjunction and interjection. Once the sounds had been—rather inadequately—described, the main emphasis was on morphology. Very little attention was paid to syntax: it was seldom carried further than elementary discussion of the agreement of adjectives or participles, and the agreement of verbs in number with their subjects. Sentence structure, and the coordination and subordination of clauses, though of fundamental importance, were almost entirely neglected. As a result, there is little in these grammars that the reader could not very quickly deduce for himself about the language by reading some sixteenth-century texts. Yet there are redeeming features. All the grammarians clearly saw, for instance, that the past tenses of French did not coincide with those of Latin, and that the Latin perfect sometimes corresponds to a French past definite, and sometimes to a French past indefinite (i.e. compound perfect tense). Indeed, on this theme the remarks of the grammarians, their examples and their attempts to indicate the limits of the tenses, are most valuable and informative. One grammarian, Louis Meigret, revealed an insight into the workings of the passive voice which could hardly be improved on today. These are exceptions, however. A work like Geoffroy Tory's *Champfleury* (1529) has little 'hard' grammatical information: indeed, only a comparatively small part of it is even relevant to grammar. It is more memorable for the faith in the future of the vernacular which it expresses. The first true grammar of French for French people, Jacques Dubois' *In linguam gallicam isagwge* ('Introduction to the French language', 1531) is extremely conserva-

---

1. Ablative, because *de* was the preposition most often used to introduce the agent in passive constructions.

tive and limited in scope; and the same is true of the *Traicté de la grammaire françoise* of Robert Estienne (1557). More enlightened are the *Tretté de la grammere françoeze* of Louis Meigret (1550) and the second of the two editions of the grammar of Pierre de la Ramée (1572: the first appeared in 1562). From time to time they express a preference—not always subjective—for one form or construction rather than another, or condemn outright some solecism, as when Meigret condemns the use of *recouvert* as the past participle of *recouvrer*.[1] Now and then, too, they mention something that one could not easily, if at all, deduce from the texts, as when they comment on the existence in speech of the *-t-* of euphony in inversions like *aime-t-on, parla-t-il*. As they could not justify it, the authors of the day did not indicate it, and continued to write *aime-(l)on, parla-il*.

Apart from grammarians strictly so called, who are in the main disappointing, there is much valuable testimony to be found in Henri Estienne's *Hypomneses de gallica lingua* ('Notes on the French language', Geneva 1582). Here there is much comment on current tendencies and hesitant usage, and Estienne is not afraid to express a preference. He has much to say about neologism in the three treatises already mentioned, *Conformité, Deux dialogues*, and *Precellence*. Some of the letters of the humanist Estienne Pasquier too throw much light on recent innovations and on verbal creation and attitudes towards them. For a truly modern grammar of French, however, in which syntax and sentence structure receive their due, we have to wait for Charles Maupas' *Grammaire françoise*, printed at Blois in 1607.

Disappointing in the amount of information they provide for us today, and in the main far more descriptive than prescriptive, the sixteenth-century grammarians nevertheless had the merit of taking the French language seriously enough to write about it and to argue about it with each other. Though their description of French as a system was inadequate and even atomistic, at least they were confident that there *was* a system, one moreover which it was perfectly proper to compare with Latin. None of them came anywhere near embracing that system in its entirety, yet they all implied in varying degrees that there was such a thing as grammatical correctness, that there were regionalisms to be avoided and solecisms to be shunned—unless and until they were so widespread as to constitute a norm. They even, occasionally, ventured opinions about aesthetic matters—the dawn of French stylistics. But they can hardly be said to have successfully laid down guide-lines for the future development of the French language.

1. Curiously enough, this use of *recouvert* was considered respectable a hundred years later, because it had become current in the best circles (see Vaugelas, *Remarques* . . . , pp. 15–16).

There is an overlap between the grammarians and the question of spelling reform, since at least two of them urged a radical change in the system of notation. The sixteenth century had inherited the heavily etymological and artificial spelling of the *praticiens*, confirmed and vulgarised by the early printers who, being for the most part foreigners, had no interest in changing the system, nor competence to change it. Those comparatively rare observations on spelling which appeared in the first decades of the century—those of Pierre Fabri in his *Grant et vray art de pleine rhetorique* (Rouen 1521) and those of an anonymous Picard from Abbeville in a pamphlet entitled *Tresutile et compendieulx traicté de l'art et science d'orthographie gallicane* (Paris 1529)—tend on the whole to justify and uphold the existing state of affairs, and to refer to Latin when in doubt. Some practical improvements were soon made. Thus in 1530 the printer Geoffroy Tory introduced the cedilla as a convenient means of attributing a sibilant value to *c* before *a, o, u* (hitherto -*ce*-, -*ss*-, -*ch*- had been used, though many printers simply used *c* ambiguously). Another printer, the humanist Robert Estienne (the father of Henri see above pp. 93 & 97), at the same time introduced the acute accent for a final 'masculine' [e]. In the following year, Jacques Dubois adopted Estienne's innovation, and also introduced the apostrophe. By 1533, *e* acute, *ç* and the apostrophe were being advocated by Montflory in his *Briefve doctrine pour deüement escripre*, together with the diaeresis used to separate vowels, which seems to have been Montflory's own invention. By 1540, some or all of these signs were being widely, though not universally or consistently, used by French printers.

An extremely important development for French spelling was the appearance in 1540 of the first French–Latin dictionary, the work of Robert Estienne. His *Dictionaire françois–latin*, a transposition of his earlier Latin–French dictionary (1531, 2nd ed. 1536), contains about 9000 words, followed first by Latin equivalents and then by illustrative examples of use, in French, followed in turn by Latin translations. If it is somewhat narrow in scope, it is because it was limited to those French words which had been used in the earlier dictionary to explain Latin ones: thus it is not surprising that many words, well attested in contemporary texts, are missing. The importance of the dictionary was that it came down heavily—though not uncritically—in favour of the etymological principle. Even when a particular spelling could *not* be justified etymologically, Estienne ratified it (sometimes under protest) if it was widely used. Thus although he considered the spelling *ung* absurd, he nonetheless adopted it throughout his dictionary, on the grounds that it was current. The spirit of the age, and undoubtedly most printers, fav oured etymological spelling. It is in the light of the fact that Estienne's dictionary already existed that we must consider the work of the would-be reformers of spelling after 1540.

The first of these was Louis Meigret, who in 1542 in a work entitled *Traité touchant le commun usage de l'escriture françoise*, argued for a phonetic spelling which would involve the use of new accents and diacritic signs, a more economic use of the existing alphabet, and the omission of all letters which were not pronounced. So much for the theory: Meigret put it into practice in 1548 in his translation of a comedy by Lucian, again in his *Tretté de la grammere françoeze* (1550), and in his bitter exchanges with Guillaume Des Autels, who went to the opposite extreme of declaring that pronunciation should be based on spelling. Meigret received partial support from Thomas Sebillet, who in his *Art poetique françois* (1548) upheld the principle that spelling should contain no letters which are not pronounced. Meigret's system was, as a matter of fact, by no means consistent, or even truly economical of the signs used. Though he made a useful distinction between *i* (vowel) and *j* (consonant) (hitherto written indifferently as *i*) he did not take the further step of distinguishing *u* from *v*, and his insistence that there were only *two* e-sounds in French was violently disputed by his contemporaries, who were certainly right in maintaining that there were three: [ɛ], [ə], [e], as in *fermeté*.

In 1550, Jacques Peletier du Mans advocated the use of a somewhat different system in his *Dialogue de l'ortografe e prononciation françoese*, a work taking the form of a debate on the spelling question, which it begs by the fact of appearing in a reformed spelling. Peletier du Mans avoids some of Meigret's errors, but falls into others. The same is true of the method employed by Pierre de la Ramée in his *Gramere* of 1562, with the difference that La Ramée at least distinguished vocalic *u* from consonantal *v*, a distinction which was eventually (in some cases more than a hundred years later) adopted by printers, together with the distinction of *i* and *j*, which, as we have seen, La Ramée had not been the first to make. By 1567, the poet Jean-Antoine de Baïf was using in manuscript a phonetic system of his own devising, involving the use of special characters for *ou, au* and *eu*. This appeared in print in his *Etrénes de poézie fransoeze an vers mezurés* in 1572, and it is not a coincidence that the spelling used in the revised edition of La Ramée's *Gramere* (this time spelled *Grammaire*) bears a striking resemblance to the system used by Baïf. Going much further, a Marseillais schoolmaster named Honorat Rambaud even abandoned the Roman alphabet altogether and devised a system of 52 signs (44 consonantal and 8 vocalic), and printed his *Declaration des abus que l'on commet en escrivant* (1578) using these signs, but hedging his bets by providing on the opposite page a key in conventional spelling. More moderate in their demands, and more practical, were Laurent Joubert (*Dialogue sur la cacographie fransoise*, 1579) and Odet de la Noue (*De l'orthographe françoise*, 1596), who both argued for some measure of rationalisation, and a greater economy in the distribution of signs.

In the meantime some simplification of spelling had in fact taken place. To some extent the worst excesses of etymologising zeal had subsided, and the worst accumulations of parasite letters had been quietly dropped by the end of the sixteenth century, in prose and verse alike. In verse, more particularly, some simplification had taken place on an experimental basis and had found, for a time at least, wide favour. The phonetic principle is, after all, not unimportant in a medium which is intended—as it was in the sixteenth century—to be read aloud and often, indeed, set to music and sung. Aware of this, and enthusiastic about Meigret's orthographic system, the poet Ronsard had intended to adopt it himself in his *Quatre premiers livres des Odes* (1550). He had, however, allowed himself to be persuaded by his friends that his poetry would not be properly appreciated if it appeared in too startlingly unfamiliar a disguise, and accordingly compromised. Ronsard's modified spelling reform, for use in verse (though there was nothing to prevent its use in prose too) amounted to the use of internal accents (acute and circumflex) to indicate the quality and length of vowels; the use of a special sign ę for an elided [ə], the replacement of final -*x* or -*z* by -*s*; the substitution of *f* for *ph*, the omission of mute *h* and of some final unpronounced consonants, frequent reduction of double consonants, and the omission of unpronounced etymological letters. Ronsard did not, however, distinguish *j* from *i* or *u* from *v*.

Ronsard soon lost interest in the spelling question, but his reforms were enthusiastically taken up by his disciples, and his modified spelling was widely used in verse, though rather less so in prose. Even so, by the end of the century, it had almost disappeared from the French scene, though in the following century it came back again, in books printed in the Lowlands, where Ronsard's system had fallen on fertile soil.

At the end of the sixteenth century then, French spelling was firmly etymological in its bias, and was consecrated in this form by the major dictionaries of the day, that is to say the derivative and successive editions and reprints of Robert Estienne's *Dictionaire françois-latin* (1st ed. 1540; 2nd ed. 1549; 3rd ed. by Jacques du Puis and Jean Thierry, 1564; 4th ed., by Du Puis, 1573; reprinted 1584; expanded version by Jean Nicot, entitled *Thresor de la langue françoyse tant ancienne que moderne*, published posthumously in

1606; several further editions up to 1628). The balance of opinion favoured a spelling which indicated etymology and family and grammatical relationships between words, rather than the pronunciation, which did not seem to the men of the Renaissance to be at all fixed. The uncertain nature of the pronunciation was partly a matter of region, partly a matter of class distinction, and partly a matter of attitude towards the phonetic implications of the written word. The 'learned' spelling was fixed in its essentials and, a not unimportant factor, enabled certain grammatical relationships to appear systematically which would have been merely sporadic had a phonetic system been adopted. The humanist Estienne Pasquier saw this very clearly when, in a letter written in 1572, he pointed out to Pierre de la Ramée (one of the reformers, as we have seen): 'Ostez de nostre escriture les lettres que nous ne prononçons pas, vous introduirez un chaos en l'ordre (= "system") de nostre grammaire.' He also pointed out the great weakness of the reformers: they all had different systems and could not agree among themselves. Who could blame the printers for taking no chances?

In their enthusiasm for their native tongue and their desire to 'illustrate' it, the authors of the age began by seeking innovation at all costs, while at the same time they were reluctant to abandon anything they already had: hence the coexistence of old and new in a more extreme form than might have been expected from the normal gradual transformation of vocabulary and syntax. They were not lacking in discrimination, as their satires on linguistic absurdities such as excessive Latinisation show, yet Ronsard's somewhat naïve remark 'Plus nous aurons de mots en notre langue, plus elle sera parfaicte' can be related to the concept of *richesse*, widely regarded at the time as a desideratum in language. Hence a certain acquisitive and quantitative attitude towards words and constructions. Bold neologisms from Latin, Greek, or French, calques of classical constructions or idioms (continuing late medieval trends, see pp. 83–4), archaisms, dialect terms, ringing the changes on suffixes—all this was grist to the mill. Italian, it was alleged, was 'rich' in diminutive suffixes: it was unthinkable that French should lag behind, and so the diminutive suffixes of French, which had been spontaneously giving way to more analytical ways of expressing the same idea, were artificially revived and self-consciously used by poets. Although the best French was recognised to be that of Paris, it was generally considered proper to use regionalisms if no suitable 'standard' term was available. Thus Ronsard, particularly in his earlier works, uses some words characteristic of Vendôme, while later Montaigne used Gasconisms, even to the point of incurring, albeit posthumously, the mild reproaches of an admirer like Estienne Pasquier.

Translation, particularly from Latin, was a common literary activity in this period, and one which encouraged other writers to use French rather than Latin, since translation, when well done, showed that French could after all express ideas hitherto confined to Latin. While Du Bellay warned his readers that every language has its own untranslatable peculiarities, on the other hand Estienne Dolet's *Maniere de bien traduire d'une langue en aultre* (1540) demanded a very high standard—translations which, if his precepts were followed, would read and sound like original compositions. On the one hand there was the danger of excessive Latinisation, but here common sense served as a bridle, and satire as a sanction; on the other lay a whole range of stylistic possibilities, plus a certain exotic flavour, which could be carried over from earlier translation to later literary composition in French.

By the end of the century, the French language, like men's minds, had shaken off the dead hand of medieval scholasticism, together with a good deal of outmoded rhetoric. Though it still showed clearly the influence of Latin, at least it had risen above jargon. New styles had been evolved, appropriate to theme and genre. A highly artificial and high-flown would-be Ciceronian prose is sometimes used in implausibly attributing speeches to historical characters (d'Aubigné); but there is also a lively conversational prose to be found in the comedies of Larivey and in the lighter narrative genres. There are still exaggerations, there is still obscurity—or, to put it another way, an over-confidence that the reader can guess the meaning from the context. Clarity sometimes suffers from the submerging of the main clause in a welter of not very clearly marked subordinate clauses and participial constructions,[1] where the author has not fully thought out his ideas or decided which is the most important, before trying to set them down in writing.

At least by now French had come of age, and was respectable: it was not something to apologise for. It was being used for a wide range of technical, scientific and literary purposes. It had proved its adaptability to changing circumstances, its suitability for conveying complex and subtle ideas, and its capacity for stylistic variation. Old words like *choir, ouïr, cuider, bailler, ains* were giving way to wider uses of *tomber, entendre, penser, donner* and *mais*. Subject pronouns were becoming increasingly inseparable from their verbs, the definite article from the substantive, *ne* from *pas* or *point*; *chaque* was replacing *cha(s)cun* as an adjective, and *que* was replacing *comme* in comparisons of equality. A host of developments were asserting themselves which were to characterise Mod.F. Earlier exuberance was

1. See the first of the two extracts at the end of this chapter.

yielding to a somewhat more sober and critical spirit: there were already some signs of a spontaneous partial reduction of super-fluity and simplification of excess, even before the moment when, as Boileau was to say, *enfin Malherbe vint.*

Examples of sixteenth-century prose:

(1) Luy voyant la grande bonté de sa femme, et que pour tant de mauvais tours qu'il luy avoit faicts, luy rendoit tant de biens, estimant sa faulte aussi grande que l'honneste tour que sa femme luy avoit faict, aprés avoir donné argent à sa mestayere, la priant pour l'avenir vouloir vivre en femme de bien, s'en retourna à sa femme, à laquelle il confessa la debte, et que sans le moyen de ceste grande doulceur et bonté, il estoit impossible qu'il eust jamais laissé la vie qu'il menoit (Marguerite de Navarre, *L'Heptaméron*, ed. of 1559).

The initial *Luy* (= the erring husband) is the subject of a nominative absolute construction and of the main verb, which is *s'en retourna* (*à sa femme*). The subject of *luy rendoit tant de biens* is an unexpressed *elle*. The subject of *estimant, aprés avoir donné,* and of course *la priant*, is again the husband. Note also *donné argent* without the partitive article, and the two examples of an asymmetrical con-struction (*voyant la grande bonté . . . et que* and *il confessa la debte, et que*) which the classical era was to condemn but which has since been revived.

(2) Ceste belle ville, capitale du plus beau royaume de la terre, le domicile de nos rois, le thrône de la justice de cest estat, et comme le temple com-mun de toute la France, perit à nostre veüe, et quasi par nos mains: les richesses de ses citoyens, la magnificence de ses bastimens, l'erudition de tant de celebres et sçavans personnages qu'elle a elevez ne l'ont peu [= *pu*] garantir ny aider. O que cet ancien parloit bien de la puissance de Dieu sous le nom de la Fortune, quand il disoit que lors qu'elle a resolu quelque chose, elle aveugle les esprits des hommes, de peur qu'ils ne luy rompent son coup! (Guillaume du Vair, *La Constance et consolation és calamitez publiques*, ed. of 1595).

The language of this passage is strikingly modern.

6

CODIFICATION AND STANDARDISATION:
CLASSICAL AND NEO-CLASSICAL FRENCH

By the early seventeenth century, spontaneous internal evolution
rather than any influence from the first grammarians had brought
the French language to a stage already approximating to its modern
form. It was understood that the norm, for the written as for the
spoken language, was the usage of educated Parisians and of the
educated citizens of major cities not too remote from Paris; yet this
norm, in the absence of any further standardisation, still allowed very
considerable latitude, for an almost infinite range of structural and
stylistic possibilities were available, and the vocabulary was as ill-
defined as it was vast. Though some of the exuberance of the sixteenth century had subsided and there was less enthusiasm for bold
experiments, individual authors, and *a fortiori* speakers, could and did
innovate freely, and it was nobody's responsibility to say that they
should not.

The seventeenth century, and particularly the second half of it,
was to be an age of increasing control and regimentation of language,
reflecting the increasingly tight control of an increasingly despotic
regime over every aspect of national life, beginning with the Court.
In the following century, some relaxation is perceptible, but by then
it was taken for granted that grammarians and lexicographers had
the right to legislate for speakers and writers, and were men to be
taken seriously, for they had come to be as authoritative for French
as their kind had been earlier for Latin. By the time of the Revolution, the grammar of French had been codified to the last detail, and
it was a codification which was to prevail, with very few modifications, down to the present day.

The history of the period 1610–1789 can be briefly summarised.
A weak king, Louis XIII (1610–43), seriously threatened by internal
unrest and feudal revolt, found a powerful ally in his minister

Richelieu, who strengthened the monarchy by suppressing rebellious nobles (Montmorency, Governor of Languedoc, executed in 1632; Cinq Mars and De Thou, executed in 1642); and by curbing the power of armed Protestants threatening to form a state within the state. After Richelieu's death, further domestic unrest ensued during the minority of Louis XIV, notably in the form of the two Frondes or insurrections (1648 and 1651), caused by the unpopularity of Richelieu's successor Mazarin and by equally unpopular fiscal measures to finance wars with Spain and Germany. Those wars themselves led to some territorial gains for France: Alsace (1648), and Artois and Roussillon (1659). From 1661 to 1714, Louis XIV ruled absolutely. Armed revolt within France had been quelled, and the nobles were kept in line by constant vigilance and by self-interest: they were allowed to keep their not inconsiderable privileges (exemption from taxation, for instance) on condition of obedience. Continual wars drained the country's resources, in spite of further territorial gains (Flanders 1668, Franche-Comté 1679, Strasbourg 1681); while the Revocation of the Edict of Nantes (1685) led to the emigration of 300 000 Protestants, a serious blow to the country's economy and a cause of hostility towards France in Protestant states. The Wars of the Spanish Succession (1701–14) led not only to the loss of Tournai, Nice and Savoy, but also to the loss of the New World territories of Hudson Bay, Acadia (i.e. Nova Scotia) and Newfoundland.

The reign of Louis XV (1715–74) is notable for a series of not very successful wars with Austria, Prussia and England, and a series of not unrelated financial crises. It is also important for the rise of the *bourgeoisie*, for the decline of the Court as an influential body in literary and linguistic matters, and for an ever-growing volume of criticism of the *status quo*. Increasing economic distress and widespread discontent led to the summoning in 1789—for the first time since 1614—of the *États-Généraux*, the representatives of the three Estates of the realm, the clergy, the nobility and the *tiers état* (i.e. the rest: *bourgeoisie*, artisans and peasants). This last body, declaring itself the National Assembly on 17 June 1789 and the Constitutive Assembly on 9 July, became the first revolutionary government of France.

The whole of this period shows an intense linguistic awareness. The first major figure with whom we must concern ourselves in this connexion is François de Malherbe (1555–1628), who from 1605 onwards was official poet at the court of Henri IV and later Louis XIII. He was not a systematic grammarian: he left no formal grammar, and his doctrine has to be deduced from his detailed commentaries on the poet Desportes. Though his main concern was the language and technique of poetry, he led the reaction against the linguistic untidiness of the previous century in verse and prose alike, by insisting that the language of poetry should resemble that of prose in one fundamental respect: ready intelligibility. He is often quoted as having said that he regarded stevedores as his masters. Since he only meant that he would consider any line of verse ill-written which could not be readily *understood* by a stevedore, it would perhaps be more appropriate to say that he regarded stevedores as what would today be termed a 'control'. At all events, his attitude can be related to his criticisms of Desportes' verse, for the things he criticises in it all interfere with comprehension, as well as being out of line with the general tendency of the spoken language of the day. He attacks archaism, whether of word-order, construction or vocabulary, and challenges the need for neologisms, loan-words, dialect words or technical terms. He advocates the regular use of the definite, indefinite or partitive articles with substantives, and of subject pronouns with verbs. For him, the negative consists of two parts, not *ne* alone, but *ne* with *pas* or *point*, and there is no doubt that this was indeed the dominant tendency at the time. He settles the gender of some nouns: *alarme, éclipse, hydre* are feminine; *espace* and *ivoire* are masculine. *Autrefois*, ambiguous for some speakers, must be used only in the sense of 'formerly' and not that of 'on another (sc. future) occasion'. Though Malherbe was nothing if not dogmatic, and somewhat narrow too,[1] his pronouncements were taken seriously not only by poets but also by other men and women of letters. If he did much to inhibit poetic language, he also struck a series of blows for clarity and sobriety by cutting away a great deal of dead wood, and he did much to inculcate a self-critical attitude in would-be writers.

The Académie Française, sponsored by Richelieu, was founded in 1635 and registered by the Parlement in 1637. Article 26 of its statutes declared: 'Il sera composé un Dictionnaire, une Grammaire, une Rhétorique et une Poétique sur les observations de l'Académie.' I shall mention the dictionary later: as for the grammar, it did not appear until 1932, and satisfied no one. However, it is fair to say that in the seventeenth century, the Academy did much to promote and sponsor grammatical and lexicographical activity.

The outstanding contribution of the century to the fixing and standardisation of the language came from Claude Favre de Vaugelas (1585–1650), although his *Remarques sur la langue françoise* (1647) do not add up to a systematic grammar, being rather a collection of scattered grammatical and lexicographical observations. In his

1. Thus, because of uncertainty about the plural forms of adjectives in *-al* (*-als* or *-aux*?), he ruled that one should simply not use them in the plural.

Preface, he insists that he is not a law-giver, but simply a recorder of usage. He has based himself, he says, not on the usage of the people at large, for that is by definition bad usage, but on the usage of 'la plus saine partie de la Cour'. Where this is confirmed by 'la plus saine partie des Autheurs de ce temps', we may speak of manifest usage. Where usage is uncertain, we can only seek evidence from authors, and, where that fails, proceed by analogy. Though his definition of usage is narrow, he readily admits that some comparatively un-educated people may have a sounder linguistic instinct than the learned, because their attitudes will not be coloured by a quite irrelevant knowledge of Greek or Latin. Thus sound usage makes *erreur* feminine, and it is only a few pedants who make it masculine on the dubious ground that *error* was masculine in Latin. He has no illusions about the role of reason or logic in language. Since 'l'usage fait beaucoup de choses par raison, beaucoup sans raison, et beau-coup contre raison', it is a futile exercise to try to rationalise every aspect of language. Thus he can see, for instance, that there are *logical* reasons for not making a relative clause depend on a sub-stantive unintroduced by the definite article, but for him a sufficient reason for not doing so is that usage—for whatever reason—avoids it. The *Remarques* were discussed and debated in the *salons*, and were on the whole taken seriously by authors, who began to revise their works in the light of Vaugelas' book. They were also debated by contemporary and later grammarians such as Ménage, Bouhours, Chapelain, Patru, and Thomas Corneille. Furthermore, they were carefully studied by the Academy, which substantially ratified them in its findings, published in 1705. The taste of the age was opposed to pedantry, and this helps to explain the vogue, not only for a book like the *Remarques*, which combined lack of system with elegance of style, but also for such works as the *Entretiens d'Ariste et d'Eugène*, by Dominique Bouhours (1671), an entertaining appreciation of the qualities of the French language and a justification of its already widespread popularity outside France—a sort of *Precellence du langage françois* (see p. 93) brought up to date; the *Remarques nouvelles sur la langue françoise* (1675) by the same author; and the *Observations sur la langue françoise* by Gilles Ménage (1672, 2nd ed. 1675).

The most important formal grammar of French to appear in the seventeenth century was the *Grammaire générale et raisonnée* of Claude Lancelot and Antoine Arnauld, commonly known as the *Grammaire de Port-Royal* (1660, frequently reprinted and re-edited in the seventeenth and eighteenth centuries). This work, based on logical if not Cartesian principles, anticipates a good deal of eight-eenth-century grammatical theory. It is interesting to note, however, that in spite of its logical bias it confirms many of the points which Vaugelas had based on the authority, not of logic, but of usage.

It must be said that the seventeenth-century grammarians, perhaps precisely because they were basing themselves on a usage which— even within the narrow limits defined by Vaugelas—was in many respects hesitant, frequently contradicted each other, and occasionally themselves. Nevertheless they all shared the conviction that French had reached a very high level of achievement—perfection is not too strong a word. They all shared the conviction that the outstanding quality of French is clarity, a virtue to be jealously guarded against anything which might compromise it, such as muddled thought, facile neologism or promiscuous derivation, careless juxtaposition, or tortuous and artificial word-order. The basic expository word-order of French, above all, was held to favour clarity, and was commonly identified with the logical processes of thought. Le Laboureur in *Les Avantages de la langue françoise* (1669), and Fr. Charpentier in *L'Excellence de la langue françoise* (1683) both praised the logical word-order of French. The grammarians, in accordance with the taste of the age, frowned upon neologisms, considering it more important to determine the precise uses of words already existing in the language. Thus it is not surprising that new metaphorical and figurative uses of existing words found greater favour than neologisms. *Préciosité* too, by no means to be identified with affectation, made for an unpedantic but sensitive and discriminating attitude to language, and a fine appreciation of nuance.

The restricted literary vocabulary of the day was enshrined first in Richelet's *Dictionnaire françois* . . . (1680: the full title is a very long one), and later in the *Dictionnaire de l'Académie françoise* (2 vols. 1694). Technical terms, though excluded from the Academy's dictionary, were relegated to the *Dictionnaire des Arts et des Sciences*, compiled by Thomas Corneille and published in the same year, a work both commissioned and sponsored by the Academy and therefore to be regarded as a semi-official supplement to that body's own dictionary. The other really important dictionary of the period, and one which contained not only the literary vocabulary but also technical terms, archaisms, colloquialisms and even some dialect terms, was the *Dictionnaire universel* of Antoine Furetière, published in three volumes in 1690, two years after the death of its compiler.

By the end of the seventeenth century, rigid codification and a fixed and hierarchised vocabulary had taken the place of the essential mobility and flexibility of the previous century. Since it was inevitable that the spoken language would continue to evolve, there was some danger of a divorce between the spoken and the written language. Incidentally, the colloquial language of the people of Paris appears only very rarely in the texts of the period. What we know of it is largely based on the usually adverse comments of grammarians and on various words and phrases which occur incidentally and in italics.

In the eighteenth century, some significant changes can be seen in current attitudes towards language. The logical principle prevails over the notion that usage should be the basis for grammar. The numerous successive editions of the *Grammaire de Port-Royal* inspired more ambitious grammars similarly based on rational principles. The most important of these are those of Régnier-Desmarais (1706), Restaut (1730), Girard (1747), De Wailly (1754), Beauzée (1767), Condillac (1775), and U. Domergue (1778). The most useful, the most enlightened and the most informative works on the French language, however, were not systematic grammars, but the grammatical dictionaries of the Abbé Féraud, *Dictionnaire grammatical de la langue françoise* (1761) and *Dictionnaire critique de la langue françoise* (3 vols. 1787–8). The earlier theorists of the century continued to display the classical distaste for neologism, and insisted on the literary use of a severely restricted vocabulary and a rigorously fixed word-order. The application of this principle to verse led Fénelon to complain in a letter to the Academy (1714) that the admittedly 'shocking excesses of Ronsard' had regrettably led to a swing to the other extreme, and he deplored, among other things, the severe restrictions placed on poetic inversion. 'On a appauvri, desséché, gêné notre langue', he wrote. The language of verse was also hampered by the insistence on general terms and periphrasis rather than *termes propres*. The great classical masters continued to be models for eighteenth-century authors, but they were liable to be criticised from time to time on points of grammar and vocabulary, where the language, or taste, had evolved in the meantime (see D'Olivet, *Remarques de grammaire sur Racine*, 1738; and Voltaire, *Commentaires sur Corneille*, 1746). The fact is that the theorists and grammarians of the age were embarrassed by the irregularity of French, perplexed to see usage so often run counter to logic, and dismayed by gallicisms which for Vaugelas could still be comfortably accommodated under the umbrella of *l'usage*. In the *Discours préliminaire* of the *Encyclopédie* (1751), d'Alembert went so far as to describe usage as a *caprice national*, and the Abbé d'Olivet showed a similar impatience with grammatical exceptions. Logical principles could of course be applied somewhat more easily to the written language than to the spoken, and this helps to account for the perceptible shift of emphasis away from *l'usage*, so far as that implied the spoken usage of a particular section of the community. Written language came to be regarded as language *par excellence*, a notion completely superseded in modern linguistic thought. The purists were more successful, though still not completely so, in their attempts to immobilise syntax, but they were unable in the long run to stifle the neologising instincts of the nation as a whole, and still less those of the intellectual *élite*. The *philosophes*, for their part, realised that to restrict vocabulary would have been to restrict thought itself, at a time when intellectual horizons were being constantly widened. Travellers were describing far-off lands, exotic products, strange customs and costumes, unfamiliar flora and fauna; discoveries were being made in natural history, physics, chemistry, political economy. Hence, in the second half of the century, there was a considerable widening of vocabulary, reflected above all in prose. Poetry, particularly verse tragedy, was far more inhibited, yet it is interesting to see Jacques Delille in a poem entitled *Les Jardins* (1782) claiming—well in advance of Victor Hugo (see p. 132) the right to use earthy, rustic and agricultural terms in verse, *la vache* rather than *la génisse*. Even the language of the lower orders won in the end a certain grudging recognition, and Marmontel (1785) was quick to point out the absurdity of eliminating from the literary language what everyone in fact says. Why should a literary queen not say *Bonjour*? Is she to be prevented from doing so by the fact that the man in the street says the same?

In one important respect the eighteenth century continued the good work of the seventeenth: it defined the meanings of words very precisely, and emphasised the importance of shades of meaning, of subtle distinctions of tone and register. We can see the modest beginnings of the study of synonymy already here and there, in Malherbe's comments on such pairs as *débile/faible*; *mot/parole*; *portail/porte*; *regard/vue*, in the *Remarques* of Vaugelas and the *Observations* of Ménage. In the eighteenth century more specialised studies of synonyms begin to appear, the first being Girard's *La Justesse de la langue françoise* (1718), (in later editions entitled *Synonymes françois*, and later still expanded with additions by Beauzée). A further important work in this field was P. J. A. Roubaud's *Synonymes françois* (1786, 2nd ed. 1796).

The successive editions of the *Dictionnaire de l'Académie françoise* (2nd ed. 1718; 3rd ed. 1740; 4th ed. 1762; 5th ed. 1798) continue to be, with some necessary readjustments notably in the 4th and 5th editions, essentially dictionaries of literary usage. Furetière's far more widely based *Dictionnaire universel* was taken over by the Jesuits in 1704 and, as the *Dictionnaire de Trévoux*, went through several editions, gradually taking on the proportions of an encyclopedia—but an orthodox one (5th ed., 6 vols. 1743; 7th ed., 8 vols. 1771). As for Diderot's *Encyclopédie* properly so called (1751–72, 17 vols.), it would hardly have been possible without the admission of a large number of technical terms, to which it then gave further currency.

The spelling reforms adopted and subsequently abandoned by Ronsard (see p. 100) had been enthusiastically taken up by the Dutch printers, whose books were imported into France in large numbers during the seventeenth century. French printers slowly followed suit and adopted this somewhat simplified spelling, which by about 1660 was widely used in France. The Academy, committed by its statutes to the production of a dictionary, finally turned its attention to the spelling question in 1673. It soon became obvious that it favoured a more learned and exclusive orthography, based on the, by then, practically superseded spelling used in the dictionaries of the Estienne tradition (see pp. 98–9). The Academy was, after all, a learned and exclusive body, and the preface to the first edition of its dictionary (1694) clearly states that it is intended for learned people and not for 'les ignorans et les simple femmes', i.e. people who, though literate, had no Latin, hence no knowledge of etymological principles, hence no knowledge of orthography as the Academy understood it. It follows that the first *Dictionnaire de l'Académie* was extremely conservative, if not retrograde, and was seriously out of step with current printers' practice. It was also inconsistent with itself, since words were considered piecemeal and without reference to other words formally and even semantically belonging to the same category. Hence *cil, ciller* versus the derivative *dessiller*; *faux* (an improvement on Estienne's *faulx*) but *le pouls, la poultre*; *cru* (Estienne: *crud*) but *le bled*. Before consonants, *s* had been mute for centuries in a large number of words, yet the Academy maintained it in spelling, though Richelet, in his dictionary published in 1680, had suppressed it in accordance with current practice. The usual graphy for *n mouillé* [ɲ] was *gn*, but in a few words it was *ign*. By failing to be consistent, the Academy unintentionally brought about the modern pronunciation of *poignard* [pwaɲar], formerly [pɔɲar] and the popular though incorrect pronunciation of *oignon* [waɲɔ̃], correctly [ɔɲɔ̃]. Some important improvements were made in the third edition (1740) thanks to the efforts of the Abbé d'Olivet. Preconsonantal *s* was suppressed except where pronounced, and the preceding vowel was given either a circumflex or an acute accent according to the stress (*escole* > *école*, but *beste* > *bête*). Many unpronounced etymological letters were removed, and double consonants simplified: *obmettre* > *omettre*; *advocat* > *avocat*; *agraffer* > *agrafer*; final -*y* was widely replaced by -*i*, hence the modern *ami, ceci, moi, gai*. The main break with seventeenth-century learned tradition lay in the use of internal accents and in the removal of some, at least, of the many superfluous consonants, even if etymology did suffer a little. No important changes took place in the fourth edition (1762), except perhaps the definitive substitution of -*és* for -*ez* in the plurals of substantives and participles. -*Ez* was maintained, however, in *le nez*, *chez* and *assez*, and in the second personal plural flexion of verbs.

As for phonology, the presence of an *élite* jealously preserving a fixed pronunciation could not in the long run check numerous spontaneous popular developments which gradually rose through the *bourgeoisie* to achieve respectability and acceptance. With the definitive establishment of the Court and seat of government at Versailles in 1682, a divergence arose between the pronunciation of the Court and that of the City, a divergence which by no means always operated to the advantage of the former.

It is unlikely that the characteristic uvular [R] of French (*r grasseyé* or *dorsal*) existed in the seventeenth century. The sound described by the Maître de Philosophie in Molière's *Bourgeois gentilhomme* (Act ii scene 4) is certainly the traditional trilled variety of [r] (*r apical*). We know, however, from the Austrian Wolfgang von Kempelen that by the eve of the Revolution an unmistakably uvular [R] was well established in Paris, where it was used, he estimated, by a quarter of the population. An earlier distinction between single and double [r] between vowels (with the geminated variety calling for a longer vibration) was lost in the course of the eighteenth century. Final [-r] was restored from about the middle of the eighteenth century to the endings -*eur*, -*ir*, and -*oir* (see p. 69), but not to -*ier* and -*er*. Popularly, the pronunciation [-ø] for [-œr] continued much longer and leaves some traces even today (*boueur/boueux*; *faucheur/faucheux*). Denasalisation made considerable progress where a nasal consonant began the following syllable. This seems to have happened first in tonic syllables, with pretonic syllables later following suit: hence the modern [ɔm], [fam], [gram(m)ɛr], [ane] for older [ɔ̃m], [fãm], [grãmɛr], [ãne] (*homme*, *femme*, *grammaire*, *année*). Final consonants which had come to be heard only in liaison were restored to many monosyllables to give them more body, thus sometimes counteracting homonymic collision, hence the modern pronunciation of *fils*, *net* and *sens* [fis], [nɛt], [sãs]. The struggle between [wɛ] and [ɛ] (written *oi* or *oy*) was finally resolved. In the seventeenth century, *droit*, *soyons*, *soyez*, for example, seem to have been commonly pronounced [drɛ(t)], [sejɔ̃], [seje], but *croire*, *boire*, *françois* [krwɛr], [bwɛr], [frãswɛ]. [wɛ] predominated in the end, in all but a few words (e.g. *la croie*, *la monnoie*, *foible*, *françois*) and in the imperfect and conditional endings of verbs. The further development of [wɛ] to [wa] (involving a slight lowering of the tongue) was well advanced in Parisian speech by the end of the seventeenth century, and by the time of the Revolution the older pronunciation was seldom heard.

Final vowels plus *e* and final vowels without *e* had long since lost any syllabic distinction (except in verse and song), but they were still distinguished in length, the tonic vowel in *finie, venue, aimée* being longer than in *fini, venu, aimé*. Obviously, this distinction was frequently of grammatical significance. The old disputes between *ouïstes* and *non-ouïstes* (see p. 71) were finally settled one way or the other: hence *profit* and no longer *proufit*; *couronne, troupe* and no longer *coronne, troppe*. 'Germanic' [h] had ceased to be pronounced in many parts of France in the sixteenth century, and by the end of the seventeenth, even in educated Parisian speech, it had become respectable not to aspirate it. *L mouillé* [lj] was being replaced by [j] in the popular speech of Paris by this time: thus many people already pronounced *bouteille, fille, grenouille* as they are pronounced today. In many words, an older pretonic [ə] had become [e] by the early eighteenth century, hence the modern pronunciation of *désormais, bénin, présent, séjourner, crécelle*. The [-t-] of euphony (see pp. 77 & 97) had everywhere become respectable and was taught by grammarians, from Vaugelas onwards, as a regular feature of the verbal system. In the seventeenth century, final *-le, -re* in words like *table, coffre* were commonly omitted. It is obviously spelling which accounts for the pronunciation, from the seventeenth century onwards, of [p] in words like *psaume, psautier*. The reduction of *cela* to *ça* is attested early in the eighteenth century, and is certainly earlier.

In the domain of morphology, comparatively little needs to be said. The forms of the demonstrative adjectives are rigorously separated from the pronominal forms. *Cettui* is eliminated; and *-ci*[1] and *-là* are regularly added to the pronouns, or to substantives introduced by the adjectival forms, to mark the near/far distinction formerly borne by the demonstratives themselves. *Dessous, dessus* and *dedans*, earlier used indifferently as adverbs and as prepositions, become almost exclusively adverbial, and *sous, sur* and *dans* largely oust them in the prepositional function. Interrogative and relative *qui* is restricted to persons: interrogative *que* is frequently expanded to *qu'est-ce que* and *qu'est-ce qui*. The earlier possibility of using relative *quoi* (after prepositions) with reference to persons, is eliminated. *Quel* (adj.) is carefully distinguished from *lequel* (pronoun); and as a relative pronoun the latter is confined to use after a preposition. Regular use of the article made it easier—as well as urgent—for grammarians to settle a number of cases of uncertain gender. Attempts to ban the partitive forms *du, de la, des* when the substantive was preceded by an adjective were for a long time unsuccessful: even the

1. The Court preferred to use *-ici* with substantives, but the City's preference for *-ci* prevailed in the end.

best classical authors use the forms incorporating the article, side by side with *de* alone. In the verbal system we may note the levelling of aberrant stems as in *pleure/plourons*, *treuve/trouvons*. *Trouver* is levelled on the pattern of the infinitive; *pleurer* is levelled on the basis of the stem-stressed forms. The older forms of the present subjunctive of *dire*: *die(s)*, *diions*, *diiez*, *dient* are soon replaced by the modern type *dise*, etc. Past definite forms such as *print*, *prindrent* and *vindrent* were considered archaic by the middle of the seventeenth century *prit*, *prirent* and *vinrent* were already normal. The past definite and the formally related imperfect subjunctive receded steadily from the spoken language and it is clear that by the time of the Revolution the complicated forms of the past definite were badly known, and that boldly analogical forms were being used, insofar as the tense was used at all in speech. It goes without saying that the forms of the imperfect subjunctive were even more badly known.

The syntax of the period echoes a growing concern for explicitness and for fixity and exclusiveness where there had previously been choice—or uncertainty. It also shows a certain readiness to sacrifice some grammatical distinctions in the interests of uniformity.

In word-order, we may note that *il en y a* had already by the middle of the seventeenth century been replaced by the modern *il y en a* Where two pronoun objects, one direct and the other indirect, are present, the modern rule 'dative before accusative except when both are third person' is already affirmed by a *remarque* of Vaugelas, and by his example *je vous le promets*, superseding the older *je le vous promets*. As for *le lui*, *la leur*, etc., it was typical of a grammatically conscious age to forbid the omission of the direct object pronoun: in both Old and Mid.F. it had been normal, no doubt for reasons of euphony, to omit *le*, *la*, *les* before (*li*), *lui*, *leur* (see p. 61). The classical age outlawed this in the interests of regularity, but it has in fact lived on in uninhibited speech down to the present day. The placing of object pronouns before finite verbs introducing dependent infinitives was still widespread in the seventeenth century, but this yielded in the eighteenth to the modern word-order, which places the pronoun before the infinitive, except when the finite verb is *laisser*, *faire* or a verb of perception, hence *je veux le voir*, no longer *je le veux voir*, but *il le laissa partir*, *on le fit venir*, *je le vis sortir*. The eighteenth century also ordained that the pronoun object should always follow the imperative: in Mid.F. and even in classical French, the pronoun preceded the second of two coordinated imperatives (see p. 78) hence Boileau's well-known line *Polissez-le sans cesse et le repolissez* The practice of placing a personal pronoun object between the two parts of the negative e.g. *pour ne le pas voir*, or of placing the infinitive itself between the two parts of the negative, e.g. *pour ne tomber pas* yielded to the modern construction *pour ne pas le voir, pour ne pas tomber*, only in the eighteenth century (see also p. 141).

Though it does not apply very well to object pronouns, there is much truth in the claim made by Rivarol in 1784: 'le français nomme d'abord le *sujet* du discours, ensuite le *verbe*, qui est l'action, et enfin *l'objet* de cette action'. We do not, of course, have to share his conviction, expressed as a comment on this statement, that this word-order necessarily corresponds to 'la logique naturelle à tous les hommes', but it is none the less true that even a hundred years before Rivarol wrote those words there was a strong tendency to place the subject close to the verb, the past participle close to the auxiliary, and complements close to the substantive or adjective on which they depend. The subject tends strongly to head the sentence, the direct noun object ceases completely to occur at the beginning of the sentence, or indeed anywhere before the verb, and the indirect object is usually placed after the verb, where clarity normally calls for it, though its relation to the direct object depends largely on the relative length of the two elements. The antecedent is kept as near to the relative pronoun as possible, and the relative clause must not qualify an indeterminate noun.

Preoccupation with synonymy (see p. 110) led to the growth of a grammatical doctrine governing the positions of adjectives, since this often affected their meaning (e.g. *même, honnête, pauvre, méchant, propre*). Grammarians reiterate that adjectives of colour must not precede the noun, that certain common adjectives normally precede it, and that certain others may precede it if they are used figuratively, or if they imply disparagement or praise—and certainly all these points are borne out by classical and neo-classical usage. The closest approximation to modern theory in this matter is to be found in Eléazar de Mauvillon's *Traité général du style* (1751). As for the separation of coordinated adjectives, so beloved of Mid.F. authors (e.g. *la principale raison et plus apparente*, cf. p. 78), this is still sometimes found in classical texts, but is more generally avoided, particularly after Vaugelas' condemnation of it (*Remarques*, pp. 156–7).

The best authors shun those abrupt changes of subject which are a well-known stumbling-block of sixteenth-century French, one which moreover an increased use of subject pronouns does not necessarily remedy—hence the corollary that one should use pronouns only when it is clear what or whom they relate to. Care must be taken in the arrangement of the elements of the sentence, so that the reader does not make wrong assumptions as to which words belong together.

Since the placing of substantival objects before the past participle in compound tenses was no longer a possibility, the question of the agreement of preceding direct objects could—and can—only concern pronoun objects. The modern rule, outlined by Clément Marot in 1538, came to be far more rigidly applied in the second half of the seventeenth century. Vaugelas (*Remarques*, pp. 175–6) distinguishes carefully between *j'ay receu vos lettres* where the participle is invariable, and *les lettres que j'ay receües*, where it agrees, while he dismisses as impossible the type *j'ai receües vos lettres*, well attested in O. and Mid.F (see pp. 79–80).

By the eighteenth century it is axiomatic that the subject of a secondary infinitive clause, or of a participial or gerundival construction, must be the same as that of the main clause: the disconcerting laxity of Mid.F. in this respect is deplored. Older dependent clauses of the type *je vous prie que* (*vous*) *me fassiez cette grâce* (see pp. 61–2 & 80), considered by Maupas in 1607 to be of equal merit with *je vous prie de me faire cette grâce*, are considered to be clumsy and archaic by Vaugelas in 1647 and by the Academy in 1705. If for aesthetic reasons classical and neo-classical authors disliked repetition, they were nevertheless urged to accept it if clarity would otherwise be threatened. Thus they avoid the normal O. and Mid.F. ellipsis of the article, demonstrative, possessive or adjective when coordinated substantives have different numbers and genders (see p. 79).

The decline of the past definite in the spoken language naturally carried with it the decline of the past anterior in speech; and the use of the compound perfect tense (past indefinite) in main clauses sometimes rendered necessary the use of the *passé surcomposé* in subordinate clauses. For example, what was in writing still *après qu'il l'eut fait, nous nous en allâmes*, became in the spoken language *après qu'il l'a eu fait, nous nous en sommes allés*. The grammarians, however, condemned this tense, which they did not find in their classical models, although it is attested in the fifteenth century, and mentioned by grammarians in the sixteenth.

Elaborate rules were formulated for the uses of the subjunctive mood, leading to a certain artificiality and arbitrariness in its application, where it had been spontaneous before. The decline in the seventeenth century of the subjunctive with verbs of thinking used affirmatively (*je crois qu'il soit parti*) is paralleled by its rise with affective verbs and expressions of emotion (*je suis content que vous soyez là*). Even in the literary language, the imperfect subjunctive loses ground to the imperfect indicative and the conditional, in hypothetical sentences, while in the spoken language it sharply declines. It was formally related to the past definite, which, as we have seen, had also declined in the spoken language; moreover, as the imperfect subjunctive was used above all in subordinate clauses, it could be argued that in most cases a present subjunctive would serve just as well, since the temporal situation was adequately indicated by the tense of the main verb. At all events, we have it on the authority of the Abbé Féraud, writing in 1788, that in Paris and in several provinces, the present subjunctive was regularly substituted in dependent clauses for the imperfect subjunctive.

Verbal periphrases of the type *estre* + present participle, *aller* + present participle; *estre après (à)* + infinitive ('to be engaged in'); *estre pour* + infinitive ('to be about to' or 'likely to') were all frowned upon by eighteenth-century grammarians, or only grudgingly admitted; but *estre en train de* has survived. The wide range of conjunctions and conjunctival expressions inherited from Mid.F. were severely pruned by the seventeenth-century grammarians. The concessives *combien que, encore que* and *malgré que* were condemned. *Parce que* triumphed over its old rival *pour ce que* before the end of the century; while, of *devant que, auparavant que* and *avant que*, only the last survived.

The vocabulary of the seventeenth century reflects the fastidiousness of the age. Such sixteenth-century features as the cult of the diminutive, hyperbolical superlatives in *-issime*, promiscuous derivation by affixation, bold compounds—all are viewed with distaste. Dialect words, technical terms, homely and earthy words were avoided in the literary language and to a considerable extent in polite conversation. To neologise was even considered to be in bad taste, a mark of ill-breeding, though it was fully recognised that a new word, however unwelcome originally, might eventually become acceptable by usage, as was the case with *exactitude*, a recent coining which had gained acceptance by the time of Vaugelas. The spontaneous evolution of the language too, as distinct from conscious attempts to regiment it, led to the gradual elimination of such words as *issir, ouïr, bailler, bouter, douloir, ramentevoir, heur* (surviving in *bonheur, malheur*) and the singular *la gent*, all to a considerable extent already compromised in Mid.F.; and to the specialisation of some words which originally had a wider meaning, e.g. *nef* 'ship', restricted to 'nave of church'. Numerous abstract nouns in *-ance* (*apercevance, demourance*) were replaced by more learned words, for it can be said that the classical age, in spite of its grudging attitude towards neologisms, more readily borrowed learned words from Latin or Greek than it formed new derivatives from native roots. Curiously enough, as regards loan-words from other languages, the Grand Siècle was less chauvinistic than has sometimes been supposed. It must be understood, however, that comparatively few of the words borrowed were admissible in the literary language. From Italian came several technical terms relating to the fine arts: *attitude, calque,* *coloris, filigrane, fresque, groupe, miniature, morbide, morbidesse, reflet, svelte* and the calque *élève*, based on *allievo*. A few relating to music: *basson, opéra, partition, récitatif, ritournelle, sonate, ténor*; and a few which might be described as miscellaneous: *bandit, café* (i.e. the beverage, transmitted from Arabic), *céleri, cortège, désinvolte, escompter, lésine, mousseline, pantalon, réussite, salon, polichinelle, volte-face.* Borrowings from other languages, however, were not numerous: from English, *yacht, paquebot, rhum, flanelle,* and *moire* (transmitted from Arabic); from Spanish, *matamore, romance*; from the Spanish colonies *chocolat, tabac*; and from the German the military terms *blocus, bivouac, sabre.*

The eighteenth century soon developed a more liberal attitude towards vocabulary. Technical terms became perfectly acceptable in conversation, and large numbers of neologisms were readily coined from Latin and Greek to keep up with the march of philosophical, political and scientific thought. The Greek element begins to loom large, particularly in the domains of history and politics, but also in science, where new 'Greek' words were made up which were unknown to the Greeks, e.g. *oxygène* and *hydrogène*. In chemistry, the Latin suffixes *-eux* and *-ique*, and the Greek suffixes *-ite* and *-ate* are used to designate new substances and their qualities. An interest in, and admiration for, English institutions led to the borrowing of the words *budget, club, congrès, comité, jury, session, vote.* Daily living and fashion provided *grog, pudding, punch, redingote. Loge* in the sense 'masonic lodge', and the word *franc-maçon* 'free-mason', are calques of English words. *Importation* and *sentimental*, in spite of appearances, are actually English loan-words from this period. German supplied a few mineralogical terms: *blende, feldspath, gneiss, quartz*; but also *blague* 'tobacco-pouch', *loustic* 'wag', 'joker' and *vasistas* 'window-fastening'; from Alsatian dialect *choucroute* 'sauerkraut', *quenelle* (< Knödel), and *schnick* 'rot-gut', 'bad brandy'; while *obus* 'shell' was transmitted from Czech and *vampire* from Serbian. Music predominates in the Italian loan-words of this period which include *adagio, aria, arpège, barcarolle, cantate, cantatrice contralto, crescendo, finale, mandoline, piano, solfège, soprano* and *violoncelle*; but a few artistic terms were also borrowed: *aquarelle camée, caricature, gouache, pittoresque*; the two banking term *discrédit* and *ristourne*; and the words *colis* and *villégiature*. Spanish borrowings were few: *cigare, embarcadère, embarcation, récife saynète, tomate*. Portuguese provided *caste, autodafé* and *fétiche* Borrowings from dialects are rare, but *nougat* (literally 'nutty') *farandole* and *amadou*, all from Provençal, may be noted.

Whether it was the style of spontaneous narrative or a more learned and self-conscious style based on Latin complex sentences sixteenth-century prose had tended to be sprawling, untidy, and often even chaotic. The same features are present in the early years of the following century, but soon a new aesthetic attitude is perceptible. Lengthy, rambling sentences where one subordinate clause, introduced by *que*, branches off into further subordinate clauses, also introduced by *que*, give way to a tighter, more selective and more vigorous syntax, in which importance is attached both to rigorous logical links between sentences and to the balance of periods, a style to be seen at its best in the writings of Guez de Balzac and Blaise Pascal. The prose of the later seventeenth century does not pretend to describe life in all its complexity: it interprets and selects, it reduces to order and presents a coherent whole. If it sometimes misleads, it is certainly not through vagueness or obscurity, qualities which the age abhorred, but because it over-simplifies in the interests of cohesion and synthesis.

The best classical authors, and still more the grammarians of the age, reveal a considerable distaste for anacoluthon and for pleonasm, and an almost morbid horror of ambiguity. Thus Bouhours objects to *Le Fils de l'homme viendra dans sa gloire* on the ground that *viendra dans* could mean 'will enter into' as well as 'will come attended by'. Anything superfluous to understanding is removed, and La Bruyère is criticised for writing *Je retombe encore dans les peintures*, where *encore* is strictly pleonastic. On the other hand, if there is any doubt, clarity must take precedence over elegance, and it must be admitted that although classical authors—like authors in every age—are good, bad and indifferent, they are nearly always clear.

Eighteenth-century prose is lighter, and even more clear. Sentences tend to be shorter and crisper, with comparatively few subordinate clauses. Harmony becomes an increasingly important factor, eventually taking precedence even over considerations of grammar. Poetic prose, already found in Fénelon's *Télémaque* (1699), may be seen later in the writings of Bernardin de Saint-Pierre and Jean-Jacques Rousseau. *Style noble* had soon ceased to be regarded as essential in serious prose, and towards the end of the century began to be challenged in verse too. The influence of the educated spoken language explains, at least to some extent, the light, unacademic but pellucid prose of Marivaux, Voltaire and Diderot.

This period sees the rapid decline of Latin in all but the most academic domains. Virtually no Latin poetry was produced after the reign of Louis XIV: most men of letters, and even scientists, wrote principally or exclusively in French. Latin was used less and less as the medium of instruction in schools and colleges.

In the seventeenth century, the frankly disparaging dictionary definitions of the word *patois*, and the comic treatment of dialect-speakers in Molière's comedies, are eloquent of the contemporary attitude of speakers of the standard language towards dialect. In the north of France, the upper classes normally spoke only French, while the lower orders spoke a French coloured by dialect, or were bilingual in French and dialect. In the south, Occitan was widely spoken but seldom written. French was still rarely heard in country districts, though it was beginning to be better known in towns, at least among the more prosperous *bourgeoisie*, who were gradually becoming bilingual, but who wrote only French. A few French schools existed in major cities of the south. Since there was as yet no scheme for universal education, it is understandable that there was no policy for the wide-scale 'conversion' to French of such newly acquired territories as Catalan-speaking Roussillon, Flemish-speaking Flanders and German-speaking Alsace-Lorraine. Even a despot like Louis XIV was content merely to impose French as the official language, for use at an administrative level, in those regions. In the following century, French made some progress in the south as a result of improved communications and the availability of yet more schools in large towns, but it was very much a language for use on special occasions, even among the better educated, while in country districts it was still a foreign language. A work like Desgrouai's *Gasconismes corrigés* (1766) was intended for a minority who spoke French, but whose French was contaminated by the Gascon dialect.

By the end of the seventeenth century, French was widely taught and cultivated as a second language among the upper classes of most European states, and widely spoken in royal and ducal courts. We may certainly attribute this in part to the aesthetic appeal of the language, and to widespread appreciation of its literary masterpieces, but we would do well to remember also that France was economically and militarily the most powerful state in Europe, and it has been calculated that its population at the time amounted to approximately a sixth of the *total* population of Europe. The prestige of French was even greater in the eighteenth century, when the Russian aristocracy, too, fell under its spell. Its adoption as a diplomatic language for use in international treaties certainly suggests that it was at last considered to be as fixed and as clear as Latin. It was used in preliminary negotiations (as in those leading up to the treaty of Nijmegen in 1678), but it was not used in treaties until that of Rastadt in 1714. Since the treaties of this period usually involved what was left of the Holy Roman Empire, there were prestige reasons why Latin could not be lightly abandoned by the Imperial diplomats (German being definitely *hors concours*). Thus the treaty of 1714 bore a postscript which stated that the use of French rather than Latin was not to be regarded as a precedent. This face-saving clause was repeated in the treaties of Vienna (1735) and Aix-la-Chapelle (1748), but was finally dropped altogether in the Treaty of Hubertusburg (1763).

Not only did French take the place of Latin as the language of diplomacy during this period; it also replaced it as the language of international communication between men of letters, heads of state, scientists and intellectuals of all nations. Frederick of Prussia, Catherine the Great of Russia, the German philosopher Grimm, the English economist Walpole and the Italian economist Galiani all wrote elegant French. Gazettes and journals were published in French in most European capitals. It is not surprising, in these circumstances, that in 1782 the Berlin Academy should have offered a prize for the best essay on the subject 'Qu'est-ce qui a rendu la langue françoise universelle?'—a title which took the *fact* of its universality completely for granted: only the causes were to be discussed. Antoine de Rivarol (1753–1801), whose essay, published in 1784 under the title *De l'universalité de la langue françoise*, shared the prize with a German entry, answered the question partly by disparaging other languages, and partly by praising the intrinsic qualities of his own. It is to him, by the way, that we owe those oft-quoted remarks 'Ce qui n'est pas clair n'est pas français' and 'La syntaxe française est incorruptible'.

In the meantime French had gained a foothold in India, in the Antilles (Guadeloupe and Martinique), and in Africa (Saint-Louis in Senegal; and Madagascar). In Canada, it is estimated that there were by 1763 some 65 000 French settlers. In that year, however, Louisiana, the colony explored in the reign of Louis XIV and settled from 1720 onwards, was ceded to Spain,[1] and although Rivarol thought that the newly-won independence of the American states (1783), with French support, was a setback for English and offered fair prospects for French, he was to be contradicted by later events.

The following passage is an example of late seventeenth-century prose. Though not consistent, the orthography is in the tradition of Ronsard, the Dutch printers, and the *Dictionnaire* of Richelet (1680).

Nous allâmes donc un Soir aprés soupé, nous promener dans le Parc. Il faisoit un frais délicieux, qui nous récompensoit d'une journée fort chaude que nous avions essuyée. Je sens, Monsieur, que je vais vous faire une Description, mais il n'y a pas moyen de vous l'épargner, la chose m'y porte necessairement. La Lune étoit levée il y avoit peut-estre une heure, et ses rayons qui ne venoient à nous qu'entre les branches des arbres, faisoient un agreable mélange d'un blanc fort vif, avec tout ce verd qui paroissoit noir. Il n'y avoit pas un nuage qui dérobât ou qui obscurcît la moindre Etoile; elles estoient toutes d'un or pur et éclatant, et qui estoit

---

1. Louisiana was returned to France in 1800, but was sold to the United States only three years later, by Napoleon.

encore relevé par le fond bleu, où elles sont attachées. (Fontenelle, *Entretiens sur la pluralité des mondes*, Amsterdam, Pierre Mortier, 1686, pp. 4–5.)

Apart from the spelling, this is already, to all intents and purposes, Modern French, down to the use of *de vous l'épargner* for earlier *de le vous épargner*. The next passage, written a hundred years later, is so modern that it calls for no further comment, except to the effect that from this point onwards no further passages will be given.

O bizare suite d'évenemens! Comment cela m'est-il arrivé? Pourquoi ces choses et non pas d'autres? Qui les a fixées sur ma tête? Forcé de parcourir la route où je suis entré sans le savoir, comme j'en sortirai sans le vouloir, je l'ai jonchée d'autant de fleurs que ma gaîté me l'a permis; encor je dis ma gaité, sans savoir si elle est à moi plus que le reste, ni même quel est ce *Moi* dont je m'occupe: un assemblage informe de parties inconnues; puis un chétif être imbécile; un petit animal folâtre; un jeune homme ardent au plaisir; ayant tous les goûts pour jouir; fesant tous les métiers pour vivre; maître ici, valet là, selon qu'il plaît à la fortune! ambitieux par vanité; laborieux par nécessité; mais paresseux ... avec délices! orateur selon le danger: poëte par délassement; musicien par occasion; amoureux par folles bouffées; j'ai tout vu, tout fait, tout usé. Puis l'illusion s'est détruite. ... (Beaumarchais, *Le Mariage de Figaro*, Act v, scene 3. London, Th. Hookham, 1785.)

7

FROM THE REVOLUTION TO THE PRESENT DAY

The period from the Revolution to the present day has, in spite of the vicissitudes of further revolutions, *coups d'état*, changes of constitution and external wars, been characterised by a highly centralised government and a highly standardised administration of a kind taken for granted in the modern world. In the course of the nineteenth century, France acquired a considerable overseas empire in Africa (Algeria, Gaboon, Ivory Coast, Senegal, Upper-Volta), in the Far East (Indochina, Cambodia, Laos), and in Oceania (New Caledonia). Although this empire, consolidated in the early twentieth century, has since been lost, the territorial losses involved have not necessarily meant losses for the French language in the areas concerned.

Linguistic unification within France has been rapid, as can be deduced from a comparison of the situation today with that which prevailed at the time of the Revolution. The population of France has approximately doubled. Nowadays, although there are linguistic minorities speaking other dialects or languages, they are nearly all bilingual. For the situation at the time of the Revolution, we are reasonably well informed. In August 1790, the revolutionary government, feeling that 'l'unité de l'idiome est une partie intégrante de la Révolution', entrusted the Abbé Henri Grégoire with the task of investigating the linguistic state of the nation. For this purpose Grégoire sent a questionnaire to parish priests all over the country, asking them to state whether dialects were spoken in their parish, and whether French was understood at all or in part. The replies enabled him to compile a report entitled *Sur la nécessité et les moyens d'anéantir les patois et d'universaliser l'usage de la langue françoise,* which he presented to the National Convention in 1794. From this report it appeared that, out of an estimated population of twenty-five million, at least six million, above all in country districts in the south, knew no French at all, while another six million had only a smattering of the language and were unable to carry on a sustained conversation in it. Only some three million, by virtue either of the region where they happened to live, or of their education, were able to speak it purely; while the number who could write it was, of course, even smaller. On the other hand, it also emerged from Grégoire's report that the dialects were themselves being influenced more and more by French, and this is certainly borne out by such scanty dialect literature as has survived from the period. Grégoire's conclusion was that 'pour extirper tous les préjugés, développer toutes les vérités, tous les talents, toutes les vertus, fondre tous les citoyens dans la masse nationale, simplifier le mécanisme et faciliter le jeu de la machine politique, il faut identité de langage'—a return, in fact, to the premise from which he had started. To bring this about, the revolutionary government proposed to provide a primary school in each *commune*, with a teacher to be paid by the State. There were, however, neither teachers nor funds available, and it was a long time before anything practical could be done. It was only in 1832 that primary state education was established by law, and it was neither free nor compulsory. Nevertheless, it prospered on a voluntary basis, and more and more teachers gradually became available. It was also established in 1832 that reading was to be taught from French texts and not Latin ones, and that for all state examinations (these were becoming increasingly important) a standard spelling and a standard grammar were to be used. The approved grammar was that of Noël and Chapsal (1823), and the approved spelling that of the Academy's dictionary, of which a new edition was imminent (6th ed. 1835).

In the course of the nineteenth century, dialect declined very rapidly. It could not withstand the inroads, not so much of French itself in the first instance, as of those material and administrative developments which inevitably brought French in their wake. The old provincial boundaries counted for less and less. For administrative purposes France had been divided in 1790 into eighty-three *départements* of approximately equal size. The new governmental machine, devised by Napoleon I and implemented and elaborated by successive governments, brought even the most remote villager, willy-nilly, into contact with the world of administration, of documents, stamps, signatures and counter-signatures. Without a knowledge of French, he was handicapped and socially incomplete. There were other factors too which made for the decline of dialect: conscription, introduced at the time of the Revolution and bringing men from all parts of France into contact with each other; improved communications, the postal service and, from 1830 onwards, the gradual spread of railways. National and regional journals, invariably in French, were another factor of linguistic unification; so was universal male suffrage (1848), and so were electoral campaigns. Since all notion of a standard Occitan language—if only for literary purposes —had long since been lost, there could be no question of southern linguistic solidarity in face of the encroachments of French. There were in fact several dialects spoken (though not written) in the south, all of them to some extent infiltrated by the national language. The Félibrige movement (1854–) of seven southern poets, led by Frédéric Mistral (1830–1914), was a worthy attempt to revive and indeed to recreate an Occitanian literary language (called Provençal), yet the enthusiasm it aroused was confined to a small number of highly literate and linguistically conscious people: it did not extend to the masses, who spoke one or other Occitan dialect but who read only French and who, even when they tried, did not find it very easy to read an artificial and archaic literary Occitan, remote from their everyday speech. It can be conceded that the Félibrige gave considerable impetus to dialect and folk-lore studies in the south of France; the fact remains that it did not stem the tide of French.

In June 1881, primary state education was made free, and in March of the following year it became both secular and compulsory. From this time onwards the decline of dialect was even more rapid, so rapid, indeed, that in an atmosphere of growing interest in the history of the French language and its relationship with other Romance languages, it was realised that no time must be lost if the already disappearing dialects were to be recorded. The first linguistic atlas of France (or for that matter of any country) was planned towards the end of the century by the Swiss philologist Jules Gilliéron (1854–1926), the founder of linguistic geography. The materials for it were collected by Edmond Edmont under Gilliéron's direction, between 1897 and 1901. Fully trained in phonetic notation and armed with a questionnaire, Edmont visited 639 localities and ascertained the local expressions of 1920 concepts. The results were published (one map per concept) as the *Atlas linguistique de la France* between 1902 and 1910. This is not the place for an assessment of the *A.L.F.* as a work throwing light on well-preserved dialects, phonetic habits and, by deduction, on previous changes which must have taken place. It is of interest to us here above all because Edmont found, only too often, that he had no option but to record what was in fact merely a phonetic variant of a standard French word, the original dialect term having been lost: e.g. *fustié* 'carpenter' (cf. O.F. *fust* 'wood'), replaced by variants of *charpentier*; *sartre* 'tailor' (Lat. and O. Provençal *sartor*), replaced by variants of *tailleur;* and *ostàu* (O.F. (*h*)*ostel*, O.Prov. *ostal* 'house') replaced by variants of *maison*. Not infrequently, Edmont had to overcome the embarrassment of dialect-speakers, and their tendency to substitute for the true local word—

when there was one—a more refined term (often French) of which they were dimly aware; or to echo, in replying, the terms in which the question was asked. Since the time of the *A.L.F.* there have been many further dialect surveys of which those of J. Séguy (Gascony, Aquitaine), Le P. Gardette (Franco-Provençal) and R. Loriot and A. Lerond (the north-east) are the most important. In the meantime, the dialects have continued to be increasingly affected by the standard language. It is understandably the older generation, particularly the menfolk, who keep them up. Women tend to be more conscious of a social stigma, real or imagined, and, since they have a great deal to do with forming the linguistic habits of young children, it is not surprising that the younger generation, today, often does not understand the local dialect at all, unless it is so like the standard language as to constitute *français régional* rather than a well-defined and systematic dialect. Today there are few dialect-speakers, or speakers of such minority languages as Basque, Breton, Catalan, Flemish and German, who cannot speak French too, and who did not receive a formal education through the medium of French.

In January 1951, in the face of considerable opposition, the proposal of a *député* named Deixonne became law. This measure authorised the study of regional languages in primary and secondary state schools, to the extent of one hour a week, on an optional basis. Occitan, Catalan, Breton and Basque are now examination subjects in the *baccalauréat*, but the results are taken into account only if the candidates have already passed in other subjects. It is unlikely that such modest activity does very much to keep dialect alive, but some teachers have stated that paying at least some attention to local dialects positively helps children's French studies, by enabling them the better to distinguish between national and local language.

Today, dialects are certainly still heard, in Auvergne, in the Massif Central, in Gascony, Languedoc and parts of the Pyrenees. Minority languages are still spoken as follows: Breton, by some 750 000 living to the west of a line running from Plouha on the bay of S. Brieuc to the eastern part of the peninsula of Rhuis on the Atlantic coast, i.e. above all in Finistère and in about a half of Côtes-du-Nord and Morbihan; Flemish, by about 100 000 living in Dunkirk and Hazebrouck; German, by well over a million people living in Bas-Rhin, Haut-Rhin and Moselle, where German enjoys a severely limited semi-official status side by side with French; Catalan, by perhaps 200 000 in Roussillon (Pyrénées-Orientales); Basque, now spoken by no more than 70 000 in Basses-Pyrénées, mostly in the *arrondissements* of Bayonne and Mauléon; and of course various forms of Occitan spoken by an unspecified number of millions. There are social and other differences. By no means all the inhabitants of a given area know the local dialect or language. Gascon might be said to have more 'prestige' than Auvergnat; Catalan has more prestige than Basque. German and Flemish obviously partake of the prestige they enjoy as national languages elsewhere.

It is nevertheless true to say that France is a country in which linguistic unification is far advanced, and linguistic standardisation too. The overwhelming majority of French people do not know—by virtue of their domicile and upbringing as distinct from their education—any language other than French, though the French they know, the common fund, may be given a local flavour, whether there is a well-defined local dialect or not. Obviously, there are regional differences of pronunciation: the trilled [r] is still widely used in the Midi and in Burgundy; the southern nasals are imperfectly assimilated; final 'feminine' e, mute in the north, is syllabic in the south [ə]; northern closed [o] is liable to be opened to [ɔ], and [ɑ] fronted to [a]; a strong aspirate [h] is heard in Béarn; [œ] is often closed to [ø] in Berry and in Lorraine (aveugle: [avœgl] > [avøgl]). Even so, it seems to be an established fact that regional accents, for whatever reason (radio, the cinema and more recently television must surely be invoked as contributory factors) have undergone considerable levelling in the last thirty or forty years. There are, however, other ways in which regional differences may manifest themselves linguistically. Standard French words may be used in a different, local sense, e.g. in Marseilles espérer = 'to wait', fatigué = 'ill', entrepris = 'embarrassed'; in Saintonge pépinière = 'apple-core'; in Normandy the preposition selon may be used (as in older French) in the sense of le long de. Non-standard constructions, too, may be used; for instance the Toulousain il se le mange 'he's eating it'; the Walloon quelque chose pour moi manger 'something for me to eat'; the Provençal nous se sommes rencontrés; the Poitevin les enfants sont après jouer (= en train de jouer); and the Gascon emphatic je l'ai vu à lui. Regionalism may be apparent too in local words, such as gone 'brat', 'urchin' (Lyons) or bouscatier 'woodsman' (Provence), not part of the vocabulary of the standard language; or in words which are part of the standard language, but which can be used only with local reference, e.g. gave 'Pyrenean mountain torrent'; mas 'Provençal farm-house'; gardian 'drover in Camargue'; manade 'herd in Camargue'; bourride 'Provençal fish-soup'; canut 'silk-worker in Lyons'; bouillabaisse 'Marseillais fish stew'; chabichou 'goat cheese' (in Poitou); calanque 'rocky inlet in Mediterranean coast'. Historically, many other such words have been assimilated to the point of losing any necessarily local associations: e.g. resquiller 'to gate-crash' and its derivative resquilleur, or esquinté 'exhausted'—all three from Marseilles; rascasse 'red mullet' from Provence; *rescapé* 'survivor' from Picardy; *crevette* 'shrimp' from Normandy. Indeed, at all times in its history, the standard language has absorbed regional words, and it will often be found that the very form of a word indicates its origin, or at least indicates that it cannot be a regular Francien word. Thus the southern flavour of *abeille* is betrayed by the presence of intervocalic [b] instead of [v]; *pelouse*, from Saintonge, would have been **peleuse* in Paris; *velours* (originally *velous*), from Provence, would have been **veleux* in the north, *jaloux *jaleux* and *amour *ameur*.

All over France, French is of course spoken in different registers. The popular, uninhibited, not to say uneducated level is much the same all over France, yet precisely because it is not the speech of the more educated classes, it is more liable to be affected by regionalisms which 'educated standard French' is better able to resist. The common features of popular spoken French will be summarised later, when it will be convenient to compare and contrast the tendencies of the written with those of the spoken language.

Turning to those phonological changes which have taken place since the Revolution, we may note that the tendency of the tonic accent to level out, i.e. to become less marked, has continued. Theory has it that in isolation or at the end of a group, the final syllable of a word bears the—admittedly slight—tonic accent. This is certainly observable, but it is also true that in practice an *accent d'intensité* may fall on any syllable of a word or group of words, e.g. *c'était AFfreux*; *c'est éPOUvantable*; *JAmais*; *ATtention!*; *D'ACcord*; *il a RAIson*; *AUjourd'hui*. The sustained accentuation of the first syllable, though seriously at variance with the normal phonetic development of the language, appears to be a rhetorical device of recent date, e.g. *la SOlution GOUvernementale CONsiste à prendre les DISpositions NÉcessaires pour PALlier les FUnestes CONséquences de cette POlitique*. A difference of accentuation may also serve to distinguish from each other pairs like *la pesanteur* 'weight' and *l'apesanteur* 'weightlessness' [lap(ə)zãtœr] versus [lápzãtœr]. It must be said, however, that French is a language which in general uses *grammatical* rather than phonetic means for the indication of emphasis.

The general slowing-down of sound-change is no doubt attributable in part to the reduction of regional influences and to the influence of the written language on the spoken. Since the Revolution, [wɛ] has everywhere become [wa] in the standard language, and the originally popular Parisian uvular [ʀ] is now standard (though not universal by any means). The difference in length between final tonic vowels according to whether they were followed or not followed by mute *e* (*voulu* [vuly]/*voulue* [vuly:]; *fini* [fini]/*finie* [fini:]) had disappeared by the end of the nineteenth century. The replacement of *l mouillé* by yod [j] in words of the type *paille, fille, bouteille, grenouille* (see p. 113) had become general by the middle of the nineteenth century, and Littré's insistence on *l mouillé* in his dictionary (1863–73) failed to reverse the trend. Today a popular tendency is observable to carry the process a stage further and to pronounce *milieu* [mijø], *escalier*, [eskaje], *million* [mijɔ̃]. This tendency, which would have the effect of obliterating certain distinctions (*rallier/railler*; *soulier/souiller*) is being vigorously combated. As for the so-called aspirate *h*, if we disregard the sub-standard tendency to ignore it altogether and precede it with elision or with liaison forms (*d'Hollande* for *de Hollande*; *des haricots* pronounced [dezaʀiko]; *sans heurts* pronounced [sɑ̃zœʀ]), we find that it is either pronounced in hiatus with a preceding vowel sound, as it should be ([deaʀiko]), or with a glottal stop [de'aʀiko]. At all events there is no aspiration.

The traditional distinction between the two nasals [œ̃] and [ɛ̃] is breaking down. A large number of French-speakers, including most Parisians, use only [ɛ̃]—[œ̃] does not exist for them. Apart from its occurrence in the indefinite article *un*, [œ̃] is not a common sound in French, and the efficiency and economy of the sound-system will not be greatly affected by its loss.

Liaison had lost considerable ground by the end of the nineteenth century and continues to decline, except between the article and the adjective or substantive and between pronouns and verbs. It is often disregarded between coordinated adjectives (*des vents faible(s) et variables*), and even between substantive and adjective, if a liaison has already been made (*des affaire(s) importantes*; *un odieu(x) assassinat*). Liaison of the verbal ending *-ent* except with a pronoun, and of the infinitive ending *-er*, is rare. Even educated speakers often seem to prefer hiatus to liaison.

The sound [ø] normally occurs only in final syllables (*-eux, -euse*) and is extremely rare in other positions. The present-day tendency is to replace it in those other positions by [œ]: thus *jeûne*, traditionally [ʒøn], tends to become identical with *jeune* [ʒœn]. The distinction between [ɛ] and [e] is in general well maintained, except in the first person of the future termination, *-ai* (traditionally [e]) which for most speakers is identical with the *-ais* of the conditional. Similarly, the *-ai* of the first person past definite of first-conjugation verbs is, so far as it is uttered, identical with the *-ais* of the imperfect. Where the sound [ɛ] is followed by a tonic [e] in the next syllable, assimilation is common and is not considered incorrect, hence *presser* [prese] or [prɛse], *aider* [ede] or [ɛde], *souhaiter* [swete] or [swɛte], *mêler* [mele] or [mɛle]. The same applies to the past participles *pressé, aidé*, etc. As has already been stated (p. 127) [ɑ] is widely fronted to [a] in the

south. It should now be added that in the north too, there is a strong
tendency among the younger generation to move [ɑ] further forward
in the direction of [a], or to pronounce both sounds as the same
'middle [a]'. This development could and indeed already does create
many homophonic pairs (e.g. *patte/pâte*). The traditional distinction
is on the whole well observed, however, by the older generation in the
north. Through the adoption of a large number of English words
ending in *-ing*, it seems that a new phoneme [ŋ] is entering the
language. It is indicated as correct in pronouncing dictionaries and
is sometimes even taught in schools.

The difference between [œ] and [ə] is to some extent compromised.
Moreover, [ɔ] tends towards [œ], a vulgarism which seems to be
rising in the social scale: *comme* [kœm]; *Médoc* [medœk]; *joli* [ʒœli].

The standard pronunciation of many words in the speech-
continuum involves reduction of syllables containing [ə] (*chemin*
[ʃəmɛ̃] but *le chemin* [ləʃmɛ̃], *un chemin* [œ̃ ʃmɛ̃]). When this process
brings into contact an unvoiced and a voiced consonant, unvoicing
of the latter is liable to result: thus *cheval* [ʃəval] becomes [ʃfal] in
groups like [ləʃfal], [œ̃ʃfal], where [v] > [f] in contact with the
voiceless [ʃ]. Similarly *jeter* [ʒəte], but *à jeter* tends to become [aʃte],
i.e. identical with *acheter*. Partial assimilations are often heard in
combinations like *en face de*, *espèce de*, *classe de*, *Place de*, where [s]
approximates to [z] in anticipation of the voiced consonant [d].

Particularly in monosyllables whose distinctiveness and usefulness
are compromised by their brevity, restoration of a final consonant is
not uncommon. To the now long-established *fils*, *net*, *sens* ([fis], [nɛt],
[sɑ̃s]) may be added the more recent *cinq*, *sept* pronounced [sɛ̃k], [sɛt]
in all positions, instead of, as previously, [sɛ̃], [sɛ] before consonants.

Since literacy is now normal, spelling has become increasingly
liable to exercise an influence on pronunciation. In some cases the
result has since come to be regarded as correct. Thus *legs*, a false
etymological spelling of what had quite rightly been *lais* before, has
come to be pronounced [lɛg], a pronunciation which was ratified in
the last edition of the Academy's dictionary. On the other hand the
popular pronunciation [gaʒœʀ] for *gageure* (correctly [gaʒyʀ], but the
spelling is misleading) is resisted. So are the not uncommon [skyl-
p(ə)te] and [dɔ̃p(ə)te] for *sculpter* and *dompter* respectively ([skylte],
[dɔ̃te]). *Compter*, being a much more common word, supported
moreover by the very frequent *se rendre compte*, does not seem to
offer the same temptation. By far the most widespread manifestation
of the influence of spelling on pronunciation, however, is to be seen,
or rather heard, in the double articulation frequently given to
orthographically geminated consonants. This is on the increase, and is
generally considered correct when the gemination occurs at the

junction of prefix and radical, as in *addition, attention, collègue, collaboration, illisible, immense, innocent*. Many speakers carry the process further, and pronounce *grammaire* [grammɛR], *littéraire* [litterɛR], and *sommet* [sɔmmɛ]. Spelling also helps to maintain *-re, -le*, frequently dropped in the final position after consonants (*aut', prop', quat', possib', troub'*).

Some popular, though condemned, simplifications of certain groups of consonants may be mentioned here: *expliquer* pronounced [ɛsplike]; *excuser* pronounced [ɛskyze]; *artiste* pronounced [aRtis].

In the field of morphology, there is little to be said. If some substantives indicating profession have no feminine form (*une femme écrivain, une femme auteur, une femme professeur, une femme docteur —doctoresse* is in restricted use), the same is true after all of many zoological terms (*un crapaud femelle, un éléphant femelle*, but also *une grenouille mâle*). The so-called diminutive suffixes are used rather for forming necessary derivatives than for the indication of smallness: *chevalet* is an easel, not a small horse. True diminutives, such as *fillette, garçonnet, sœurette*, tend to be in severely restricted use: in general, analytical means have come to be preferred for the expression of smallness. The morphology of the plural is in some respects unsatisfactory, since, when substantives are indeterminate (i.e. not preceded by an article), the pronunciation may well not indicate plurality: *sans histoire(s)*; *sans bagage(s)*; *des prêtres en bonnet(s) carré(s)*. This is, it is true, more often a difficulty in dictation than a source of serious semantic confusion, but the 'visual' nature of much of French grammar is brought home to us when we consider a sentence like *les grands garçons mangeaient des pommes vertes*, in which plurality is expressed seven times in writing, but only twice (yet sufficiently) in speech. There is much hesitation about the plural forms of foreign words: *sandwich(e)(s); flash(e)(s); barmans/barmen*. The stressed forms of the possessives *mien(ne), tien(n)e, sien(ne)* have virtually ceased to be used in the attributive function (*un mien ami*, etc.), and the spoken language makes little use of them predicatively, as pronouns.

In the verbal system, the following points are to be noted. Uncertainty of conjugation has led and is still leading to the replacement of some irregular verbs by regular ones: thus *tirer* may replace *traire* 'to milk', and *solutionner* may replace *résoudre*. In the case of *frire*, a factitive periphrasis, *faire frire*, is the remedy. Because of complications of form, plus the fact that the paradigms depend on a visual memory unsupported by auditive memory, mistakes are frequent in the conjugation of the past definite of irregular and sometimes regular verbs: *je sentai* for *je sentis, il lit* for *il lut, il souria* for *il sourit*; and in the conjugation of the imperfect subjunctive: *qu'il dusse* for *qu'il dût, qu'il allasse* for *qu'il allât*. There is widespread confusion in writing between the past anterior and the pluperfect subjunctive. The *passé surcomposé* type *j'ai eu fait* is in common use in the spoken language, and this is duly reflected in the written language when it is stylistically or realistically relevant—and sometimes when it is not.

The progressive emancipation of the vocabulary, traceable throughout the eighteenth century, continued with increasing momentum after the Revolution. That upheaval itself, and the reorganisation of society which followed it, rendered archaic a large number of terms associated with the semi-feudal administration of pre-Revolutionary days. The metric system, introduced in 1793, led to the general use of *mètre, kilomètre, gramme, litre*. A vogue for Greek words, born to some extent of admiration for the Greek city-states, gave a new currency to some terms coined earlier: *aristocrate, aristocratie, démocrate, démocratie, physiocrate, physiocratie*. Incidentally, an awareness of *-cratie* as a suffix (or as the second element in a compound, as it really is) led later to the creation of *ploutocratie* (Renan, 1848) and *voyoucratie* (Flaubert, 1865). The word *organisation*, hitherto used only of plant life, had its meaning extended and led to the creation of further derivatives: *réorganiser, réorganisation, organisateur, désorganisateur*. Political activity, and a new administration, produced or gave further currency to such terms as *affameur, anarchiste, arrondissement, civisme, département, préfet, sous-préfet, municipalité, législature, motion, amendement, recrutement, conscription, conscrit, la gauche, la droite*. A new need for political and ideological 'labels' led to considerable use of certain prefixes, as in *antidémocratique, antirévolutionnaire, contre-révolution, non-votant, ex-prêtre, ultra-patriote, ultra-royaliste, archi-ministériel*; and suffixes, as in *réactionnaire, républicide, nationicide, liberticide*, not to mention the extremely productive suffixes *-isme, -iste, -iser*. Some revolutionary neologisms proved to be short-lived, witness the revolutionary calendar with its evocative months: *thermidor, prairial, pluviôse, vendémiaire*, etc., devised by the poet Fabre d'Églantine, and its rather unimaginative ten-day week or *décade*, in which the days simply suggested numbers: *primidi, duodi, tridi, quartidi*, etc.

In one respect the Revolution was not revolutionary, and that was in the linguistic and prosodic conventions for classical and neo-classical tragedy, where a highly artificial vocabulary and a set of elaborate periphrases prevailed until the late 1820s, when that citadel was successfully stormed by the Romantics led by Victor Hugo. Hugo's account of his part in this may be seen in the poem *Réponse à un acte d'accusation*, written in 1856 but given the date 1834 (*Les Contemplations*, No. 7: but see also p. 110 above).

The industrial and commercial expansion of France in the course of the nineteenth century led to the creation or borrowing of a large number of technical terms. Since the Industrial Revolution took place much earlier in England than it did in France, many of the words borrowed in the early—and in the later—stages were English. In railway terminology alone, *ballast, rail, tender, ticket, tunnel* and *wagon* were early borrowings, the words *rail, ticket* and *tunnel* being of French origin (O.F. *reille*, Mod.F. *étiquette, tonnelle*), so that they were in fact being borrowed back. English primacy in the textile industry, too, is reflected in some loan-words from this period: *chéviote* (1872), *jersey* (1881), *lasting* (1837), *mackintosh* (1842), *smoking* (= 'dinner-jacket', 1890), *spencer* (1800), *ulster* (1872). Sporting terms include: *handicap* (1831), *match* (1828), *record* (1883), *ring* (1872), *sport* (1828: of O.F. origin), *sportsman* (1823), *starter* (sc. of race, 1862), *tennis* (1836: of O.F. origin), *turf* (1828). Fashion provided *clubman* (1888), *dandy* (1820), *fashion* (1830), *fashionable* (1804), *festival* (1838), *garden-party* (1885), *keep-sake* (1829), *snob* (1857). Where necessary, verbs were coined from substantives: *boycotter, flirter, handicaper*. One borrowing from this period rests on a misunderstanding: *shake-hand*, found in French long before 'hand-shake' is attested in English! Calques of English words at this time include *entraîner*, extended to denote the training of athletes, and *bas-bleu* 'blue-stocking' (originally made feminine).

The conquest of Algeria (1830–) led to the introduction, via military slang, of a number of Arabic words: *bled* 'open country'; *casbah* 'citadel, or native quarter in vicinity of citadel'; *goum* 'tribal contingent'; *gourbi* 'shack', 'hut'; *smala(h)* 'hangers-on', 'numerous following'; *toubib* 'doc'. The publication in 1828 of the memoirs of Vidocq, ex-criminal and ex-chief of the Sûreté, led indirectly to the acceptance into the standard language of a small number of terms originating in thieves' slang: e.g. *escarpe, cambrioleur, pince-monseigneur, boniment*. Cultural and political contacts with Italy led to the borrowing of some eighty Italian words—not a very impressive number when we compare it with the figure for the sixteenth century (see p. 93): but by the nineteenth century, the main traffic was flowing in the opposite direction. However, such words as *biscotte, crinoline, désinvolture, fantoche, fiasco, ferroviaire, malaria, pile, trémolo, vasque* and *vendetta* date from this period.

In the twentieth century, Anglicisms have continued to enter the language at an ever-increasing tempo, to the extent of giving rise to serious concern in purist circles. Sport and entertainment are particularly conspicuous domains of Anglicism, but gadgetry and daily living also show this influence, which is to be seen at its worst in advertising. The brevity of English words is often a recommendation: many of them are monosyllabic yet full-bodied in the sense that they end in a consonant. It is to be noted that for the most part the English words borrowed have, or are given, an extremely precise and even narrow meaning. After all, French does not lack general terms, but sometimes a loan-word relieves a French word of one of a cluster of meanings which it would otherwise have to bear; and purists would do well to remember that the adoption of an English word does not necessarily eliminate a French *word*: it often simply means that *one* of the meanings of a French word has a competitor. Thus *le test* is in competition with *l'épreuve* only in one of its senses, not in other respects, and *la star* is in competition with *la vedette* only in one of its meanings: *vedette* continues to mean also 'motor-launch' and 'mounted sentry'. French does not need to borrow English words to express the concepts 'puzzle', 'boy' or 'girl': if *puzzle*, *boy* and *girl* are all three used in French, it is only in the respective senses 'jigsaw puzzle', 'native servant' and 'chorus girl'. Since they are for the most part 'opaque' or unmotivated words for French people (i.e. are not readily analysable in terms of French roots), English words can be given whatever meaning may be deemed appropriate. Many borrowings are elliptical, or rather *would be* elliptical if they were so used in English, e.g. *rocking* 'rocking-chair', *parking*[1] 'parking-place', 'car park', *cross* 'cross-country running or race'. Some are frankly unnecessary and are used for snobbish reasons: *feeling*, *drink*, *glass*. *Timing* seems completely superfluous in the light of *minutage*, *chronométrage*, *synchronisation* and *synchronisme*. Potentially more insidious, though in most cases harmless enough, are loan-translations or calques based on English words and phrases: *poids mouche* 'fly-weight', *demi de mêlée* 'scrum-half', *boucler la boucle* 'to loop the loop'. In general such calques amount to no more than a reasonable extension of the existing meaning or meanings of a word or phrase. Only occasionally does the calque seem inherently undesirable, when the extended meaning is incompatible with the traditional meaning, so that misunderstanding or serious ambiguity could arise, as with *réaliser*, *contrôler* and *ignorer* used in the sense of English 'to realise', 'to control' and 'to ignore'. It is true that, without the slightest English influence, some French words already possess incompatible meanings, e.g. *chasser* 'to drive away' and 'to pursue with a view to capture', or *défendre* 'to defend' and 'to forbid'—but that is no good argument for adding gratuitously to the number of such words.

By far the most common sources of neologism, however, today and yesterday, are Latin and Greek. Indeed, so much is this the case that

---

1. Not all loan-words in *-ing* are elliptical, however, witness *dumping*, *marketing*, *shopping*.

there has been some neglect of the traditional resources available for the formation of 'native' words from French roots by means of affixation. These resources are often passed over: instead, a neologism is forged *de toutes pièces* from Latin or Greek, or a mixture of the two. Historically, this process has often given rise to a wide gulf between a basic term and a semantically closely related word: an adjective may be popular and the corresponding substantive learned, or the adjective may be learned and the corresponding substantive popular. The first type may be seen in the pairs *boiteux/claudication, bossu/gibbosité, aveugle/cécité* (*aveuglement* being used only of *moral* blindness): the second is represented by *semaine/hebdomadaire, foie/hépatique, oie/ansérine, suie/fuligineux*. Even where there is an etymological relationship, this may be anything but immediately apparent, e.g. *mûr/maturité, dimanche/dominical*.

Some traditional affixes are still 'alive' in the sense that they are used to form new words as needed, e.g. *dé-, -ier, -ard, -eux* and the infinitive ending *-er*. New verbs, it must be added, almost automatically belong nowadays to the first conjugation, rare exceptions being *mincir* 'to slim' (*mincer* exists but has a different meaning), *atterrir* 'to land' (of aircraft; *atterrer* exists but has a different meaning), *amerrir* (based on *atterrir*) 'to touch down on water' and still more recently, *alunir* 'to land on the moon', based on the previous two (*aluner* exists but means 'to treat with alum'). Many older affixes are no longer productive today; they simply exist, occurring in inherited words, but are not used to form new ones. Thus we may contrast certain pairs, of which one member is popular but unproductive, while the other is learned but productive: *outre-/ultra-; entre-/inter-; -aison, -oison/-ation; r + vowel/ré + vowel*. Composition, the formation of compound words by combining hitherto independent entities, is another fruitful source of word-formation, though far less important for French than it is for such a language as German. A traditional type which is still common is the combination of a verb-form (which some identify as the imperative, others as a descriptive third person present indicative) with a substantive regarded as the complement of the verb. Thus on the pattern of *tire-bouchon* 'corkscrew', we find the more recent formations *ouvre-boîtes* 'tin-opener', *remonte-pente* 'ski-lift', *lave-vaisselle* 'dishwasher', *amuse-gueule* 'cocktail snack' and many others. *Ad hoc* compound concepts may be expressed by means of simple juxtaposition, with the second element serving to qualify the first: *cas limite* 'borderline case', *fermeture éclair* 'zip-fastener', *état tampon* 'buffer state', *état providence* 'welfare state', *argument massue* 'knockdown argument', 'clincher'. This is in reality merely an extension of traditional combinations of noun and qualifying adjective. Many of these formations eventually acquire a hyphen, e.g. *industrie-clé* 'key industry'; *facteur-clé* 'key factor'.

Many learned words are polysyllabic, and some of them are abbreviated when in frequent use: *auto*(*mobile*), *bac*(*calauréat*), *ciné*(*ma*)(*tographe*), *météo*(*rologique*), *métro*(*politain*), *oto-rhino-*(*laryngologiste*) 'ears, nose and throat specialist', *sana*(*torium*), *vélo*(*cipède*). Popular speech goes further, with *impec*(*cable*), *imper-*(*méable*), *sensas*(*s*) (= *sensationnel*), *fortif*(*ication*), *manif*(*estation*), *bénéf*(*ice*). On the other hand many long words are *not* abbreviated: *antiparlementarisme, compétitivité, incommunicabilité, inintelligibilité, multilatéralisation, pluridisciplinarité*. A traditional source of brevity which has lost none of its usefulness is ellipsis, permitting, through constant association, the omission of one element, e.g. (*camion*) *poids lourd* 'heavy lorry', (*auto*) *traction* (*avant*) 'car with front-wheel drive', *des* (*étudiants de*) *première année* 'first-year students', *un* (*café*) *crème*. In France as elsewhere, groups of initial letters can form words: e.g. *un P-D.G.* [pedeʒe] (*Président-Directeur général*); *l'O.N.U.* [ɔny] (*Organisation des Nations unies*); *l'O.T.A.N.* [ɔtã] (*Organisation du traité de l'Atlantique du nord*), *une B.A.* [bea] (*bonne action*); *un O.S.* [ɔɛs] (*ouvrier spécialisé*). Further derivatives may be formed from words created in this way: thus *C.G.T.* (*Confédération générale du travail*) gives rise to *cégétiste*, and *J.O.C.* (*Jeunesse ouvrière chrétienne*) to *jociste*.

Major events in the history of French lexicography were the appearance between 1863 and 1873 (with a supplement in 1877) of Émile Littré's *Dictionnaire de la langue française*, in four volumes, a work still widely used today; and in this century Paul Robert's *Dictionnaire analogique et alphabétique de la langue française* (1951–64, in six volumes, with a supplement in 1970). More recently still, the vast lexicographical project known as *Le Trésor de la langue française* (*T.L.F.*), undertaken by the Centre national de la Recherche Scientifique under the direction of Paul Imbs, and based on the computerisation of a documentation far wider than anything of the kind employed hitherto, has begun to publish the first part of its material, relating to the language of the nineteenth and twentieth centuries. Two volumes, of the fourteen envisaged, had appeared by the spring of 1973.

Of the grammars of the nineteenth century, that of Noël and Chapsal (1823) has already been mentioned. There were in all eighty editions of this work, the last appearing in 1889. Another grammar frequently re-edited and reprinted during the period was that of Charles-François Lhomond, originally published in 1780. By far the most complete and at the same time influential grammar, however, was the *Grammaire des Grammaires* of Charles-Pierre Girault-

Duvivier (1763–1832). First published in 1812, and running into twenty-two editions, of which the last appeared in 1886, it was essentially in the normative and rationalist tradition of the grammar of Port-Royal (see p. 107) and the derivative eighteenth-century grammarians. The result is that the dominant note is a reasoned justification for the 'rules' in terms of logic, and a selective attitude towards those classical and neo-classical examples which do not confirm the rules. The actual usage of the early nineteenth century is viewed even more selectively. The influence of this work in shaping grammatical attitudes and in determining the usage of nineteenth-century men of letters cannot be overestimated.

The outstanding grammar of French in this century is *Le Bon Usage*, by Maurice Grevisse. First published in 1936, and regularly revised since (5th ed. 1953, 8th ed. 1964, 9th ed. 1969), it has become a standard work of reference in France and Belgium. The title is aptly chosen, for though Grevisse formulates the inherited rules, and supports them with apposite examples, he also indicates where good usage is perfectly compatible with non-observance of rules, and musters an impressive array of examples from modern authors of merit, who have on occasion chosen to disregard them.

Few changes have been made in the official spelling of French. The fifth edition of the Academy's dictionary was in preparation when the Revolution broke out. The Academy was dissolved, but eventually publication of the dictionary was authorised by the National Convention. The 'fifth edition' of 1798 was to all intents and purposes a reprint of the fourth edition of 1762. It included, however, a supplement of revolutionary and post-revolutionary words. The sixth edition (1835) is remarkable for the long overdue adjustment of spelling to pronunciation in one important respect. Where *oi* was pronounced [ɛ], as distinct from the far more usual [wa], the spelling was changed to *ai*, as in *craie, monnaie, faible, raide*[1] and in the imperfect and conditional endings of verbs, officially *-ois, -oit -oient* until 1835. In the seventh edition, only insignificant changes were made. *Rhythme* lost the first of its *h*'s but not the second, and the hyphen linking *très* to adjectives and adverbs was suppressed. The latest edition, the eighth, appeared in 1932–5, and shows only minor adjustments: *abatis, abatage* were given an extra *t* to bring them into line with *abattre*; words of the type *grand'mère* were henceforward to be written with a hyphen instead of an apostrophe; the hyphen was suppressed in a few words (*contrecoup*), and a few alternative spellings were somewhat illiberally suppressed: *flegmon* and *gaieté* still stand,

1. *Roide* remained as an alternative, corresponding to the alternative pronunciation [rwad].

but *phlegmon* and *gaîté* were eliminated. In its Preface, the Academy disclaimed any responsibility for innovation, whether in spelling or in grammar, and reiterated that its traditional role has been to record usage, not to create it. It is, then, clearly not to the Academy that we must look for spelling reform, if there is to be any. For this, projects have not been lacking in the present century. In February 1901 a ministerial decree allowed certain *tolérances* which concern both grammar and spelling. These *tolérances* did not go far and in any case are widely disregarded. Proposals for spelling-reform were made by Ferdinand Brunot in 1907, by Albert Dauzat in 1940, by Lafitte-Houssat in 1950, by Charles Beaulieux in 1952, and, also in 1952, by a commission under the chairmanship of M. Aristide Beslais—but all to no avail. The problem is an acute one, of great complexity. French spelling is an inconsistent mixture of etymology and phonetics, a considerable burden on the memory and further complicated by grammar. Not for nothing did Charles Bally once write 'Le français est une langue faite pour l'œil.' The spelling and grammar of French are inseparable.[1] Not only is the system an almost impossible one to master perfectly: school syllabuses no longer allow as much time for the study of spelling and grammar as they did in the days when children learned little else. The result has been an alarming decline in standards. A fresh commission, again under the chairmanship of M. Beslais, was set up by the Minister of Education in July 1961, and published in 1965 a detailed report entitled *Rapport général sur les modalités d'une simplification éventuelle de l'orthographe française.* The proposals made include: some simplification of double conso-nants; simplification of Greek letters: *rh > r, th > t, ph > f, y* (in Greek words) *> i;* change of final *-x* to *-s;* rationalisation of *-ance/ -ence, -ant/-ent;* suppression of some unpronounced etymological letters; and some rationalisation of accents. The proposals have been studied, but not adopted, and the problem remains in all its acuteness.

We must now turn to the syntactical and stylistic changes which the language has undergone since the end of the eighteenth century.

In the eighteenth century, the rigidity of French word-order was a matter of congratulation for grammarians and for Rivarol, though a matter of regret for Fénelon and Diderot, since it seemed to the one to inhibit poetic elegance and to the other to hinder spontaneity. Syntactically, word-order has not changed: stylistically, it has. Pro-vided that one does not violate certain fundamental grammatical

---

1. This aspect of French is in contrast with English. English spelling too is disconcertingly unphonetic and irregular, yet, with the notable exception of the apostrophe, the connexion between spelling and grammar is nil.

prohibitions, considerable variety is in fact possible, as has been discovered by a succession of enterprising authors.

There are circumstances in which inversion of verb and subject is a matter of grammatical rule, for example in interrogation, in *incise* after direct speech (e.g. '*Non*', *répondit-il*), and after a very limited number of initial adverbs: *peut-être, aussi, à peine, encore, toujours*. Apart from those circumstances, inversion was frowned upon in the classical and neo-classical language. Nevertheless, concern for rhythm and for balance, for the *phrase nombreuse* and for the avoidance of *cadence mineure*, it was often felt—and is still felt—to be desirable to invert verb and subject in subordinate clauses where the subject is a long one and the verb short and/or semantically weak. Inversion was—and is—also felt to make for clarity when it enables a relative immediately to follow its antecedent. Not only for such considerations as these, but for a variety of stylistic reasons, there has been a considerable rise in inversion since the Revolution. It is true that inversion is still more common in subordinate than in main clauses, because the factors indicated above are quite compelling, though of an aesthetic rather than a strictly grammatical order. There has, however, been a considerable rise in the use of inversion in main clauses too, after a wide range of unspecified and unspecifiable adverbs and adverbial expressions. On the face of it, this marks a partial return to the O.F. state of affairs, but this must surely be coincidental. Since we are here still in the domain of aesthetics (whereas O.F. inversion after an initial adverb was a matter of grammar), no hard and fast rules can be laid down. It is certain, at any rate, that inversion skilfully wielded can produce a wide range of effects: solemnity, finality, harmony, balance, chiasmus, emphasis, and even, by keeping the reader guessing as to the identity of the agent of the action already revealed, mystification or surprise.

Where the fixity of French word-order does not ideally suit the requirements of logical exposition or of emphasis, certain remedies are possible, in both the spoken and the written language. One is the device known as *reprise*, the 'taking up' of a substantive by means of a pronoun, a device which increased in frequency through the centuries as word-order became increasingly fixed and stereotyped: e.g. *Ces contraintes, on s'y heurte . . . , Ses amis on les choisit, sa famille on la subit; Cette activité, il peut l'exercer sans trop de défaillances.* Another is the isolating device *c'est . . . qui* or *c'est . . . que*, e.g. *c'est cet employé que le patron a chassé hier* or *c'est le patron qui a chassé cet employé hier*—two different ways of viewing and analysing the same basic sentence *le patron a chassé cet employé hier.*

There are yet other ways of varying the word-order of French. If one wishes to avoid (or to break up) a succession of sentences in

which the subject comes first, one can use an impersonal construction
whose logical subject comes later: *il s'est produit un grave accident,
il est prévu de nouvelles mesures.*

Turning to sentence structure in general, we shall find that subordination is often avoided by turning into a parenthesis what might
otherwise have been a main clause calling for *que* and a subordinate
clause: e.g. *nous sommes, pourrait-on dire, notre propre interlocuteur
de tous les instants*—the equivalent of *on pourrait dire que nous
sommes,* etc.; or *Cette règle, avouons-le, n'a rien d'absolu*; or *Ces
dérogations sont, répétons-le, bien rares.* Various kinds of suspension
and *découpage* are possible by means of punctuation (*style parcel-
laire*). Supplementary or even fundamental information can be given
much emphasis by placing it after a full stop. The element thus added
appears completely isolated grammatically from what has gone
before, though it is obviously linked with it logically and semantically, e.g. *Il s'est mis à chanter. Faux. De sa voix enrouée.* Elements
thus added are often, even usually, verbless. Elements normally and
indeed logically belonging together are often artificially separated for
convenience, for effect, or for variety: *il avait, pour s'en débarrasser
fait une infinité de démarches*; *on distinguait, qui s'estompaient, des
palmiers*; *doué sur elle d'une excellente influence*; *la voix en lui per-
pétuellement qui sanglote.*

Verbless sentences, attested even in Classical French, come into
their own in the second half of the nineteenth century, largely under
the stimulus of the Goncourt brothers, and are now commonplace,
e.g. *Mugissement continu du torrent . . . Clochettes de mulets chargés
de charbon . . . Psalmodie nasillarde des psaumes avec éclipses de
lanternes* (Goncourt). Aragon's sentence *Une infiltration de roues et de
bonshommes* is the equivalent of *Des roues et des bonshommes s'infil-
trèrent/s'infiltraient.* The Goncourt brothers also developed a related
phenomenon: the use of a semantically weak verb which leaves the
main emphasis on a substantive or series of substantives: *Pendant
une heure, ce sont des piaffements, des roulements, des bruits de
portières mêlés à des ruissellements d'eau* (Goncourt). *Puis ce fut
l'abandon,* as a comment on a cycle race, is another way of writing
Puis il dut/ils durent abandonner; or *Puis il abandonna/ils aban-
donnèrent.*

Some features of word-order which were once a matter of grammar and therefore stylistically neutral have, used as archaisms, come
to be stylistically positive. Thus not infrequently one finds pronoun
objects in modern writing placed before the finite verb rather than
the infinitive, just as they were in the seventeenth century: *Je
désespère de vous pouvoir livrer les pages*; *on en peut parler*; *il y devait
rester.* Archaism is also apparent in the placing of adverbs and other

complements directly after pronoun objects but before the infinitive: *pour le bien imaginer*; *de lui tout raconter*. Both parts of the negative, *ne pas, ne point, ne plus* precede the infinitive in modern French and, if there is also an object pronoun present, come before the pronoun: yet one finds the older *pour ne le perdre pas* and *pour ne le pas perdre* as well as *pour ne pas le perdre* (see also pp. 114–5).

There are basic principles which govern the position of adjectives. Truly discriminatory adjectives of size, colour, nationality, species, basic category, and technical adjectives, with very few exceptions, occur after the noun, whereas those which merely recall a quality already inherent in the substantive (e.g., *la blanche neige, la verte Érin*), those which are used figuratively, those which merely recall a quality already indicated and established, or known to the reader or hearer, precede the noun. For reasons of euphony, however, or for sheer love of variety, adjectives which normally follow the noun may precede it, even when they appear to have their full semantic value. There are also factors of convenience and practicality to be reckoned with, particularly when an adjective qualifies the first of a linked pair of substantives: *un pâle matin de septembre*; *une subite baisse de régime*; *son relatif manque d'objectivité*. In the general tendency to place the adjective more and more often before the noun, some would see an English influence. It is true that this order is particularly conspicuous in translations from English, but there is nothing un-French about the underlying principle.

Another common stylistic device of Mod.F. is to isolate the adjective by means of punctuation and thus give it particular emphasis, e.g., *il chercha autour de lui, indistincts, les objets familiers*; *les semaines se succédèrent, identiques*; *foudroyante, la sirène retentit*. In the last two examples, the effect is to convey to the adjective much of the modifying force of an adverb. This last type of construction was in fact advocated by Joachim du Bellay as early as the sixteenth century, but it was little used, and then mainly in verse.

Other comparatively modern stylistic developments in French include the use of abstract nouns in a concrete sense, often in the plural, a feature introduced by Gustave Flaubert in the nineteenth century and carried further, to the point of being almost systematically used, by the Goncourt brothers. It is now taken entirely for granted (*la fraîcheur > une fraîcheur > des fraîcheurs*). A device used and in fact overworked by the Goncourt brothers, but nonetheless effective when discreetly applied, is the emphasising of the quality of an object by using an abstract noun rather than an adjective or a relative clause, e.g., *la fugitivité de l'eau = l'eau qui coule*; *des blancheurs de draps = des draps blancs*; *la blancheur d'une main = une main blanche*. Maupassant made a disparaging reference to this device when he wrote of 'ceux qui font tomber la grêle ou la pluie sur *la propreté des vitres'*.

Between direct and indirect speech lies a third possibility, known in French as *style indirect libre*. It amounts to the conveying of information in the third person exactly as if it were indirect speech, while nevertheless omitting the normal framework of indirect speech, i.e. by omitting phrases of the type *il dit que, il répondit que, il lui assura que*. This third possibility of presentation seems to have existed even in medieval French, but it was little used until Flaubert made it an important feature of his style, e.g., *Binet donc avait deviné d'où elle venait, et il ne se tairait pas, il bavarderait, c'était certain*—which does not come as a statement directly vouched for by Flaubert, but which presupposes: *Emma* (*Bovary*) *se dit/se disait que* . . . , which Flaubert has suppressed.

With regard to Latinism, much of the self-conscious artificiality of the sixteenth century has subsided. Certain constructions of Latin origin have, however, become in an attenuated form so much a part of French syntax that they appear normal and certainly not learned. Thus absolute constructions are still in use, though they tend to be short and immediately transparent: *Ceci dit . . . ; Cela posé. . . . ; Ceci rappelé . . . ; Tout bien considéré; Sa lettre écrite, il sortit; Les vendanges passées, on est rentré à Paris*. The accusative and infinitive construction has undergone a considerable reduction in use (except of course with verbs of perception, with *laisser* and with *faire*): nevertheless it is not uncommon with *dire, croire*, and *savoir*, usually in relative clauses introduced by *que*: e.g., *une affaire qu'il savait l'intéresser; des gens qu'il disait fréquenter le quartier*.

As for the use of tenses, the most important stylistic innovation since the Revolution has been the so-called narrative imperfect (*l'imparfait de narration*), which amounts to the use of the imperfect in circumstances where, to say the least, the past definite would have been perfectly appropriate and within its traditional role. By substituting an imperfect for the past definite in *Le 21 janvier, le roi mourut sur l'échafaud*, an author is being more vivid; he is describing rather than narrating. This function of the imperfect is above all associated with precise dates and other indications of time, and consequently often occurs in the narrating of *faits-divers* in newspapers, and in those condensed biographies which encyclopaedias so readily provide. This is not to disparage its stylistic value. This use was unknown in classical and neo-classical French. In the language of the seventeenth and eighteenth centuries, a clause like *la guerre éclatait* could imply only a repeated or habitual action, an incomplete action in the past, or an action described or thought by someone (indirect speech). The innovation, which dates from the first half of the nineteenth century, lies in the use of the imperfect in a succession of events forming the narrative itself, and not as part of the secondary, 'background' information or commentary on the narrative. In Classical French, a statement like *Le 15 juillet, il quittait Paris* could not be considered complete in itself: it would be taken to be mere background information, and the reader would expect to be told next what happened *while* the man was leaving Paris: in other words he would expect a new clause containing a verb in the past definite or the past indefinite. Only since the nineteenth century could a sentence of the type *Le lendemain il quittait Paris* be interpreted as complete in itself. Nothing is now more commonplace than this use of the imperfect in accounts of events, e.g., *Soudain, une roue se détachait du camion*; *Deux jours après, le malheureux se suicidait*. It is, I think, not irrelevant to mention in this connexion that the imperfect happens to be an admirably regular tense, whereas the past definite is not. It must be added that the narrative imperfect is *not* used in the spoken language.

The rules for the correct use of the subjunctive mood are extremely complicated, and there is in fact a not inconsiderable area where it is nowadays correct to use either the subjunctive or the indicative. Modern French writing shows considerable hesitation and uncertainty with regard to the expression of modality. The imperfect subjunctive, though found in all its forms, is mainly used in the third person, and in practice the present subjunctive is often substituted for it, in defiance of the traditional rules governing the sequence of tenses (see also pp. 116–17). The rule which says that dependent noun clauses opening a sentence should have their verb in the subjunctive is widely disregarded. There is confusion between *il semble que* + subjunctive and *il me, lui, nous*, etc., *semble que* + indicative. Elegant variation may explain, though not condone, the not uncommon use of the subjunctive in the second of two linked subordinate clauses, in circumstances where the subjunctive is not called for at all (e.g. *puisque* + indic. *et que* + subjunctive). Irrelevant analogy with *avant que* is invoked to explain the use of the subjunctive with *après que*. Historically, there is little doubt that the subjunctive here owes its encroachment to uncertainty of spelling, in Classical French, when the past anterior was *correctly* used with *après que*. Visual and phonetic confusion of *eust, eut, eût* + past participle, and of *fust, fut, fût* + past participle, led to the supposition that the pluperfect subjunctive was being used, and that it was therefore correct to use the subjunctive after *après que* in all circumstances; hence, in Mod.F., the common use even in the spoken language of *après qu'il soit parti*; *après qu'il l'ait fait*, etc. Analogy with *il est possible que* leads to the incorrect use of the subjunctive with *il est probable que*; and analogy with *souhaiter que* leads to its equally incorrect use with *espérer que*. These extensions of the traditional role of the subjunctive are hardly a sign of the strength or vitality of this mood, as some grammarians have optimistically supposed. They spring from widespread confusion, and merely serve to emphasise the conventional and a-semantic nature of the subjunctive in the overwhelming majority of its uses. In practice the relationship of subordinate clauses to main clauses is indicated either by the nature of the main clause itself (*je pense que* + indic.; *il faut que* + subj.) or by the nature of the subordinating conjunction (*parce que, puisque* + indic.; *avant que, pourvu que* + subj.). Whether a distinctive form of the verb is used or not (and this depends very much on the conjugation and tense of the subordinate verb), sufficient information has already been conveyed to the reader or hearer. Only rarely does it make a difference to the meaning whether one uses the subjunctive or not—which is another way of saying that certain verbs used in main clauses are ambiguous (e.g., *supposer, admettre, prétendre, entendre*) or that certain subordinating conjunctions are ambiguous (*de sorte que, de façon que*). Frequent formal identity of the indicative and the subjunctive has rendered it essential to introduce with a grammatical marker (*que*) the admittedly no longer common optative or third person imperative subjunctive in a main clause. The difference illustrated by *il s'arrange* (statement) and *qu'il s'arrange* (wish) is an extremely important one, and one which cannot be left to the mere accident of distinctive verb-forms. Hence the need for a permanent marker, indicating the modality of the expression. In the seventeenth century, it is true, M. Jourdain could still exclaim: *La peste étouffe le tailleur!* (*Le Bourgeois gentilhomme*, Act ii, scene 4), but, given the context, it is unlikely that his audience imagined he was stating a fact!

The objective relative *qui*, introduced by a preposition, is sometimes used of things in modern writing. This marks a return to pre-classical usage. In general, *qui* has been replaced by *lequel, laquelle* and *quoi* in this function. *Quoi*, moreover, perhaps because it is both monosyllabic and invariable, tends more and more to replace *lequel, laquelle* and their plural forms.

The use of the reflexive for the passive, in the third person (see p. 80 and note), originally used with human as well as inanimate subjects, is widespread today, but is now confined to the inanimate. Many verbs which were, and still are, intransitive, have come to be used occasionally as transitives, e.g. *penser* and *repenser*. Many transitive verbs are used absolutely, i.e. with ellipsis of the object, e.g., *exposer* 'to exhibit (sc. pictures)'; *abandonner* 'to give up (sc. a contest, an enterprise)'; *conduire* 'to drive (sc. a car)'; *porter, livrer à domicile* (sc. *des marchandises*). Some present participles used adjectivally have taken on a passive meaning: *voyant* 'conspicuous'; *rue passante* 'busy street'; *spectacle payant* 'show for which admission is charged'.

There are at all times differences between the spoken and the written forms of a language. Writing *always* implies a measure of deliberation and critical self-observation. Speech *may* imply the same, but we must distinguish here between spontaneous and prepared utterance. News bulletins and a good many broadcast speeches and public addresses do not constitute spontaneous utterance: even so-called free discussions may not be truly spontaneous, in that the participants have usually had an opportunity of thinking over, and even talking over, what they are going to say. In this century, recorded speech has enabled the spoken language to be scientifically studied for the first time. Yet if there is one thing which emerges very clearly from the analysis of the spoken language of a highly literate society, it is that the written language and the educational system have an influence on the spoken word which sometimes goes far beyond the mere influence of spelling on pronunciation, or the choice of word or phrase. This is in no way to deny the general influence of spoken French on written French *in the long run*.

Thus there are few features of the written language which do not occur *to some extent* in the spoken language, and vice versa. For realism, an author may reproduce the ungrammatical (though none the less spontaneous and comprehensible) utterances of near-illiterates. For elegance, for effect, and as a part of a rhetorical tradition by no means dead in France, an educated speaker, particularly in a prepared speech, may use inversion, may cultivate the *phrase nombreuse*, may even use the past definite or the imperfect subjunctive. Yet it is, in general, true to say that there are many tendencies which sharply separate written from spoken French. The inversion of verb and subject, kept up as a matter of grammar, and greatly cultivated as a matter of style, is almost systematically avoided in the spoken language, even when strict grammar calls for its use. Archaisms such as the placing of pronoun objects in 'classical' or pre-classical positions in relation to the infinitive, are not features which the man in the street feels called upon to imitate. Bold experiments in sentence structure are not his *forte* either. Spontaneous utterance follows structures which are by no means always orthodox. The descriptive grammarian may note them: the normative grammarian prefers to pretend they do not exist. Even educated speech often makes use of paratactic constructions, simple juxtapositions of clauses which are perfectly transparent, given the added aids of context, modulation and gesture. After all, *vous viendrez, j'espère* is a perfectly serviceable way of saying *j'espère que vous viendrez*. Into *Il n'a pas fermé la porte*:

il est pressé or *J'ai klaxonné: il n'a pas freiné* we may 'read' formal hypotactic structures of the type *il n'a pas fermé la porte, car il est pressé* or *bien que j'aie klaxonné, il n'a pas freiné.* Some dominant tendencies of the spoken language can be listed: it is difficult to classify them rigorously in terms of educated/uneducated. Some, like the types just mentioned, are shared by the educated and the uneducated: others are found only (or normally) in uneducated speech.

In speech, one would expect grammatical inversion to occur chiefly in one of two ways: in *incise* after direct speech has been quoted; and in interrogation. In practice, *incise* is often avoided by using the 'presentative' words *il m'a dit, elle m'a répondu* and so forth, before the direct speech is given. When the direct speech occurs first, however, uneducated speakers often use after it a direct word order introduced by *que,* e.g. *J'sais pas, qu'i(l) m'a dit.* In interrogation, failure to invert is not necessarily ungrammatical: it is often strictly correct to use an affirmative word-order with an interrogative intonation: *Tu viens? Vous trouvez?*—a type which is extremely common. Also, by using *est-ce que,* itself an inversion, though a stereotyped one, it is possible to continue with the affirmative word-order: *Est-ce que je le sais, moi?* Incorrect speech on the other hand may avoid inversion by more questionable means, such as: interrogative word followed by *que,* then affirmative word-order: *comment que t'as fait? où qu'elle est?*; interrogative word(s) followed by affirmative word-order: *où il est? à quoi tu joues?*; interrogative word followed by *c'est que,* then affirmative word-order: *où c'est qu'il l'a vu?*; and lastly affirmative word-order with *-ti, -t'i, -ty* after the verb. This last type arose through the stereotyping (in the eighteenth century, it seems) of a correctly used *-t-il* in an interrogative sentence containing a substantival subject. In a correct sentence like *Son père a-t-il été en Allemagne?* it is to be noted that the word-order could be read as affirmative if one were to disregard *-t-il,* but could nevertheless be understood as a question, in view of context and intonation. Historically, what has happened is that *-t-il,* pronounced [ti], has in the minds of some speakers come to be dissociated from the subject in sentences of this kind, and regarded simply as a sign—an *additional* sign—of interrogation: thus it can occur in uneducated speech with pronoun subjects of *any* person, number or sex. A correct *Vous avez été en Allemagne?* simply becomes *Vous avez-ti été en Allemagne?*

There is also considerable confusion between direct and indirect interrogation, and this is sometimes (by no means always out of concern for realism) reflected in the written language: e.g., *on (ne) savait pas qu'est-ce qu'il voulait dire* for *on (ne) savait pas ce qu'il voulait dire; on va savoir d'où vient-il* for *on va savoir d'où il vient.*

In compound tenses, even well-educated people often fail to make the past participle of a transitive verb agree in number and gender with a preceding direct object, e.g. *les mesures que nous avons pris.* Colloquial speech makes very wide use of the impersonal *on* as the equivalent of *nous.* Indeed, *nous* is often prefixed, for emphasis: *nous, on était partis plus tôt* (note the 'logical' agreement of the participle in writing). In the negation of verbs, *ne*, phonetically unimpressive, is often omitted, even by educated speakers in their more uninhibited moments, so that the negation is borne by *pas* or *plus* alone (or *rien* or *personne*: *point* is very little used in conversation). Negative final clauses are often introduced by the uneducated by means of the incorrect *pour ne pas que.* The subjunctive is well preserved in statistically frequent constructions like *il faut que, vouloir que* and *avoir peur que*, and after the conjunctions *pour que* (*afin que* is literary) and *avant que*: so well preserved, in fact, that incorrect though distinctive forms of the subjunctive of the dependent verb are sometimes heard in these contexts: *aye* [ej], *soye* [swaj], *voye* [vwaj], *croye* [krwaj]. The less common, and more subtle, uses of the subjunctive are widely disregarded. The periphrastic future, formed from *aller* + infinitive, is often used in preference to the future tense properly so called, in circumstances where the latter would be more appropriate. As has already been mentioned, liaison is on the decline. A corollary of this is the hypercorrect use of *false* liaison where it is not called for, e.g. between verb and adverb: *il viendra-t-aujourd'hui*; or elsewhere: *son état continue-t-à être satisfaisant.*

Pronominal verbs such as *se fier*, and intransitive verbs such as *profiter* (*de*), are sometimes used in such a way as to imply transitivity, e.g., *un homme à fier*; *une occasion à profiter. Se rappeler quelqu'un* or *quelque chose* becomes *se rappeler de* by analogy with *se souvenir de*: hence *je m'en rappelle.*[1]

Uneducated speech uses the objective relative *que* as a kind of grammatical *passe-partout*: e.g., *le type que* (= *dont*) *je vous ai causé* (also *le type que je vous en ai causé*); *les outils que* (= *dont*) *j'ai besoin*; *le type que je causais avec* (= *avec qui je causais*). *Avoir* is sometimes used instead of *être* as the auxiliary in the compound tenses of intransitive and pronominal verbs: *on a descendu*; *il a tombé*; *je m'ai trompé.*

Extremely characteristic of uninhibited speech is the pleonastic use of subject pronouns where a substantival subject is already present, e.g., *Marcel i(l)* (*ne*) *tient pas le coup*; *sa sœur elle est malade*; *le patron i(l) m'a dit.* Spoken French is full of anticipations and back-references which sometimes enable the face of grammar to be saved, and sometimes not. A common form of anticipation is to use

1. *Je me rappelle de toi; il se rappelle de vous* are, however, correct.

a pronoun first and identify it later: *Je le regardais l'agent*; *elle (n)'y est pas allée, sa sœur, en Suisse*; *il l'a-t-il jamais attrapé, le gendarme, son voleur?*; *parce que je l'ai pas connu, moi, son fils, hein!*

*   *   *

With all its recent changes, whether at the literary or at the colloquial level, French continues to be, like any inherited language, the repository and accretion of what has been said and written by previous generations, minus what has been lost. As a system, it is like all living languages, highly irregular, not least because it continues to carry along with it many features which were more truly characteristic of an earlier stage in its evolution, but which, for one reason or another, still live on. The reader who has persevered thus far will be able to guess what is archaic, or idiomatic, or atypical, in at least some survivals still current in Mod. F. and not necessarily having an archaic flavour.

The set expressions *les us et coutumes, au fur et à mesure* contain two words (*us* and *fur*) which no longer have any independent existence. The phrase *à demeure* perpetuates a sense long since lost from *la demeure* as used in other contexts. In *sans coup férir, sans bourse délier, sans mot dire* we have reminders of a lost word-order; in *l'appétit vient en mangeant* we have the tolerated survival of a construction usually considered highly ungrammatical today. In the exclusively nominative use of the indefinite pronoun *on*, we are reminded that it is the surviving nominative form of an O.F. substantive. A sentence like *les vieilles gens sont soupçonneux* recalls— and perpetuates—the historical tug-of-war between the feminine gender of the singular substantive *la gent* and the common-sense tendency to make it both plural and masculine as the equivalent of *les hommes*. In *elle était toute contente* but *tout heureuse* we have the uneasy outcome of the conflict between the medieval tendency to treat *tout* as an adjective in this function and the bad conscience of classical grammarians who thought that a word modifying an adjective must be an adverb and therefore invariable, but who lacked the courage to carry their conviction to its logical conclusion. In the tolerated omission of *pas* with *cesser, oser, pouvoir* and *savoir*, we are reminded that in O.F. *ne* alone was sufficient negation with *any* verb. The highly literary *d'aucuns* ('some') is a lone survival of the positive uses of the otherwise exclusively negative *aucun*. Liaison—when correctly applied—recalls the early O.F. period, when final consonants were still pronounced in all circumstances. *La douleur* and the corresponding adjective *douloureux*, representing the inevitable outcome of far-distant sound changes, stand in contrast to *la chaleur* and its adjective *chaleureux*, where analogy intervened. Pairs like *la mer/la marée*, *le foin/le fenil*, and verb forms like *il meurt/nous mourons, je viens/nous venons* are survivals of a widespread but regular pattern, now substantially reduced by analogy. *L'hôtel-Dieu* and *la Saint-Michel* recall one of the uses of the oblique case of O.F. substantives. French place-names, notoriously conservative, also contain lessons and reminders for us. Orly/Aurillac and Châteauneuf/Castelnau are eloquent of the wide phonetic differences which could exist between *langue d'oïl* and *langue d'oc*. Plessis-lez-Tours, in spite of appearances, perpetuates the O.F. preposition *lés* 'near' (< *latus*). Juan-les-Pins does not! Laval and Vaucluse recall the early Romance gender of *val*, now masculine. Rochefort, and Roquefort too for that matter, remind us, like *grand-mère*, of the O.F. undifferentiated forms of certain adjectives.

8

THE DEFENCE OF FRENCH

The distribution of the French language in the world today (see Appendix, pp. 156–7), whether as a first or second language, is impressive when we compare it with the position of French at the time of the Revolution; but such a comparison is of limited validity, for French, which had no serious rival then as an international language, has a serious rival now. If today it is the native language of some seventy-five million people, and if as a second language it reaches some two hundred million more, those figures have to be considered in relation to English, the native language of over three hundred million, and the second language of at least as many again.

At the time when French reigned unchallenged as an international language, it was of course international only in the sense that it was spoken and cultivated by a largely aristocratic *élite*. Since the French Revolution, there have been other revolutions in other countries, and royal and ducal families and courts have largely vanished from the scene. Nationalisms have been asserted, and the equality of all languages as vehicles of a national culture and of national education has been affirmed. In spite of the growing rivalry of English in the nineteenth century, French continued nevertheless to be the normal diplomatic language. In the twentieth, however, it has met with serious setbacks in this function. In 1919, on the insistence of President Wilson of the USA and Lloyd George, Prime Minister of Great Britain, the Treaty of Versailles was drawn up in English *as well as French*—a severe blow to the exclusivity which French had enjoyed since the eighteenth century (see pp. 120–1). A further setback, which might easily have been even more serious, occurred when at the foundation of the United Nations Organisation (San Francisco, April–June 1945), only English, Spanish and Russian were proposed as working languages. French—and Chinese—were added only as a result of energetic protest and a vote which gave French a majority of one. English and French have since become joint working languages, yet in December 1967 a special debate was needed before *equal* publication of communications in French and English was secured. English is also today overwhelmingly the language of all scientific publication. In view of the fact that French has unquestionably lost ground as an international language, certain remedies—or palliatives—have been proposed as a result of growing concern.

(1) *Spelling reform.* Since French spelling is so difficult, it would, so the argument runs, make French more attractive to foreigners (as well as easier for French school-children) if its notation were simplified, not to the extent of becoming phonetic or even phonemic (against which there are overwhelming arguments) but to the extent of some reduction of the anomalies in the system. As we have already seen (pp. 137–8), it has not been found possible to change French spelling in any worth-while way. In any case one wonders whether, if the motivation to learn French in the first place is there, the would-be learner would really be put off by French spelling. There is no evidence that English spelling has deterred people from learning English.

(2) *Le Bilinguisme mondial.* The organisation *Le Monde bilingue*, founded in 1951, proposed that all French-speakers should be taught English, that all English-speakers should be taught French, and that all others should be taught *either* English *or* French. Since the number of those whose native language is English greatly exceeds the number of those whose native language is French, the gain for French would obviously be very much greater than the gain for English. Moreover, if, of those whose native language was neither English nor French, some learned English while others learned French, how would the two groups be able to communicate with each other? The scheme was, for understandable reasons, not adopted. Since then *Le Monde bilingue* has devoted its attention with rather more success to the matter of *jumelages* or the twinning of French and English towns.

(3) *Le français fondamental.* This, first launched in 1954 as *le français élémentaire*, is a new method for teaching French, based on a system of priorities deduced from recorded conversations and from some empirical tests. This method has been further elaborated and has been widely applied, with a considerable degree of success. As its organisers have always insisted, the French it purports to teach is, from the outset, completely authentic; the learner does not have to un-learn anything at a later stage. Thus the comparison with Basic English, made by the opponents of the scheme to discredit it, was quite unfair. The early stages of learning French are simplified, in the sense that a great deal of *provisionally* unnecessary material is postponed. By this kind of stream-lining, the organisers of the scheme

have contrived to some extent to reduce the advantage which English, by virtue of its very simple morphology, has over French in the initial stages of learning; but the fact remains that the morphological detail to be mastered, even for *le français fondamental 1er degré*, is considerable.

In addition to initiatives and activities such as these, numerous organisations exist which are concerned in one way or another with the purity and with the propagation of the French language. It will be convenient to deal first with those which exist in order to maintain or restore high standards in speaking and writing French, and in order to ensure that its development is in conformity with its best traditions.

The French Academy must be mentioned first, for it is a venerable institution, whose role from its inception has been to regulate the French language. Yet it must be admitted that at the present day its influence is slight, save with a small *élite* of professional writers. The Academy's grammar, finally produced in 1932, nearly three hundred years after that body first undertook to produce one, was quite inadequate and aroused a storm of protest. The Academy insists that its role is essentially *to record usage*, but it is obviously able to exercise some discrimination (and, one hopes, influence) in deciding which, of conflicting usages, is to be recorded, and which rejected. Since the eighth edition of the Dictionary appeared in 1932–5, it has been preparing the next edition, but so far it has reached only the letter *C*, and at the present rate of progress, by the time the end of the alphabet is reached, the first part of it will already be seriously out of date. Indeed, the Dictionary has lost considerable ground as an authoritative and practical work of reference, partly because the still current eighth edition is unobtainable, and partly because the Academy is so slow in revising it. The work most readily consulted by printers all over France is in fact not the *Dictionnaire de l'Académie Française*, but the *Petit Larousse Illustré*, which is both easily obtainable and frequently revised and brought up to date.

The *Office du vocabulaire français*, founded in 1957, is an active body which seeks above all to regulate and filter neologisms and to check the improper use of existing French words. Both are delicate tasks. Through its official organ the monthly journal *Vie et Langage*, and also by occasionally enlisting the aid of national newspapers, it organises referenda on specific questions. It is not on principle opposed to loan-words from other languages, among which English naturally looms large. It invites those interested to indicate whether they accept a given neologism, and if not, to suggest alternatives. If the public disapproves of *pipeline*, for instance, what should take its place? *Oléoduc? Artère?* And if the word is in itself acceptable, how should it be pronounced: [piplin] or [paiplain]? If not *best-seller,* then what? *Livre à succès? Succès de librairie?* If not *speaker* (fem. *speakerine,* 'announcer') then what? *Spiqueur? Diseur? Annonceur?* If not *bulldozer,* then what? *Bouteur?* or *bouldozeur?* The O.V.F. also calls attention to current misuses of traditional terms, for example *avatars = aventures, vicissitudes; errements = erreurs; réticence = objection, bien achalandé = bien pourvu de marchandises.*

Another useful organisation is the *Comité d'étude des termes techniques français,* which has been in existence since April 1954 and which plays an important part in deciding both the form and the precise meaning of new technical terms as and when the need for them arises, and in deciding what the French equivalents of foreign technical terms are to be.

Of the three commissions grouped together under the *Haut Comité pour la défense et l'expansion de la langue française* (1966), only one, the *Commission du bon langage,* under the chairmanship of the permanent secretary of the French Academy, is concerned with maintaining standards. This, and the avoidance of jargon, is also the main preoccupation of the *Association pour le bon usage du français dans l'administration* (1967–).

The traditional interest of educated French people in linguistic questions is reflected not only in the existence and activity of such bodies as have just been mentioned. It is reflected also in those semi-popular articles on questions of language which have long been a regular feature of national journals and newspapers, for example those of R. Le Bidois and more recently Jacques Cellard in *Le Monde,* those of Marcel Cohen in *L'Humanité,* and those of Louis Piéchaud and more recently Fernand Feugère in *Le Figaro.* In Canada, René de Chantal has similarly published articles in the Ottawa journal *Le Droit,* and Jean-Louis Darbelnet in the Montreal journal *Notre Temps.* In response to popular demand, articles such as these often appear subsequently in book form.

For specialists of the French language, there are such journals as the quarterly *Le français moderne* (1933–) and the more recent *Langue française* (1969–) of which each number is devoted to a particular aspect of the language. Yet another quarterly periodical, *Défense de la langue française* (1959–), specialises in the denunciation of slackness and error. The more popular *Vie et Langage,* already mentioned as the organ of the *Office du vocabulaire français,* performs a useful service also in providing, well in advance of their appearance in dictionaries, precise definitions of numerous neologisms in current use.

For the propagation of French language and culture outside France, the most important organisation is *Alliance Française*, a private association founded in 1883. It has twelve hundred centres, distributed all over the world, and its own monthly journal *L'Enseignement du français aux étrangers*. Another journal of relevance in this connexion is the pedagogical *Le français dans le monde* (1961–) of which eight numbers appear each year.

Founded in 1963, the *Fédération internationale pour la sauvegarde du français universel*, generally known as the *Fédération du français universel*, concerns itself above all with coordinating linguistic and cultural activities all over the French-speaking world, and with countering centrifugal tendencies. Two commissions of the *Haut Comité* (see p. 153) are concerned principally with the diffusion of French in the world: they are the *Commission de l'expansion culturelle à l'étranger* and the *Commission de la coopération culturelle et technique entre pays de langue française*. In Canada there is the *Académie canadienne française* (Montreal), which has been publishing a monthly bulletin since 1957. Quebec province has its own *Office de la langue française*, founded in March 1961. In the United States, Louisiana has its *CODOFIL* (*Conseil pour le développement du français en Louisiane*) and, since the summer of 1972, a *Revue de Louisiane* which appears twice yearly.

International congresses, bringing together delegates from different French-speaking areas and serving to reaffirm and ideally to implement common aims, are held from time to time: e.g., *Le Congrès des Amériques francophones*, Lafayette (Louisiana), April 1972; and the *Biennale de la langue française*, Namur 1965; Quebec 1967; Liège 1969; Menton 1971. At each *Biennale*, a different theme is studied: at Menton it was 'Le français, langue des affaires'. The fifth *Biennale* was held at Dakar in December 1973: its theme was 'Le français hors de France'.

It is clear, then, that the French-speaking world takes seriously the quality of the French language itself and its position in the world today. Complacency and insularity, at one time a serious threat, have been largely overcome. In the last few years there has been a considerable rallying of the forces of preservation, and the defence and propagation of the French language have been organised on an international basis. It is generally recognised that the real threat comes from the competition of English, but some see any change in the French language itself as a threat. Yet fixity is impossible in any living language. Curiously enough, it is often those who are perfectly aware of this as a matter of historical fact who protest when the language changes to the slightest degree in their own lifetime. If traditionalists had their way, the already considerable gulf between written and spoken French would yawn even wider. French will be doing itself a disservice if it misguidedly resists the need to adapt itself to the ever-changing requirements of a highly technical and industrialised society: it will only place itself at an even greater disadvantage in relation to English. Fortunately this is widely realised, and it is also fortunate that the French language today shows itself to be more resilient and adaptable than it has been at any time since the sixteenth century. The encroachments of English are, in the last analysis, slight. If French is indeed the Romance language which has moved furthest away from Latin, that is the measure of its originality: it has nothing to do with such superficialities as English loan-words.

Spoken language continues to evolve, as it has always done, and to adjust itself to changing needs in a changing world. Though we have seen that there are—and always have been—many differences between the spoken and the written word, we must not underestimate the power and influence of the written language, of a highly organised and standardised system of education, and of a strong tradition which attaches importance to accuracy, if not elegance, of expression. On the other hand the rapid tempo of modern living, and the pressure in school syllabuses of subjects other than grammar, spelling, and literary appreciation, may favour rapid change. Two points need to be made here. One is that change does not necessarily mean decline, or decadence, or deterioration. The other is that whatever changes take place, it is certain that they will be nation-wide, at least as far as France is concerned. And though empires come and go, Paris is still unquestionably the capital of the French-speaking world, and its linguistic standards and linguistic initiatives are heeded in Geneva, Brussels and Montreal. The centripetal forces are stronger than the centrifugal ones. A conscious linguistic policy, cultural contacts, educational standardisation, and the international availability of the printed and spoken word, all contribute to an intense awareness and proud sense of belonging to *la Francophonie*.

APPENDIX

THE DISTRIBUTION OF THE FRENCH
LANGUAGE IN THE WORLD TODAY

France. Population 50 770 000.

Belgium. French is the native language of slightly over half of the population (five million out of nine and a half million). It is spoken in the southern provinces—Hainaut, Liège, Luxembourg, Namur, the southern part of Brabant and, of course, in Brussels. Brussels is officially bilingual though it lies, in fact, within the Flemish-speaking part of Brabant.

Switzerland. French, one of four official languages, is spoken above all by the inhabitants of the western cantons—Vaud, Neuchâtel, Geneva, and parts of Berne, Fribourg and Valais. It is the native language of approximately one million out of a total population of 6 270 000.

Luxemburg. Population 340 000. French is the official language.

Italy. French is spoken by about 100 000 inhabitants of the Valley of Aosta in Piedmont, and theoretically, though not, it seems, in practice, has equal rights with Italian in that area.

Canada. French and English have equal rights as official languages. Out of a total population of just over twenty million, six and a half million are French-speaking. Of these about two-thirds live in Quebec province. The remainder live chiefly in parts of Ontario, New Brunswick, Nova Scotia and Cape Breton Island.

S. Pierre et Miquelon. French is the language of the five thousand inhabitants of this small group of islands off the coast of Newfoundland.

Louisiana. French is the native language of about 800 000 people in this state, whose total population is about 3 500 000.

Haïti. French is the official language and the medium of instruction of the 4 500 000 inhabitants.

Guadeloupe (Antilles). French is the official language of the 323 000 inhabitants.

Martinique (Antilles). French is the official language of the 332 000 inhabitants.

French Guiana (Guyane française). French is the official language of the 34 000 inhabitants.

Africa. French is the official language of Réunion (436 000) and joint official language with English in Mauritius (834 000). It is an official language (sometimes jointly with other languages) spoken by a minority in the following territories: Algeria, Burundi, Cameroon, Central African Republic, Chad, Comorese Islands, Congo, Congolese Republic, Dahomey, Gaboon, Guinea, Ivory Coast, Madagascar, Mali, Morocco, Mauritania, Niger, Rwanda, Senegal, Togo, Tunisia and Upper Volta: also in the territory known until 1967 as French Somaliland, now the 'Territoire français des Afars et des Issas'.

Far East. French is an official language (spoken by a small minority) in the Khmer Republic (Cambodia), Vietnam and Laos.

Oceania. French is the official language of New Caledonia (98 000), and of French Polynesia, which includes Tahiti, the Society Islands and the Marquesas (total population: 109 000).

SUGGESTIONS FOR FURTHER READING

General

Sturtevant E. H., *Linguistic change. An introduction to the historical study of language* (New York 1917).

Ewert A., *The French language* (London 1933).

Price G., *The French language: present and past* (London 1971).

Chapter 1

Elcock W. D. *The Romance languages* (London 1960), chs. 1–3.

Väänänen V., *Introduction au latin vulgaire* (Paris 1964).

Muller H. F., *L'Époque mérovingienne, essai de synthèse de philologie et d'histoire* (New York 1945).

Pei M., *The language of the eighth-century texts in Northern France* (New York 1932).

Sas L. F., *The noun declension system in Merovingian Latin* (Paris 1937).

Lot F., 'A quelle époque a-t-on cessé de parler latin?', *Bulletin Du Cange* 6 (1931), pp. 97–159.

Chapter 2

Ewert A., 'The Strasbourg Oaths', *Transactions of the Philological Society* (1935), pp. 16–35.

Tabachowitz A., *Étude sur la langue de la version française des Serments de Strasbourg* (Upsala 1932).

Porter L. S., 'The *Cantilène de Sainte Eulalie*, phonology and graphemics', *Studies in Philology* 57 (1960), pp. 587–96.

De Poerck G., 'Le sermon bilingue sur Jonas du ms. Valenciennes 521 (475)', *Romanica Gandensia* 4 (1956), pp. 31–66.

Linskill J., *La Vie de Saint Léger, étude sur la langue du ms. de Clermont-Ferrand* (Paris 1937).

Meunier J-M., (Ed.) *La Vie de Saint Alexis* (Paris 1933).

Whitehead F., (Ed.) *La Chanson de Roland* (Oxford 1942).

Chapter 3

Anglade J., *Grammaire élémentaire de l'ancien français* (Paris 1965).

Foulet L., *Petite syntaxe de l'ancien français* (Paris 1930).

Ménard P., *Manuel d'ancien français. 3. Syntaxe* (Bordeaux 1968).

Greimas A., *Dictionnaire de l'ancien français* (Paris 1969).

Delbouille M., 'La notion de "bon usage" en ancien français', *Cahiers de l'Association internationale des études françaises* **14** (1962), pp. 9–24.

Delbouille M., 'Comment naquit la langue française', *Mélanges Georges Straka*, Lyons and Strasbourg, 1970, **1**, pp. 187–99.

Brunot F., *Histoire de la langue française* (Nouvelle édition, Paris 1966), vol. i, Livre deuxième, ch. vi, 'Les dialectes de l'ancien français'.

Chapter 4

Brunot F., *H.L.F.* vol. i, Livre deuxième, ch. ix, 'Le français en France du XIIIe siècle à 1500'.

Brunot F., *H.L.F.* vol. i, Livre troisième, 'Le moyen français'.

Rasmussen J., *La Prose narrative française du XVe siècle* (Copenhagen 1958).

Huguet E., *Étude sur la syntaxe de Rabelais comparée à celle des autres prosateurs de 1450 à 1550* (Paris 1894).

Nykrog P., 'L'influence latine savante sur la syntaxe du français', in vol. v of *Actes du deuxième congrès international des études classiques* (Copenhagen 1957), pp. 89–114.

Lorian A., 'Les Latinismes de syntaxe en français', *Zeitschrift für französische Sprache und Literatur* **77** (1967), pp. 155–69.

Monfrin J., 'Humanisme et traducteurs au moyen âge', *Journal des Savants* (1963), pp. 161–90.

Monfrin J., 'Les Traducteurs et leur public en France au moyen âge', *Journal des Savants* (1964), pp. 5–20.

Chapter 5

Brunot F., *H.L.F.* vol. iii, 'Le Seizième Siècle'.

Gougenheim G., *Grammaire de la langue française du XVIe siècle* (Lyons 1951).

Catach N., *L'Orthographe française à l'époque de la Renaissance* (Geneva 1968).

Rickard P., *La Langue française au XVIe siècle. Étude suivie de textes* (Cambridge 1968).

Darmesteter A. and Hatzfeld A., *Le Seizième Siècle en France. Tableau de la littérature et de la langue* (Paris, 11e édition, 1914), pp. 183–301.

Neumann S. G., *Recherches sur le français des XVe et XVIe siècles et sur sa codification par les théoriciens de l'époque* (Lund and Copenhagen 1959).

Chapter 6

Brunot F., *H.L.F.* vol. iii, Pts. 1 and 2, 'La formation de la langue classique: 1600–1660'.

Brunot F., *H.L.F.* vol. iv, Pts. 1 and 2, 'La langue classique: 1660–1715'.

Brunot F., *La Doctrine de Malherbe* (Paris 1901).

Vaugelas C. F. de, *Remarques sur la langue françoise*, Ed. J. Streicher (Paris 1934).

François A., *La Grammaire du purisme et l'Académie française au XVIIIe siècle* (Paris 1905).

Gohin F., *Les Transformations de la langue française pendant la deuxième moitié du XVIIIe siècle (1740–1789)* (Paris 1903).

Rivarol A., *De l'Universalité de la langue françoise*, Ed. Th. Suran (Paris, 1930).

Seguin J-P., *La Langue française au XVIIIe siècle* (Paris 1972).

Chapter 7

Lettres à Grégoire sur les patois de France, 1790–1794. Documents inédits, Ed. A. Gazier (Paris 1880).

Gougenheim G., *La Langue populaire dans le premier quart du XIXe siècle d'après le Petit Dictionnaire du peuple de J-C. Desgranges* (Paris 1929).

Levitt J., *The 'Grammaire des Grammaires' of Girault-Duvivier. A Study of 19th-century French*, Janua Linguarum, Series Major 19 (The Hague 1968).

Harmer L. C., *The French language today. Its characteristics and tendencies* (London 1954).

Sauvageot A., *Français écrit, français parlé* (Paris 1962).

Sauvageot A., *Analyse du français parlé* (Paris 1972).

Brun A., *Parlers régionaux* (Paris and Toulouse 1946) Ch. 6.

Chapter 8

Bengtsson S., *La Défense organisée de la langue française* (Upsala 1968).

Viatte A., *La Francophonie* (Paris 1969).

Balous S., *L'Action culturelle de la France dans le monde* (Paris 1970).

Burney P., *Les Langues internationales* (Paris 1962).

Gougenheim G., et al., *L'Élaboration du français fondamental (1er degré)* (2e édition, Paris 1964).

Cohen M., et al., *Français élémentaire? Non!* (Paris 1955).

INDEX

INDEX